THE INNER WORLD OF TRAUMA

One of the most outstanding and important contributions to the practice of Jungian analysis (and psychoanalysis altogether) that I have encountered in the last few years.

Mario Jacoby, C. G. Jung Institute, Switzerland

The 'rediscovery' of childhood physical and sexual abuse has again revived psychiatric interest in disorders which arise from traumatic experience. In *The Inner World of Trauma* Donald Kalsched explores the interior world of dream and fantasy images encountered in therapy with people who have suffered unbearable life experiences. In order to examine the inner world, the author focuses on certain archaic and typical dream-images which occur in response to critical moments in therapy. He shows how, in an ironical twist of psychical life, the very images which are generated to defend the self can become malevolent and destructive, resulting in further trauma for the person. Why and how this happens are the questions the book sets out to answer.

Drawing on detailed clinical material, the author gives special attention to the problems of addiction and psychosomatic disorder, as well as the broad topic of dissociation and its treatment. Donald Kalsched here brings together Jung's views on trauma and redefines classical interpretations of Jungian theories. By focusing on the archaic defenses of the self and the mythopoetic language of dream and fairy tale, he connects Jungian theory and practice with contemporary object relations theory and dissociation theory. At the same time, he shows how a Jungian understanding of the universal images of myth and folklore can illuminate treatment of the traumatized patient.

Trauma is about the rupture of those developmental transitions that make life worth living. Donald Kalsched sees this as a spiritual problem as well as a psychological one, and in *The Inner World of Trauma* he provides a compelling insight into how an inner self-care system tries to save the personal spirit.

Donald Kalsched is an analyst in private practice and a teaching member of the C. G. Jung Institute, New York.

THE
INNER WORLD OF
TRAUMA

Archetypal Defenses of the Personal Spirit

Donald Kalsched

London and New York

First published 1996
by Routledge
11 New Fetter Lane, London EC4P 4EE

Simultaneously published in the USA and Canada
by Routledge
29 West 35th Street, New York, NY 10001

Typeset in Times by
Ponting–Green Publishing Services, Chesham, Bucks
Printed and bound in Great Britain by
Mackays of Chatham PLC, Chatham, Kent

British Library Cataloguing in Publication Data
A catalogue record for this book is available from the
British Library

Library of Congress Cataloging in Publication Data
Kalsched, Donald,
The inner world of trauma: archetypal defenses of the personal
spirit / Donald Kalsched.
p.   cm.
Includes bibliographical references and index.
1. Psychic trauma.   2. Psychic trauma–Case studies.   3. Defense
mechanisms (Psychology)   4. Dreams.   5. Jungian psychology.
6. Freud, Sigmund, 1856–1939.   I. Title.
BF175.5.P75K35   1997
616.85'21–dc20   96–13507
CIP

ISBN 0–415–12328–3 (hbk)
ISBN 0–415–12329–1 (pbk)

To Robin

CONTENTS

Part II

ACKNOWLEDGEMENTS

Many people have suffered through with me the ever-shifting kaleidoscope of ideas which take shape in the following pages – none more intimately or helpfully than my patients themselves, especially those individuals whose curiosity matched my own about the angelic/daimonic "presences" appearing on the stage of dreams. I wish especially to thank those of my patients who have kindly given me permission to use dreams and other aspects of their therapy process. All the clinical material described in the book is based on actual cases, but identifying-details and certain other aspects of the therapeutic context have been changed in order to preserve confidentiality. In a few instances I have "fictionalized" the data by creating an amalgam of material from more than one patient.

In addition to my patients, I am also especially grateful to the faculty, staff, and participants of the Professional Enrichment Program in Jungian Theory and Practice, a study community for professionals sponsored from 1988 through 1995 by the Center for Depth Psychology and Jungian Studies in Katonah, New York. Within this group I owe special thanks to my co-director Sidney Mackenzie, who helped so ably to create the kind of enabling space that makes intellectual work a pleasure, and to other members of the core faculty, El Mattern, Alton Wasson, Loren Stell, and Robin van Loben Sels, for their patience and encouragement over the many years during which my ideas were gestating and reaching the "surface" of our study group in one form or another.

It remains for me to express my gratitude to Mario Jacoby of the C. G. Jung Institute in Zurich for his encouragement of my ideas, to David Stonestreet at Routledge for his enthusiastic response to a preliminary proposal for the book, and to Edwina Welham, Commissioning Editor, without whose openness and flexibility this project would have never been completed. Finally, my deepest thanks are to my wife Robin for her understanding and support, even during the many "lost weekends" that were taken up in the various stages of writing and editing the final manuscript.

INTRODUCTION

This is a book about the inner world of trauma as it has been revealed to me in the dreams, fantasies, and interpersonal struggles of patients involved in the psychoanalytic process. By focusing on the "inner world" of trauma I hope to illustrate how the psyche responds *inwardly* to overwhelming life events. What happens in the inner world, for example, when life in the outer world becomes unbearable? What do dreams tell us about the inner "object-images" of the psyche? And how do these "inner objects" compensate for the catastrophic experience with "outer objects"? What patterns of unconscious fantasy provide an inner meaning to the trauma victim when life-shattering events destroy outer meaning altogether? Finally, what do these inner images and fantasy structures tell us about the miraculous life-saving *defenses* that assure the survival of the human spirit when it is threatened by the annihilating blow of trauma? These are some of the questions I will attempt to answer in the following pages.

Throughout the discussion that follows, I will be using the word "trauma" to mean any experience that causes the child unbearable psychic pain or anxiety. For an experience to be "unbearable" means that it overwhelms the usual defensive measures which Freud (1920b: 27) described as a "protective shield against stimuli." Trauma of this magnitude varies from the acute, shattering experiences of child abuse so prominent in the literature today to the more "cumulative traumas" of unmet dependency-needs that mount up to devastating effect in some children's development (Khan, 1963), including the more acute deprivations of infancy described by Winnicott as "primitive agonies," the experience of which is "unthinkable" (1963: 90). The distinguishing feature of such trauma is what Heinz Kohut (1977: 104) called "disintegration anxiety," an unnameable dread associated with the threatened dissolution of a coherent self.

To experience such anxiety threatens the total annihilation of the human personality, the destruction of the personal spirit. This must be avoided at all costs and so, because such trauma often occurs in early infancy before a coherent ego (and its defenses) is formed, *a second line of defenses* comes into play to prevent the "unthinkable" from being *experienced*. These defenses and their elaboration in unconscious fantasy will be the focus of my investigation. In psychoanalytic language, they are variously known as the "primitive" or "dissociative"

1

defenses; for example, splitting, projective identification, idealization or dia-bolization, trance-states, switching among multiple centers of identity, de-personalization, psychic numbing, etc. Psychoanalysis has long understood that these primitive defenses both *characterize* severe psychopathology and also (once in place) *cause* it. But rarely in our contemporary literature do these defenses get any "credit," so to speak, for having accomplished anything in the preservation of life for the person whose heart is broken by trauma. And while everyone agrees how maladaptive these defenses are in the later life of the patient, few writers have acknowledged the miraculous nature of these defenses – their life-saving sophis-tication or their archetypal nature and meaning.

For insights into these matters we turn to C. G. Jung and to dreams – but not to Jung as he has classically been interpreted, and not to dream images as they are understood by many clinicians today. Instead, in Chapter 3 we go back to the early dialogue between Freud and Jung where both were struggling to understand the "mythopoetic"[1] fantasy images that were thrown up by the psyche as the sequelae of trauma. During this fruitful time, and before their tragic split and the subsequent reification of their theories, they each brought an experimental openness to the psyche's mysteries – an openness we must try to recover if we are to understand trauma and its meaning. In Chapter 3 we follow their dialogue to the point where it came apart, and we discover that it did so around the question of how to understand the "daimonic" and "uncanny" images of trauma-linked dream and fantasy.

If we study the impact of trauma on the psyche with one eye on traumatic outer events and one eye on dreams and other spontaneous fantasy-products that occur *in response* to outer trauma, we discover the remarkable mythopoetic imagery that makes up the "inner world of trauma" and that proved to be so exciting to both Freud and Jung. And yet neither Freud's nor Jung's *interpretations* of this imagery have proven entirely satisfactory to many clinicians today, including the present author. For this reason, a new interpretation of trauma-linked fantasy follows in the ensuing pages – one that combines elements from both Freud and Jung. This "new" interpretation relies a great deal on dreams that immediately follow some traumatic moment in the patient's life. Careful study of such dreams in the clinical situation leads to our main hypothesis that the archaic defenses associated with trauma are *personified as archetypal daimonic images*. In other words, trauma-linked dream imagery represents *the psyche's self-portrait of its own archaic defensive operations*.

In the clinical material to follow we will find examples of this imagery in the dreams of contemporary patients, all of whom have struggled with the devastating impact of trauma on their lives. We will see how, at certain critical times in the working through of trauma, dreams give us a spontaneous picture of the psyche's "second line of defenses" against the annihilation of the personal spirit. In providing these "self-portraits" of the psyche's own defensive operations, dreams aid in the healing process by symbolizing affects and fragments of personal experience that have been heretofore unrepresentable to consciousness. The idea that dreams should be capable, in this way, of representing the psyche's dissociative activities and holding its fragmented pieces together in one dramatic story is a kind of miracle of psychological life which we may too easily take for granted. Usually, when dreams do this, no-one is listening. In depth psychotherapy, we try to listen.

What dreams reveal and what recent clinical research has shown are that when trauma strikes the developing psyche of a child, a fragmentation of consciousness occurs in which the different "pieces" (Jung called them splinter-psyches or complexes) organize themselves according to certain archaic and typical (archetypal) patterns, most commonly dyads or syzygies made up of personified "beings." Typically, one part of the ego *regresses* to the infantile period, and another part *progresses*, i.e., grows up too fast and becomes precociously adapted to the outer world, often as a "false self" (Winnicott, 1960a). The *progressed part* of the personality then caretakes the *regressed part*. This dyadic structure has been independently discovered by clinicians of many different theoretical persuasions – a fact that indirectly supports its archetypal basis. We explore the writings of these clinicians in more detail in Chapters 5 and 6.

In dreams, the regressed part of the personality is usually represented as a vulnerable, young, innocent (often feminine) *child- or animal-self* who remains shamefully hidden. Occasionally it appears as a special animal – a favorite pet, a kitten, puppy, or bird. Whatever its particular incarnation, this "innocent" remainder of the whole self seems to represent a core of the individual's imperishable personal spirit – what the ancient Egyptians called the "Ba-soul," or Alchemy, the winged animating spirit of the transformation process, i.e., Hermes/Mercurius. This spirit has always been a mystery – an essence of selfhood never to be fully comprehended. It is the imperishable essence of the personality – that which Winnicott referred to as the "True Self" (Winnicott, 1960a) and which Jung, seeking a construct that would honor its transpersonal origins, called the *Self*.[2] The violation of this inner core of the personality is *unthinkable*. When other defenses fail, archetypal defenses will go to any length to protect the Self – even to the point of killing the host personality in which this personal spirit is housed (suicide).

Meanwhile, the progressed part of the personality is represented in dreams by a powerful *benevolent or malevolent great being* who protects or persecutes its vulnerable partner, sometimes keeping it imprisoned within. Occasionally, in its protective guise, the benevolent/malevolent being appears as an angel or a miraculous wild animal such as a special horse or a dolphin. More often the "caretaking" figure is daimonic and terrifying to the dream-ego. In the clinical material of Chapters 1 and 2 we will explore cases in which it presents itself as a diabolical axeman, a murderer with a shotgun, a mad doctor, a menacing "cloud," a seductive "food demon," or as the Devil himself. Sometimes the malevolent inner tormenter turns another face and presents a more benevolent aspect, thereby identifying himself as a "duplex" figure, a protector and persecutor in one. Examples of this are found in Chapter 2.

Together, the "mythologized" images of the "progressed vs. regressed" parts of the self make up what I call *the psyche's archetypal self-care system*. The "system" is archetypal because it is both archaic and typical of the psyche's self-preservative operations, and because it is developmentally earlier and more primitive than normal ego-defenses. Because these defenses seem to be "co-ordinated" by a deeper center in the personality than the ego, they have been referred to as "defenses of the Self" (Stein, 1967). We will see that this is an apt theoretical designation because it underscores the "numinous,"[3] awesome character of this "mythopoetic" structure and because the malevolent figure in the self-care system presents a compelling image of what Jung called *the dark side of the ambivalent Self*. In exploring this imagery in dream, transference, and myth, we will see that Jung's original idea of the Self as the central regulatory and ordering principle of the unconscious psyche requires revision under conditions of severe trauma.

The self-care system performs the self-regulatory and inner/outer mediational functions that, under normal conditions, are performed by the person's functioning ego. Here is where a problem arises. Once the trauma defense is organized, all relations with the outer world are "screened" by the self-care system. What was intended to be a defense against further trauma becomes a major resistance to all unguarded spontaneous expressions of self in the world. The person survives but cannot live creatively. Psychotherapy becomes necessary.

However, psychotherapy with the victims of early trauma is not easy, either for the patient or the therapist. The resistance thrown up by the self-care system in the treatment of trauma victims is legendary. As early as 1920, Freud was shaken by the extent to which a "daimonic" force in some patients resisted change and made the usual work of analysis impossible (Freud 1920b: 35). So pessimistic was he about this "repetition compulsion" that he attributed its origin to an instinctive aim in all life towards death (Freud, 1920b: 38–41) Subsequently, clinicians working with the victims of trauma or abuse have readily recognized the "daimonic" figure or forces to which Freud alludes. Fairbairn (1981) described it as an "Internal Saboteur" and Guntrip (1969) as the "anti-libidinal ego" attacking the "libidinal ego." Melanie Klein (1934) described the child's fantasies of a cruel, attacking, "bad breast;" Jung (1951) described the "negative Animus," and more recently, Jeffrey Seinfeld (1990) has written about an internal structure called simply the "Bad Object."

Most contemporary analytic writers are inclined to see this attacking figure as an internalized version of the actual perpetrator of the trauma, who has "possessed" the inner world of the trauma victim. But this popularized view is only half correct. The diabolical inner figure is often far more sadistic and brutal than any outer perpetrator, indicating that we are dealing here with a *psychological* factor set loose in the inner world by trauma – an archetypal traumatogenic agency within the psyche itself.

No matter how frightening his or her brutality, the function of this ambivalent caretaker always seems to be the protection of the traumatized remainder of the personal spirit and its *isolation from reality*. It functions, if we can imagine its inner rationale, as a kind of inner "Jewish Defense League" (whose slogan, after the Holocaust, reads "Never Again!"). "Never again," says our tyrannical caretaker, "will the traumatized personal spirit of this child suffer this badly! Never again will it be this helpless in the face of cruel reality.... before this happens I will disperse it into fragments [dissociation], or encapsulate it and soothe it with fantasy [schizoid withdrawal], or numb it with intoxicating substances [addiction], or persecute it to keep it from hoping for life in this world [depression].... In this way I will preserve what is left of this prematurely amputated childhood – of an innocence that has suffered too much too soon!"

Despite the otherwise well-intentioned nature of our Protector/Persecutor, there is a tragedy lurking in these archetypal defenses. And here we come to the crux of the problem for the traumatized individual and simultaneously the crux of the problem for the psychotherapist trying to help. This incipient tragedy results from the fact that the Protector/Persecutor is not educable. The primitive defense does not learn anything about realistic danger as the child grows up. It functions on the magical level of consciousness with the same level of awareness it had when the original trauma or traumas occurred. Each new life opportunity is mistakenly seen as a dangerous threat of re-traumatization and is therefore attacked. In this way, the archaic defenses become anti-life forces which Freud understandably thought of as part of the death instinct.

These discoveries made by exploring the inner world help us to explain two of the most disturbing findings in the literature about trauma. The first of these findings is that *the traumatized psyche is self-traumatizing*. Trauma doesn't end with the cessation of outer violation, but continues unabated in the inner world of the trauma victim, whose dreams are often haunted by persecutory inner figures. The second finding is the seemingly perverse fact that *the victim of psychological trauma continually finds himself or herself in life situations where he or she is re-traumatized*. As much as he or she wants to change, as hard as he or she tries to improve life or relationships, something more powerful than the ego continually undermines progress and destroys hope. It is as though the persecutory inner world somehow finds its outer mirror in repeated self-defeating "re-enactments" – almost as if the individual were *possessed* by some diabolical power or pursued by a malignant fate.

In the first chapter of the book we will anchor these preliminary ideas in three clinical cases and several important dreams which illustrate the diabolical side of the Self in early trauma. In Chapter 2 further examples enrich the picture by showing the self-soothing aspects of the self-care system in addition to its diabolical aspects. In Chapter 3 we will trace Freud and Jung's initial explorations of trauma's inner world and show that Jung had independently "discovered" our dyadic defensive structure as early as 1910, although he did not label it as such. In Chapter 4 we provide a compilation of Jung's views as they relate to trauma, beginning with Jung's personal boyhood trauma and how it informed his later theory. Chapter 5 reviews and critiques additional Jungian contributors to a clinical theory of trauma, and Chapter 6 surveys psychoanalytic theorists, focusing on those who describe a structure similar to our trauma defense.

By the end of Part I, the reader should have a good sense of how the dyadic defense functions in the inner world as seen from a variety of theoretical perspectives, and also an awareness of its recurrent, universal features. Given the mythopoetic features described in Part I, it will come as no surprise that these primordial defenses of the Self frequently appear in mythological material, and the demonstration of this fact is the purpose of Part II of the book. In these chapters, we will interpret several fairy tales and a short myth, the tale of Eros and Psyche (Chapter 8), in order to show how the personified imagery of the self-care system appears in mythological material. Readers unacquainted with Jung's approach may find such attention to folklore and mythology somewhat strange in a psychological work, but we must remember, as Jung has repeatedly pointed out, that *mythology is where the psyche "was" before psychology made it an object of scientific investigation.* By drawing attention to the parallels between the findings of clinical psychoanalysis and ancient religious ideation we demonstrate how the psychological struggle of contemporary patients (and those of us trying to help them) runs rather deeper into the symbolic phenomenology of the human soul than recent psychoanalytic discussions of trauma or the "dissociative disorders" are inclined to acknowledge. Not everyone is helped by an understanding of these parallels, but some people are, and for them, this "binocular" way of viewing, simultaneously, the psychological and religious phenomena is equivalent to finding a deeper meaning to their suffering, and this in itself can be healing. It is not an accident that our discipline is called "depth psychology," but for psychology to remain deep, it must keep one "eye," so to speak, on the life of man's spirit, and the vicissitudes of the spirit (including its dark manifestations) are nowhere so well documented as in the great symbol-systems of religion, mythology, and folklore. In this way, psychology and religion share, as it were, a common concern with the dynamics of human interiority.

In Chapter 7, we find our self-care system personified in the Grimms' fairy tale of the innocent Rapunzel under the protective but persecutory guardianship of the witch, and we explore some of the clinical implications of how to get this psychical "child" out of her tower. Chapter 8 describes a similar "captivity story," i.e., that of Eros and Psyche: and in Chapter 9, we explore an especially violent rendition of the Self's dark aspect in the fairy tale of Fitcher's Bird, one of the popular Bluebeard cycle of tales. Chapter Ten concludes the book with an analysis of a Scandinavian tale of Prince Lindworm, and emphasizes the role of sacrifice and choice in the resolution of the trauma defense. Throughout there latter chapters, implications for the treatment of trauma victims are interspersed in the mythic material.

By focusing the following investigation on the *inner* world of trauma, especially on unconscious fantasy as illustrated in dreams, transference, and mythology, we will be attempting to honor the *reality of the psyche* in ways that much current literature about trauma fails to do, or does only secondarily. By the reality of the psyche, I mean an intermediate realm of experience which serves as a ligament connecting the inner self and the outer world by means of symbolic processes which communicate a sense of "meaning." In my experience, a sense of the reality of the psyche is extremely elusive and hard to maintain, even for the experienced psychotherapist, because it means staying open to the unknown – to a mystery at the center of our work – and this is very difficult, especially in the area of trauma, where moral outrage is so easily aroused and with it the need for simple answers.

In an effort to place the present study in context, we should note that psychoanalysis began in a study of trauma almost one 100 years ago, but it then suffered a kind of professional amnesia on the subject. In recent years there is some indication that the profession is returning to a "trauma paradigm" once again. This renaissance of interest in trauma has been motivated by the cultural "rediscovery" of childhood physical and sexual abuse, and psychiatry's revived interest in the dissociative disorders, especially Multiple Personality Disorder and Post-traumatic Stress Disorder. Unfortunately, with very few exceptions, this literature has escaped comment by Jungian writers.[4] This fact is all the more peculiar given Jung's relevant model of the psyche's dissociability and his emphasis on ego–Self "indivisibility" (individuation). I believe that Jung's insights into the *inner* world of the traumatized psyche are especially important for contemporary psychoanalysis while, at the same time, contemporary work on trauma requires a revision of Jungian theory. The present work is an effort, on the one hand, to illustrate the value of Jung's contributions, while attempting, on the other hand, to offer certain theoretical revisions made necessary in my judgment by the findings of trauma researchers and clinicians, especially those of contemporary object-relations and self-psychologists.

The reader should be forewarned that at least two different psychoanalytic "dialects" define the language of the present investigation and the argument moves freely back and forth between them. On the one side is British object-relations – especially Winnicott – together with some of Heinz Kohut's self-psychology and, on the other, is the mythopoetic language of C. G. Jung and his followers. I consider both of these idioms essential for an understanding of trauma and its treatment.

Some of the observations in these chapters have appeared elsewhere in print (Kalsched, 1980, 1981, 1985, 1991) and others have been the subject of extended lectures at the C. G. Jung Institute in Zurich and at the Center for Depth Psychology and Jungian Studies in Katonah, New York. But the full implications of my earlier ideas for a theory of trauma and its treatment were not clear until recently. Even so, the present volume should be considered as little more than provisional – a preliminary effort to cast some light into that dark background of unconscious imagery making up the "inner world of trauma."

Part I

1

THE INNER WORLD OF TRAUMA IN ITS DIABOLICAL FORM

When innocence has been deprived of its entitlement, it becomes a diabolical spirit.

(Grotstein, 1984: 211)

In this and the following chapter, I will offer a series of clinical vignetttes and theoretical commentary in order to explore the phenomenology of a "daimonic" figure whose appearance I have encountered repeatedly in the unconscious material of patients with a history of early childhood trauma. The word "daimonic" comes from *daiomai*, which means to divide, and originally referred to moments of divided consciousness such as occur in slips of the tongue, failures in attention, or other breakthroughs from another realm of existence which we would call "the unconscious" (see von Franz, 1980a). Indeed, dividing up the inner world seems to be the intention of our figure. Jung's word for this was "dissociation," and our daimon *appears to personify the psyche's dissociative defenses in those cases where early trauma has made psychic integration impossible.*

I can best approach this topic by sharing with the reader how I became interested in it. Over the last twenty-five years of clinical work I have had a number of individuals in analysis who, after an initial period of growth and improvement, reached a kind of plateau where they seemed to stagnate in therapy and, instead of getting better as a result of the treatment, seemed instead to get stuck in a "repetition compulsion" of earlier behavior, which left them feeling defeated and hopeless. These were individuals who might be described as "schizoid" in the sense that they had suffered traumatic experiences in childhood which had overwhelmed their often unusual sensitivities and driven them inward. Often, the interior worlds into which they retreated were childlike worlds, rich in fantasy but with a very wistful, melancholy cast. In this museum-like "sanctuary of innocence" these patients clung to a remnant of their childhood experience which had been magical and sustaining at one time, but which did not grow along with the rest of them. Although they had come to therapy out of need, they did not really want to grow or change in ways that would truly satisfy that need. To be more precise, one part of them wanted to change and a stronger part *resisted* this change. They were divided within themselves.

In most cases these patients were extremely bright, sensitive individuals who had suffered, on account of this very sensitivity, some acute or cumulative emotional trauma in early life. All of them had become prematurely self-sufficient in their childhoods, cutting off genuine relations with their parents during their developing years and caretaking themselves in a cocoon of fantasy instead. They tended to see themselves as the victims of others' aggression and could not mobilize effective self-assertion when it was needed to defend themselves or to individuate. Their outward facade of toughness and self-sufficiency often concealed a secret dependency they were ashamed of, so in psychotherapy they found it very difficult to relinquish their own self-care protection and allow themselves to depend on a real person.

What gradually became clear to me through the analysis of these patients' dreams, was that they were in the grip of an internal figure who jealously cut them off from the outer world, while at the same time attacking them with merciless self-criticism and abuse. Moreover, this inner figure was such a powerful "force" that the term *daimonic* seemed an apt characterization. Sometimes in the dreams of my patients, this inner daimonic figure violently dissociated the inner world by actively attacking the dream-ego or some "innocent" part of the self with which the dream-ego was identified. At other times its goal seemed to be the encapsulation of some fragile, vulnerable part of the patient which it ruthlessly "divided off" from reality, as if to prevent it from ever being violated again. At still other times, the daimonic being was a kind of guardian angel, soothing and protecting a childlike part of the self inwardly while at the same time hiding it shamefully from the world. It could play a protective or a persecutory role – sometimes alternating back and forth between them. And to further complicate matters, this duplex image usually made its appearance in what James Hillman has called a "tandem" (Hillman, 1983). It usually did not appear alone, but was paired with an inner child or with some other more helpless or vulnerable "partner." In turn, this innocent "child" had a duplex aspect – sometimes it was "bad" and "deserved" persecution, so to speak; at other times it was "good" and received protection.

In summary, these duplex imagos, yoked together as an internal "structure," make up what I call the *archetypal self-care system*. As I hope to demonstrate in the ensuing pages, we have reason to believe this structure is a universal inner "system" in the psyche, whose role seems to be the defense and preservation of an inviolable personal spirit at the core of an individual's true self.

The question I began to ask myself, then, was: "How did the internal guardian figures of this 'system' and their vulnerable child 'clients' get organized in the unconscious, and from whence did they derive their awesome power over the patient's well-intentioned ego?"

JUNG AND DISSOCIATION

The psyche's normal reaction to a traumatic experience is to withdraw from the scene of the injury. If withdrawal is not possible, then a part of the self must be withdrawn, and for this to happen the otherwise integrated ego must split into fragments or *dissociate*. Dissociation is a normal part of the psyche's defenses against trauma's potentially damaging impact – as Jung demonstrated many years ago with his word association test (Jung, 1904). Dissociation is a trick the psyche plays on itself. It allows life to go on by dividing up the unbearable experience and distributing it to different compartments of the mind and body, especially the "unconscious" aspects of the mind and body. This means that the normally unified elements of consciousness (i.e., cognitive awareness, affect, sensation, imagery) are not allowed to integrate. Experience itself becomes discontinuous. Mental imagery may be split from affect, or both affect and image may be dissociated from conscious knowledge. Flashbacks of sensation seemingly disconnected from a behavioral context occur. The memory of one's life has holes in it – a full narrative history cannot be told by the person whose life has been interrupted by trauma.

For the person who has experienced unbearable pain, the psychological defense of dissociation allows external life to go on but at a great internal cost. The outer trauma ends and its effects may be largely "forgotten," but the psychological sequelae of the trauma continue to haunt the inner world, and they do this, Jung discovered, in the form of certain images which cluster around a strong affect – what Jung called the "feeling-toned complexes." These complexes tend to behave autonomously as frightening inner "beings," and are represented in dreams as attacking "enemies," vicious animals, etc. In his only essay explicitly about trauma, Jung wrote:

> a traumatic complex brings about dissociation of the psyche. The complex is not under the control of the will and for this reason it possesses the quality of psychic autonomy. Its autonomy consists in its power to manifest itself independently of the will and even in direct opposition to conscious tendencies: it forces itself tyrannically upon the conscious mind. The explosion of affect is a complete invasion of the individual, it pounces upon him like an enemy or a wild animal. I have frequently observed that the typical traumatic affect is represented in dreams as a wild and dangerous animal – a striking illustration of its autonomous nature when split off from consciousness.
>
> (Jung, 1928a: paras 266–7)

The nature and functioning of those dissociative mechanisms responsible for complex-formation were not clear to Jung in his early experiments, but subsequent research with patients suffering from the so-called "dissociative disorders" showed that it is not a passive, benign process whereby different parts of the mind become disconnected and "drift apart." Instead, dissociation appears to involve a good deal of aggression – apparently it involves an active attack by one part of the psyche on other parts. It is as though the normally integrative tendencies in the psyche must be interrupted by force. Splitting is a violent affair – like the splitting of an atom. This is a fact that strangely eluded Jung. Despite his awareness

13

that traumatic affect may appear in dreams as a "wild animal," he did not include violent affect in his understanding of the psyche's primitive defenses themselves. Contemporary psychoanalysis recognizes that where the inner world is filled with violent aggression, primitive defenses are present also. More specifically, we now know that *the energy for dissociation comes from this aggression.*

In the dream material of the cases below, the violent nature of these self-attacking dissociative processes is illustrated. In psychotherapy with trauma victims, it seems that as the unbearable (traumatic) childhood experience, or something resembling it in the transference, begins to emerge into consciousness, an intra-psychic figure or "force," witnessed in the patient's dreams, violently intervenes and dissociates the psyche. This figure's diabolical "purpose" seems to be to prevent the dream-ego from experiencing the "unthinkable" affect associated with the trauma. For example, in the cases below "he" cuts off the dreamer's head with an axe, shoots a helpless woman in the face with a shotgun, feeds crushed glass to a helpless animal, and "tricks" the helpless ego into captivity in a diabolical "hospital." These actions appear to fragment the patient's affective experience in such a way as to disperse the awareness of pain that has emerged or is about to emerge. In effect, the diabolical figure traumatizes the inner object world in order to prevent re-traumatization in the outer one. If this impression is correct, it means that a traumatogenic imago haunts these patient's psyches, supervising dissociative activities, reminding one of Jung's early suspicion that "fantasies can be just as traumatic in their effects as real traumata" (Jung, 1912a: para. 217). In other words, the full pathological effect of trauma requires an outer event *and a psychological factor.* Outer trauma alone doesn't split the psyche. *An inner psychological agency – occasioned by the trauma – does the splitting.*

CLINICAL EXAMPLE: THE AXEMAN

I will not soon forget the first case where these possibilities began to dawn on me. The patient was a young female artist who, later treatment revealed, had suffered repeated physical and sexual abuse by her alcoholic father, who was her only living parent and someone who, as a little girl, she had loved deeply. When this woman came to her first therapy appointment she arrived on a motorcycle, dressed in black leather, and spent the entire hour in cynical condemnation of her roommate who had recently gotten married and had a child. She was tough, contemptuous toward others, cynical about life in general, and extremely armored against any acknowledgement of her own pain. As close as she could get to acknowledging any difficulties of her own was to mention a whole bundle of psychosomatic complaints – chronic back pain, incapacitating pre-menstrual cramps, episodic asthma, and recurrent epileptic-like symptoms where she would "go blank" for several minutes. This had frightened her enough for her to seek help. Her inner life was haunted by morbid feelings of being a living dead-person and was full of overwhelming rage, portrayed in horrifying images of mutilation and dismemberment. These images of amputees, of chopped-off hands, arms, and heads, kept spontaneously appearing in her artwork, and everyone but the patient was appalled by them.

The following dream occurred about one year into her treatment immediately after a session in which, for the first time, this very self-sufficient patient had allowed herself to feel small and vulnerable in response to my departure for a summer vacation. In an unguarded moment and with the coquettish smile of an adolescent girl, she had grudgingly acknowledged she would miss me and her therapy hour. That night, after writing a long letter to me about how she could not continue her treatment (!) because she was becoming "too dependent," she had this dream.

> I am in my room, in bed. I suddenly realize I have forgotten to lock the doors to my apartment. I hear someone come into the building downstairs, walk to my apartment door – then walk in. I hear the footsteps approach the door of my room ... then open it. A very tall man with a white ghost-like face and black holes for eyes walks in with an axe. He raises it over my neck and brings it down!. . . I wake up in terror.

Interpretation and theoretical commentary

Here we have an image of a violent decapitation – an intended split between mind and body. The neck, as an integrating and connecting link between the two, is about to be severed. The room in which the dream took place was her current bedroom in an apartment she shared with a roommate. Usually afraid of the dark, she always double-locked the door to this room before retiring. The unlocked outer door was the door to her apartment, and this door she also compulsively checked whenever she was home alone. In the dream, the ghost-like man apparently has access to both doors, just as her father had had unrestricted access to the bedroom where she slept and also to her body. Often my patient – when only 8 years old – had heard his footsteps approach her room before his regular sexual violations of her.

Clearly her "unguarded" moment of neediness within the transference during the previous hour was equivalent to her "forgetting" to lock the door in her dream and constituted a breach in her usual ego-defenses. Through this breach comes a kind of "death spirit," an image of unmitigated horror – the ghost-like man with black holes for his eyes. The patient recognized this dream as one version of a repetitive nightmare from her childhood in which she would be attacked by threatening figures. But why, I wondered, had she dreamed about such a horrific image the very night she felt emotionally open and vulnerable in relation to me and her therapy?

In keeping with our prior hypotheses about the function of the self-care system, the explanation seems clear enough. Apparently, the vulnerable admission of feelings of dependency in the previous hour was experienced by some part of the patient's psyche (the ghost-like man) as a dire threat – the threat of re-experiencing the unbearable pain of needing an outer object (her father) and having this need traumatically rejected. In other words, the patient's emergent feeling for me in the transference was linked associatively with her childhood devastation – the unbearable suffering she had experienced in desperately loving a man who then beat her and sexually abused her. As this "love" and neediness came into consciousness, associated with *unthinkable* despair from her unremembered childhood, it triggered overwhelming anxiety, which in turn triggered her dissociative defenses. And so she was going to "split" this off and leave her therapy! This splitting behavior was further represented in her dream as the axe with which the murderous figure prepared to sever the connections (links) between her body (where many of her traumatic memories were stored) and her mind. This figure, then, represents the patient's *resistance* to re-experiencing feelings of dependency and probably to vulnerable feelings in general. He represents a "second line" of defense, when the usual ego-defenses have been penetrated and unacceptable levels of anxiety have been constellated. As a truly daimonic figure, he would cut her off from her embodied, feeling self – in the world – in order to keep her in her persecutory "mind," where he would have total control over her unrealized personal spirit. Such is the perverse "goal" of the self-care system when early trauma has simply broken the heart too many times.

The self-care system and the psyche's auto-immune reaction

In the intervening years since my experience with this patient, I have come to see it as almost axiomatic that in the inner world of the trauma victim we will find such diabolized personifications of self-attack and abuse. In the dreams of trauma patients I have analyzed over the years, the diabolical Trickster has performed the following acts: he or she has tried to cut the dreamer's head off with an axe, has brutally raped the dreamer, petrified the dreamer's pet animals, buried a child alive, seduced the patient into performing sado-masochistic sexual favors, trapped the dream-ego in a concentration camp, tortured the patient by breaking his knees in three places, shot a beautiful woman in the face with a shotgun, and performed a variety of other destructive acts, the purpose of which seems to be nothing less than driving the patient's terrified dream-ego into a state of horror, anxiety, and despair.

How do we understand this? It is bad enough that our hapless patient suffered unbearable outer trauma in early childhood. Now the psyche seems to perpetuate this trauma in unconscious fantasy, flooding the patient with continued anxiety, tension and dread – even in sleep. What could possibly be the purpose or telos of such diabolical self-torture?

One hint at a possible understanding comes from the derivation of the word "diabolical," from the Greek *dia* (across) and *ballein* (to throw) (*OED*), hence, "to throw across or apart." From this derives the common meaning of "diabolos" as the Devil, i.e., he who crosses, thwarts, or dis-integrates (dissociation). The antonym of diabolic is "symbolic," from *sym-ballein*, meaning "to throw together." We know that both processes – throwing apart and throwing together – are essential to psychological life and that in their apparently antagonistic activities we have a pair of opposites which, when optimally balanced, character- ize the homeostatic processes of the psyche's self-regulation. Without "throwing apart" we would have no differentiation, and without "throwing together" there would be no synthetic integration into larger wholes. These regulatory processes are especially active at the transitional interface between the psyche and outer reality – precisely the threshold at which defense is necessary. We might imagine this self-regulatory activity, then, as the *psyche's self-care system, analagous to the body's immune system.*

Like the body's immune system, these complementary dynamisms of dis- integration/re-integration are involved in complicated gatekeeping functions at the thresholds between inner and outer worlds and between the conscious and unconscious inner systems. Strong currents of affect reaching the psyche from the outside world or from the body must be metabolized by symbolic processes, rendered into language, and integrated into the narrative "identity" of the developing child. "Not-me" elements of experience must be distinguished from "me" elements and must be rejected aggressively (outwardly) and repressed firmly (inwardly).

In the trauma response, we might imagine that something goes wrong in these naturally protective "immune responses." It is an almost universal finding in the trauma literature that children who have been abused cannot mobilize aggression to expel noxious, "bad", or "not-me" elements of experience, such as our young artist's hatred of the abusive father. The child is unable to hate the loved parent – and instead identifies with the father as "good" and, through a process which Sandor Ferenczi (1933) called "identification with the aggressor," the child takes the father's aggression into the inner world and *comes to hate itself and its own need.*

If we apply this analysis to our case, we can see that as her vulnerable need within the transference began to emerge, the patient's introjected hatred (now amplified by archetypal energy) attacked the links between body and mind in an effort to cut the affective connections. The white-faced, black-eyed "terminator" in her psyche is, however, much more than the introjected father. He is a primitive, archaic, archetypal figure, personifying the terrifying dismembering rage of the collective psyche and, as such, represents *the dark side of the Self.* The outer catalyst for this inner figure may be the personal father, but the damage to the inner world is done by the psyche's Yahweh-like rage, directed back upon the self. It was for this reason that neither Freud nor Jung were convinced that outer trauma alone was responsible for splitting the psyche. It was rather an interior, psychological factor that ultimately did the worst damage – witness the diabolical axeman.

Developmental hypotheses on the origin of the Dark Self

Why, then, does the primordial ambivalent Self, both light and dark, good and evil, appear with such regularity in the inner world – even for patients who have not suffered outright physical or sexual abuse? The following is a brief description of how I understand this issue developmentally, in light of clinical experience with patients like our young artist with her horrifying inner world.

We must assume that the inner world of the very young infant is one in which painful, agitated, or uncomfortable feeling-states oscillate with feelings of comfort, satisfaction, and safety in such a way that gradually two images of the self and the object gradually build up. These early self- and object-representations tend to be structured in opposites and to embody opposing affects. One is "good," the other "bad;" one is loving, the other hateful, and so on. In their original condition, affects are primal and archaic like volcanic storms, quickly dissipating or giving way to their opposite, depending on the nature of environmental provision. Negative, aggressive affects tend to fragment the psyche (dissociation), whereas positive, soothing affects accompanying adequate mediation by the mother, have the effect of integrating these fragments and restoring homeostatic balance.

The mediational capacities that later become the ego are, at the beginning of life, totally vested in the maternal self-object who serves as a kind of external metabolizing organ for the infant's experience. Through her empathy, the mother senses the infant's agitation, picks up and comforts her infant, helps to name and give form to its feeling-states, and restores homeostatic balance. As this happens repeatedly over time, the infant psyche gradually differentiates and he or she begins to contain his or her affects, i.e., to develop an ego capable of experiencing strong emotion and tolerating conflict among emotions. Until this occurs, the infant's inner self- and object-representations are split, archaic and typical (archetypal). Archetypal inner objects are numinous, overwhelming, and mytho-logical. They exist in the psyche as antinomies or opposites, which gradually come together in the unconscious as dual unities which are alternately blissful or terrifying, such as the Good Mother and her "tandem," the Terrible Mother. Among the many such *coincidenta oppositora* in the deep unconscious is one central archetype which seems to stand for the very principle of unity among all the opposing elements of the psyche and which participates in their volcanic dynamism. This central organizing agency in the collective psyche is what Jung called the archetype of the Self, both light and dark. It is characterized by extraordinary numinosity, and an encounter with it can involve either salvation or dismemberment, depending upon which side of the Self's numinosity is ex-perienced by the ego. As the "unity of unities," the Self stands for the image of God in the human psyche, although the God embodied in the Self is primitive, a *mysterium tremendum*, combining both love and hate, like the Old Testament Yahweh. Until the ego develops, the unified Self cannot actualize – but once constellated, it becomes the "ground" of the ego and its "guide" in the rhythmic unfolding of the individual's inborn personality potential. Michael Fordham (1976) described this as the de-integration/re-integration cycle of the Self.

In healthy psychological development, everything depends upon humanization and integration of the archetypal opposites inherent in th. the infant and young child wrestles with tolerable experiences of frustration. in the context of a good-enough (not perfect) primary relationship. The ch. ruthless aggression does not destroy his object and he can work through to gu. reparation, and what Klein called the "depressive position." However, inasmuch as the traumatized child has *intolerable* experiences in the object world, the negative side of the Self does not personalize, remaining archaic. The internal world continues to be menaced by a diabolical, inhuman figure. Aggressive, destructive energies – ordinarily available for reality-adaptation and for healthy defense against toxic not-self objects – are directed back into the inner world. This leads to a continuation of trauma and abuse by inner objects long after the outer persecutory activity has stopped. We turn now to a second case in which such inner persecution is starkly illustrated.

MRS. Y. AND THE SHOTGUNNER

Mrs. Y, an attractive, likeable, professionally accomplished divorced woman in her early 60s, sought analysis because of generalized depression and an awareness that some part of her was withheld in all her relationships – leaving her with an underlying sense of loneliness. From previous therapy, she knew that the roots of this "schizoid" problem lay deeply buried somewhere in a childhood of which she had almost no happy memories. Her history revealed an early family situation of emotional poverty in the midst of material luxury. Her narcissistic mother, already symbiotically attached to the first-born 3-year-old brain-damaged son, paid the patient little or no attention – never physically touching her except for rigidly routinized feedings and toilet training. A younger sister was born when the patient was 2 years old. Whatever emotional life Mrs. Y. could eke out as the middle child in this family came from a succession of nurses and nannies. With them she remembered crying, raging, spitting, and rebelling. Nothing of this ever happened with her mother. Instead, the mother was "untouchable" – remote – tied to the other two siblings or to the father. A repeated childhood nightmare showed the mother watching indifferently from the porch while the patient was run down by the laundry truck in the driveway of her house.

The patient's father, whom she adored, was preoccupied with business. He seemed to prefer her younger sister (also the mother's favorite) and was otherwise in orbit around the narcissistic, controlling mother. Although he took care of the patient when she was sick, and spent time alone with her, he was also subject to attacks of rage which were terrifying. When Mrs. Y. was 8 years old, her father developed a chronic illness and was home in bed for six years until he died. During these years the patient was afraid to disturb him. All emotion around his death – indeed, even the reality of the illness itself – was denied. The result was that the patient could never make her needs or feelings known to either parent for her entire childhood. To have a childhood in which needs cannot be expressed to primary caretakers is tantamount to losing one's childhood altogether, and such was Mrs. Y.'s experience. She retreated into an inner world of unconscious fantasy, convinced that some unfathomable "badness" had condemned her to despair in this world. For reasons unknown to her, she felt chronically ashamed and, despite her constant efforts to please people through her considerable school achievements, she never felt that she made anyone very happy.

The psyche's natural anesthesia for the "cumulative trauma" in a childhood such as this renders most patients incapable of remembering specific traumatic events, much less experiencing them on an emotional level in analysis. Such was the case for Mrs. Y. We talked *about* the deprivation in her early life, but we could not recover it *experientially*. Often, in my experience, it is not until some aspect of the early traumatic situation emerges in the *transference* that analyst and patient are given emotional access to the real problem, and it is just such an incident I wish to report.

While at her mother's home one day, Mrs. Y. found some old home movies taken when she was 2 years old. In one of the films, taken at a family party, she saw her knee-high, 2-year-old, skinny self, crying and desperately running from one pair of legs to another, looking up imploringly for help, being ignored and then rushing to another pair of legs where she pleaded again, until finally, overcome by grief and rage, the nanny came and dragged her off kicking and screaming. At her analytic session the next day, Mrs. Y. reported all this in her usual dispassionate way, covering her sadness with humor and sarcasm. Inwardly, she seemed very upset.

To capitalize on this fortuitous access to strong feeling about her childhood self, I suggested that we schedule a special session and watch the film together. Obviously pleased but embarrassed by this offer (she had never heard of such a thing in therapy) and protesting that she could never presume upon my time like that, offering various reasons why this would be too much to ask, etc., she nevertheless accepted the idea and we set up an extra "movie-session."

As expected, this new situation was somewhat awkward for both the patient and myself, but after some joking and laughter around our mutual awkwardness with this new experience, she relaxed as we talked about the various people in the film leading up to the moment she had described. And then together we witnessed the horrific despairing trauma captured some 55 years earlier on film. We watched this part a second time and during this second review, Mrs. Y. started to cry. I too found my eyes full of tears which, as far as I could tell, the patient didn't notice. Mrs. Y. quickly recovered her composure but then broke down again and we struggled together with her mixture of genuine grief and empathy for her despairing childhood self, and her efforts to recover her composure with self-demeaning remarks about her "weakness" and "hysteria" together with awkward efforts to reassure me that she was all right and would soon leave.

The following session, through many awkward silences, we processed what had happened. "You became a human being last time," she said:

"I had neutralized you until you offered to see that movie with me and then I saw your tears. My first reaction was 'Oh God, I didn't mean to do that . . . to upset you. Please, I'll never do it again!' – As though affecting you in any way was a terrible, thing. But secretly I was pleased and deeply moved inside. You were so human. I couldn't get over it," she continued. "I kept saying over and over 'you affected him! you affected him! He cares about you!' It was very moving. I'll never forget that session! It felt like the beginning of something new. All my armor fell away. I was up late into the night writing about it in my journal."

But that same night Mrs. Y. also reported an alarming dream. In this dream, an ominous male figure we had both come to know from previous dreams, made his dark appearance again. Here is the dream she reported:

The scene is somber, with many dim male figures lurking in the shadows. The colors are muted, sepia tones. There was going to be a joyful reunion between two women. Perhaps they are sisters, long separated. I am in a happy, anticipatory mood, and am waiting in a hall overlooking a double staircase and balcony. The first woman appears on the ground floor. She's wearing an incredibly bright kelly-green suit. Suddenly a dim figure, a man, jumps out from behind a curtain and shoots her in the face with a shotgun! She falls, the colors are startling: bright green and blood red. The other woman, eager to see her friend, appears entering from the left onto the balcony. She is dressed in bright bright red. She leans over the balcony to see the green/red body. Her shock is great. She vomits great gushes of red blood in her grief and falls over backwards.

The patient's main reaction to this dream was horror and revulsion. She could not understand this dream in light of her experience in the session, although she knew it was linked somehow. In working with the dream, I started with the anticipated joyful reunion between the sisters and asked her to associate to that feeling. She came up with nothing. Suspecting, then, that she was avoiding the transferential "union" of the previous hour, I wondered out loud whether perhaps she was in great conflict about allowing the feelings for me that had come up the previous hour to surface again, or to even entertain them within an inner space inside herself. She blushed and agreed that this might be so. She then began to get in touch with the part of her that minimized and contemptuously dismissed this feeling (the shotgunner). Its negative and frightening voice sometimes spoke to her with phrases like: "That's all bullshit – his feelings weren't real – it was just a technique – it's all just a business relationship anyway – he shows you out and then the next one comes in for the same treatment."

Further associations emerged. The shotgunner's cruelty in response to a hoped-for connection reminded her of earlier male figure from a dream the previous year who had ruthlessly killed a primitive octopus-like creature that was also trying to make contact. She thought the double staircase and balcony created a shape like a uterus, while the red and green reminded her of Christmas, which in turn reminded her of Rubens' painting *The Slaughter of the Innocents*, depicting King Herod's envious attempt to murder the Christ-child by having his soldiers kill all male children under two years of age. This biblical event had always partially spoiled the Christmas story for her and filled her with dread whenever she heard it or saw Rubens' painting. She also mentioned that red and green are complementary colors – if you close your eyes after seeing one of them, the inner after-image is its complement. Finally, she was reminded that she had had bright red hair as a girl and that her mother had never let her wear red.

I had forgotten her previous dream, so I looked it up. It was from a period six months earlier in her analysis at a time when she had just met an interesting man and become emotionally and sexually involved with him. We had not worked on this dream, but my notes indicated that she was very hopeful about this new relationship and excited about the rekindled sexual feelings she was having. The night after her first rendezvous with this man she had the octopus dream as follows:

> I'm lying in that childhood bed of mine. I'm screaming in fear, having some nightmare. I hear this very faint whisper saying that I've been heard by somebody. I feel terribly guilty because I've woken up the person or interrupted them. Then, somehow related to this scene, a big trash-can has spilled. In its there's a slug-like octopus creature. At first I am disgusted with this thing, but then I begin to play with it. I tap the floor in front of the can and this tentacle reaches out playfully – kitten-like – and touches a pencil I'm holding. At this point two men come in. One is wearing dark glasses with mirrored lenses. He takes them off, grinds up the lenses and feeds the crushed glass to this animal so it'll die a long slow death. I'm appalled at the cruelty. I turn my back on it.

Interpretation and theoretical commentary

So here we have two important affect-laden relational events in Mrs. Y.'s life – one in the transference, another with her new male friend – followed by dramatic "statements" from the unconscious in response: a shotgun blast in the face of the green-dressed woman seeking reunion with her long-lost sister, on the one hand, and the cruel man who feeds crushed glass to the octopus on the other. The patient notes that the shotgunner dream so horrified her that she was numb and could hardly remember the events from the previous session. In other words, the dream itself was a trauma and had the same effect as a real-life trauma, i.e., dissociation from affect. This seemed like re-traumatization by fantasy. Why, I wondered. would her dream do this?

Developmental considerations

To understand this we have to go back to her childhood situation. From observing the film and exploring her memories, the patient and I were already aware that all

22

dependency-needs in her childhood had been denied. Given that childhood is by definition a dependent period of life, this meant my patient had been made ashamed of her own needs repeatedly and was repeatedly frustrated to the point of raging temper tantrums. These also could not be tolerated, so the result was a split in her inner world where the rage she felt toward her neglectful parents was used to repress the neediness about which now even she had grown intolerant. So the aggressive energies of the psyche are turned back upon the dependent aspects and we have an internal environment where self-attack for neediness is a constant occurrence. This internal attack becomes what Bion (1959) called an "attack against linking," and so the archetypal aggressive energies that rage through the psyche dismember it *in order to keep the ego from feeling its own pain.*

When the linkages are attacked within the inner world, the natural processes of symbolic integration cannot occur. The psyche cannot metabolize its own experience and render it meaningful. This is what Winnicott meant when he said that severe trauma could not be encompassed within the area of symbolic illusion or the child's omnipotence (Winnicott, 1965: 145). We see this problem illustrated in the dreams of soldiers who suffer an acute trauma in wartime – such as a soldier who lights his buddy's cigarette in a foxhole and sees his head blown off by sniper fire. These soldiers' nightmares are pure repetition of the unbearable event (see Wilmer, 1986). The psyche cannot symbolize something this unbearable until much later. Slowly, if such a traumatic event can be told and retold, the dreams start to symbolize the experience until eventually it is metabolized. But for sustained, unbearable childhood trauma, the archaic defensive system must come into play, and this system annihilates the architecture of the inner psychological world. Experience is rendered meaningless. Thoughts and images are disconnected from affect. The resulting state is what Joyce McDougall (1985) calls "alexithymia," or having no words for feelings.

This process might be imagined as analogous to the circuit-breaker in a house. If too much electricity comes in, i.e., more than the wires of the house can carry without burning up, then the circuit blows and the connection to the outside world is annihilated. But in the psyche the process is more complicated because there are two sources of energy – both the outside world and inner world, the unconscious. So when the psychological circuit-breaker trips, it shuts off both. The person must be defended against dangerous stimulation from the outer world, but also from those needs and longings which arise from deep within.

Shame and self-attack

As I interpreted this material, it seemed that my offer of the special session, as well as my empathic tears in response to the movie we watched, had opened up a level of need or longing in the transference, and had also opened up my patient's unconscious *feeling of shame about this need,* (i.e., she felt the need was "bad," "weak," etc.) which had heretofore been unavailable in the analysis. She was at first terribly ashamed at having "upset me" with her "bad" (because needy) tearful feelings. (The extent of the patient's feeling of shame appears in the octopus dream as the guilt for having been heard and awakened someone with her screaming.) Yet my own unintended self-disclosure of feeling (tears) reduced her shame and made it easier for her to experience her own "bad" vulnerability.

There was a price to be paid for this, however, and here is where the dreams present a fuller picture of her intra-psychic state. It seems that a very important inner figure connected to her shame did not like this exposure of vulnerability and possibly mistook it as a signal for immanent re-traumatization. In other words, vulnerable longings presumably preceded earlier traumatic ruptures and now, fifty-five years later, a recurrence of such vulnerability serves as a warning to the guardian shotgunner that the trauma may occur again. This would be unbearable, so the diablical introject dissociates the ego from its emerging affect (shotgun blast).

If we understand "killing" in dreams as an obliteration of awareness or profound dissociation, then we see that the psyche of the traumatized person cannot countenance re-exposure of the same vulnerable part-self representation as (apparently) occurred in the original traumatic situation. The original humiliating shame must be avoided at all costs. The price, however, is severance from the potentially "corrective" influence of reality. Here we have the psyche's self-care system gone mad.

Like the immune system of the body, the self-care system carries out its functions by actively attacking what it takes to be "foreign" or "dangerous" elements. Vulnerable parts of the self's experience in reality are seen as just such "dangerous" elements and are attacked accordingly. These attacks serve to undermine the hope in real object-relations and to drive the patient more deeply into fantasy. And just as the immune system can be tricked into attacking the very life it is trying to protect (auto-immune disease), so the self-care system can turn into a "self-destruct system" which turns the inner world into a nightmare of persecution and self-attack.

Both the "shotgunner" dream and the "octopus" dream associated with it give eloquent testimony to the annihilating self-attack suffered by the patient as she tried to reach out for a real object in the world in the hope of meeting a need. Many analysts would interpret these figures as "introjections of the perpetrator" (although there was no single perpetrator here) or perhaps as introjections of the mother's sadism or "negative animus." It would be more correct to say that these malicious killers *captured rather the mythological level of the patient's childhood experience of shame*. The resulting image is an *archetypal inner object*, a feature of the inner world of trauma that only an archetypal understanding can encompass adequately.

In the dream featuring the shotgunner, Mrs. Y.'s nascent renewed hope for connection within the transference was symbolized by the long-awaited reunion between two women, which I would interpret as complementary aspects of her feminine self-identity (green, the color of vegetative life, and red, the color of blood, are both symbols of life-energy) which the dream says "belonged together" but which had been separated previously (early dissociation from the mother in infancy?). This reunion, says the dream, will take place in a womb-like structure (the two stairways and balcony), indicating a revival of the maternal containing environment, presumably in the transference. The response of the unconscious to this anticipated connection is shocking – a traumatic "death" to the vulnerable figure reaching out for contact (the woman in green).

Even in her associations to the red and green of Christmas (King Herod's slaughter of the innocents) the same theme emerges: potential new life is snuffed out by a tyrannical masculine "ruling principle" who cannot countenance the threat to his powerful control by the miraculous child of light. Similarly, in the octopus dream (also occasioned by a new, hoped-for relationship) the undefended, archaic, "disgusting" trash-can part of the self reaches out "kitten-like" to make contact. This again is the apparent signal for the arrival of the violent, sadistic male image who emerges at the critical moment to bring death into the dream and traumatically end the "reaching out" process. It is interesting that he does this with crushed glass from a "polarized" lens – the fragmented remnants of the ocular lens which allows him to see "out" but no-one to see "in." Given that consciousness means literally "knowing with another," our octopus-killer might be thought of as a kind of anti-consciousness factor in the psyche. The dreamer "turns her back" on the scene, i.e., dissociates herself from the violence of this inner process. She cannot "look at" it.

Trauma and the repetition compulsion

With such a terrifying sadistic figure lurking in her psyche, it was of course no surprise when, following the romantic evening with her new friend, Mrs. Y. had a great deal of difficulty pursuing the relationship afterwards – despite the friend's initial interest in her. She found great resistance in herself which she could not rationally explain but which, we were able to discover, represented her resistance to being re-exposed to the potentially annihilating shame originating in her "forgotten" childhood trauma. It was as though her psyche was "remembering" an unthinkable similar event from long ago.

The reader will note that these assumptions about the dangers inherent in hoping for new life or relationship seem to be the same assumptions by which the patient's inner terminator operates. In other words, in killing off her own feeling of hope, the patient acts in "identification with the aggressor" in herself – as if she is "possessed" by him. In this way the persecutory, anxiety-ridden inner world of trauma is recapitulated in outer life and the trauma victim is "compelled to repeat" the self-defeating behavior.

Such is the devastating nature of the trauma cycle and the resistance it throws up to psychotherapy. As Mrs. Y. and I worked through the resolution of her "trauma-complex" we encountered again and again the cycle of hope, vulner-ability, fear, shame, and self-attack that always led to the predictable repetition of depression. Every moment of intimacy or personal accomplishment was an occasion for her daimon to whisper that it would all be taken from her, or that she didn't deserve it, or that she was an imposter and a fraud and would soon be humiliated. Fortunately, we were able to work on this cycle in the intimacy of the transference/counter-transference relationship and could thereby "catch" the daimon at his tricks in the moment-to-moment changes of feeling during the sessions.

Without the consciousness that can only come in such a process of working through, the inner world of trauma, with its archetypal defensive processes, duplicates itself in the patient's outer life (repetition compulsion) in a pattern which Freud justly called *daimonic*. In Jung's language, we might say that the original traumatic situation posed such danger to personality survival that it was not retained in memorable *personal* form but only in *daimonic* archetypal form. This is the collective or "magical" layer of the unconscious and cannot be assimilated by the ego until it has been "incarnated" in a human interaction. As archetypal dynamism it "exists" in a form that cannot be recovered by the ego *except as an experience of re-traumatization.* Or, to put it another way, the unconscious repetition of traumatization in the inner world which goes on incessantly must become a *real* traumatization with an object in the world if the inner system is to be "unlocked."

This is why a careful monitoring of transference/counter-transference dynamics is so important in our work with severe trauma. The patient wishes to depend upon the analyst, to "let go" of the self-care system, and get well again, but the system itself is much more powerful than the ego – at least initially, and so the patient inadvertently resists the very surrender to the process that would restore a feeling of spontaneity and aliveness. To hold these patients responsible for this resistance is a terrible mistake, not just technically but structurally and psycho-dynamically as well. The patient is already feeling blamed for some nameless "badness" inside, so interpretations which emphasize the patient's "acting out" or avoidance of responsibility merely drive home the conviction of failure. In many respects, it is not "they," the patients, who resist the process at an ego level. Rather, their psyches are battlegrounds on which the titanic forces of dissociation and integration are at war over the traumatized personal spirit. The patient must, of course, become more conscious and responsible for a relationship to his or her tyrannical defenses, but this consciousness must include the humble realization that archetypal defenses are much more powerful than the ego.

The prominence of the archetypal defense system explains why the "negative therapeutic reaction" is such a prominent feature in our work with these patients. Unlike the usual analytic patient, we must remember that for the person carrying around a dissociated trauma experience, integration or "wholeness" is initially experienced as the worst thing imaginable. These patients do not experience an increase of power or enhanced functioning when the repressed affect or traumatogenic experience first emerges into consciousness. They go numb, or split, or act out, somatize, or abuse substances. Their very survival as cohesive "selves" has depended upon primitive dissociative operations which *resist* integration of the trauma and its associated affects – even to the point of dividing up the ego's "selves" into part-personalities. Analytic work with them, therefore, must involve "softer" techniques than the usual interpretations and reconstructions we consider mutative in analysis. Great attention must be given to the creation of a safe physical space and a safe interpersonal environment within which dreams and fantasies can emerge and be worked with in a more playful, open-ended fashion than the usual analytic interpretation allows. All forms of the so-called "creative-arts" psychotherapies are extremely helpful toward this end and often these will open up traumatic affect much faster than purely verbal exploration.

Grief and the process of working through

To return to our case, it is worth noting that instead of dissociated awareness (turning her back in the octopus dream), it is the emotion of overwhelming grief that characterizes the shotgunner dream. This grief over the lost union is felt by the woman in red (clearly an identity figure for the patient) as she witnesses the lost friend, now killed by the shotgun blast. If we consider what Masud Khan (1983: 47) means by the "space potential of the dream towards self-experience," we might speculate that this grief is the patient's previously unfelt mourning for all the lost satisfactions and unmet needs of her childhood, presented in a dream image – now that a positive transference is encouraging the opening up of her inner world and its trauma – so she can "see" it and relate to it. Her grief unites, as it were, the hope of anticipation and the violent disappointment of loss. Both sides of the archetype – the "tearing apart" and the "throwing together" – are held together in the overarching symbolic narrative of the dream. This is an important reminder of the healing efficacy of dream experience, quite apart from the interpretive meaning our analysis may give it.

The inability to mourn is the single most telling symptom of a patient's early trauma. Normal mourning requires an idealized self-object with whom the young child merges and around whom the child's omnipotence can first be experienced – then slowly given up through what Heinz Kohut called the mother's "tolerable failures in empathy" (see Kohut, 1971: 64). This process of normal mourning is, according to Kohut, how internal psychic structure is built and how the archetypal world is humanized. If this empathically attuned self-object is never experienced by the child, or is experienced inadequately, then the archaic idealized and diabolized figures we have described in this chapter haunt the child's inner world in archetypal form and substitute for the ego-structure that would otherwise have been consolidated.

In the two previous cases, the diabolical figure has appeared as a true *agent of death*, attempting to murder the dream-ego or its identificatory object. In this form he seems to represent a truly perverse factor in psychological life. His dis-integrative activity constitutes a formidable resistance to psychotherapy or, for that matter, to any form of personality change, growth, or vital living. While it is not necessary to propose a "death instinct" in the psyche, I believe it was this diabolical factor in the psyche which Freud and Klein were concerned about when they elaborated the notion of an intra-psychic anti-life force (Thanatos) and its "repetition compulsion" (see Freud, 1926).

It would not be appropriate to attribute the archaic violent energies of this figure to the "shadow" – at least not in the way Jung intended the shadow to represent the coherent ego's dark alter-personality, split off in moral development and later integrated in the interest of the "wholeness" of personality. Clearly, this figure belongs to a more primitive level of ego development and corresponds to what Jung designated as the "archetypal shadow" or the "magic demon with mysterious powers" (Jung, 1916: para. 153). If anything, this figure, whose unfeeling murderous acts assure psychic disintegration, is closer to incarnate evil in the personality – the dark side of the Godhead or Self.

In addition to killing, this diabolical figure accomplishes its purposes by encapsulating a part of the psyche and sealing it off. Our next case illustrates this role of the inner daimon. By thus imprisoning a relatively "innocent" part of the personality, it seeks to assure its protection from further abuse. In order to accomplish this, our daimon now appears as a Trickster, seducing the ego into addictive behaviors and other aberrant distractive activities which bring on a variety of "altered states." He is the true "oblivion-seeker" in the psyche, personifying the psyche's undertow toward regression. He becomes the inner voice that tempts the ego with intoxicating substances, including food or alcohol, away from any struggle with outer reality.

MARY AND THE FOOD DAIMON

Jung once said that "compulsion is the great mystery of human life" (Jung, 1955: para. 151) – an involuntary motive force in the psyche ranging all the way from mild interest to possession by a diabolical spirit. Freud was also deeply impressed by the "uncanny" aspect of what he called the "compulsion to repeat," a seemingly universal destructive tendency in the psyche of his very resistant patients (see Freud, 1919: 238). In the case of Mary we will be exploring the world of compulsive addiction and will see how the diabolical figure of our previous two cases appears again as a seductive "food daimon" and also as a diabolical "doctor," seducing the patient's ego into oblivion and anesthetizing it against feeling.

Mary, an overweight middle-aged Catholic woman came to see me for psychotherapy during the final stages of her mother's terminal illness. In addition to her grief over this impending loss, she complained of a sometimes desperate loneliness made worse by what she called "binge eating," and she was worried about the fact that she had had no sexual experience and that, indeed, she had no sexual desire that she was aware of. On the outside she presented a kind of rough and ready, no-nonsense exterior, with a keen – albeit self-deprecatory – sense of humor. I found myself liking her immediately. She was a pediatric nurse – a very competent one – and held leadership roles in various public groups. But underneath she felt like a fragile bird without feathers. As the oldest child in a very large rural family from Pennsylvania, she had taken care of the younger siblings and become the caretaking confidante of her alcoholic, phobic mother, who spent most of her time in bed crying and bitterly complaining about their lack of money or the father's cruelty. Instead of getting solace and mirroring for her developing self, Mary had been forced to mirror and caretake the mother.

This went on until she left for the convent at the age of 16. She then embarked upon an ascetic life of prayer and service to the various mother superiors, until twenty years later when her religious order lost most of its members and she no longer felt needed – at which point she left. By the time she came to see me ten years later she was an established workaholic, and when she was not working she was caring for what was left of her extended family. The father, a benign figure, but uninvolved in her life, had died some years earlier. A positive transference soon developed and I rapidly assumed the role of the dead mother – once a week this very delightful woman with a keen sense of humor would come to her session and "take care" of me. She did this by regaling me with outrageously entertaining stories about her very disturbed family and the extraordinarily incestuous goings-on that regularly transpired on the farm among her brothers and sisters, aunts, uncles, nephews, nieces, and a menagerie of farm animals, each and everyone with their own eccentric personality. These stories were punctuated with stories from her Overeaters Anonymous meetings – always about other people – and the closest we could get to her inner life were descriptions of her struggle to lose weight.

After several months of this family gossip, I began, ever so gently, to share with Mary my impression that all this talk about other people might be avoiding the deeper personal feelings which were the reason for her having come into therapy in the first place. I recalled Winnicott's comment that patients like this, in presenting a false self, are rather like a nurse who brings a sick baby for treatment. The nurse chats with the doctor about all sorts of pleasantries, but the therapy doesn't start until the child-part is contacted and starts to play (see Winnicott, 1960a). At one point, I said that her stories seemed to me like the broken wing display of a mother bird whose nest of eggs is being approached by a dangerous intruder and that I was being "led away" from *her own* psychic pain and vulnerability by her entertaining descriptions of everyone else's. Her response to this was to feel criticized – even humiliated – and confused about what she was supposed to do. What did I want? Maybe therapy was not going to work for her after all. But despite her protests, I could tell that another part of her – her healthier part – was peeking out, curious – and that this part of her liked my comment.

Slowly, as we worked through this injury in the transference, Mary began to grope for a language with which to open up the great undifferentiated mass of psychic pain that lived in her body. At first she could not locate this as psychological pain in *herself*. The only "place" this pain was housed was in her archaic identification with the emotionally disturbed and abused children she treated in hospital. We began to talk about these children and her deep feeling for them, and I started to treat these stories about her child-patients as if they were a dream about aspects of herself. In other words, I began to treat them as if they were parts of herself. I would say things like: "You know, your empathy for that child is obviously so powerful, so compelling, and so accurate – it's as though some part of you has experienced their suffering in your own life". This was the only way I could approach *her* pain. She would usually look at me like a stunned fish after such interpretations, having no memories of such pain, but gradually it began to dawn on her that maybe there was more to her life than she thought.

In fact, Mary had no "memories" of her life before the age of 5 or 6 – only vague feelings of anxiety whenever she tried to think about it. She had heard from a beloved Aunt that at the age of 2 she had severe excema, was subject to temper tantrums and beatings by both parents, and had often been locked in her room for hours on end when she was "bad." Reportedly, she had toilet trained herself by the age of 12 months. Before her mother died Mary asked about these rumors, but the mother denied it all and claimed Mary had had a happy childhood. I asked her to bring in pictures of herself and family members and gradually we began to get some vague memories or proto-memories of how impossible it had been for her to be the dependent child she in fact was and how, suffering what self-psychologists call the "trauma of unshared emotionality," she had grown up much too fast, sacrificing her true self's need, identifying with the caretaking adults, adopting a false facade of invulnerability and "independence."

Behind this independence there lay a fragile world in which Mary took *care of herself in fantasy.* She was a melancholy child, and spent much of her time alone, reading or on long walks. Nature was a special sanctuary for her and, as analysis progressed, she began to remember a kindergarten daydream about the Lord Jesus and the Virgin Mary who lived in heaven on a cloud and watched over her from on high. These idealized inner figures were the only support Mary had from within. Her life of prayer and devotion could sustain her only for a limited time.

A great sadness enveloped these memories as Mary slowly realized that she had been totally unable to depend on anyone in the real world, and that while cared for physically, emotionally she had been abandoned. During this period of analytic exploration, she had the following dream image:

> I see a little girl floating away from a space ship without an umbilical cord, arms outstretched in terror, eyes and mouth distorted as if by a silent scream for her mother.

When Mary allowed herself to feel this frightening image, her grief was overwhelming and typically she felt shortness of breath in the session, just like the asthma she had suffered as a child. Each time we approached this anxiety and despair, she would need to cut off her feeling, sometimes with a sarcastic remark or by "going blank." To complicate the matter, I was leaving in a month for vacation and Mary had begun to realize for the first time, and to her horror, that she was feeling very dependent on me and was already missing me! She thought this was inappropriate and "sick."

In one particular session, approaching the summer break, she was especially courageous about this new-found vulnerability, worrying out loud that her old defenses might freeze her up again and undo all the progress we had made. She asked if she might be in touch with me over the summer if she needed to be. I said yes, and for the first time, her gruff humorous facade melted and her eyes filled up with tears. We discussed the realities of how this phone contact would work, and of course, she said, she would never abuse it, and I said that I knew she wouldn't, and we parted that day with a mutual feeling of deep connection.

She appeared for her next session looking bloated, flushed and depressed. With great embarrassment and fear of my disapproval she reported that immediately upon leaving my office, she had stopped at a bakery, purchased a whole chocolate cake and a quart of ice cream, gone home in state of possession, with her heart pounding, and eaten everything in one sitting. Five hours later, upon awakening from a stuporous sleep she had gone out to the local deli, bought more food and consumed that also. She was up all night eating. Since the last session she had gained 10 pounds. She was disgusted and ashamed. She had an impulse to call me during the binge, but was afraid she'd get out of control with her neediness.

This is an experience of *resistance,* and we psychotherapists all have strong counter-transference reactions to moments like this in our work. As I reflected on my personal response to Mary's self-destructive act, I became aware of a sense of irritation – even a feeling of anger that she had just destroyed what had clearly been an important breakthrough in our work together. This interested me. I had never felt these reactions toward this patient before. The "screw you" message in her action was clearly coming from a different place than Mary's usual ingratiating ego-attitude. Underneath my irritation, I also became aware of disappointment – almost a feeling of betrayal, as though she had cheated on me and "had an affair with somebody else." As I was musing on these "mad" counter-transference reactions, Mary said something like this:

> You know, it's exactly like I'm possessed by the Devil. Food is the only sensual pleasure I have. It's the only place I can lose control. I savor each spoonful of chocolate like it's the touch of a lover. I'm compelled to do it. I search it out – there's a feeling of dark excitement just approaching the bakery! The Devil says "C'mon – you've done all this work, why don't you be 'bad' for once – you need this. There's no sense fighting it, Mary. It's hopeless to resist. I'm too strong for you. You can always lose the weight if you really want to – that'll happen when you're ready, but right now you need this comfort and you know it. You're too stressed out. I want you all to myself. Leave your world behind and come into my world. You know how good it tastes, how good it feels. C'mon, Mary. You belong to me. Good girls don't say no!"

Perhaps the reader can imagine my shock and dismay hearing this erotic language from my very asexual patient. So she *did* have an affair, I thought to myself, but with an *inner* figure. Who was this speaking through her? Certainly not her highly "spiritual," sweet, ingratiating ego, busy pleasing people all the time. This was truly a diabolical seductive voice – a part of her inner world that neither of us had really known about. "He" was very clever, a veritable shape-shifter, a Trickster. He would use the truth about her excessive "goodness" to seduce her into being "bad" – clearly something Mary needed to risk in her life – but the result was always an even deeper sense of worthlessness and a vicious circle of trying to be extra good to atone for her compulsion. This figure's crafty seductiveness is what intrigued me. He personified a bodily sensuality, a sexuality, and an aggression that gave Mary's otherwise pale ingratiating ego much-needed color and depth. Submission to her "Daimon-lover" was the only place she could lose control, and what's more, this "surrender" was to her much-neglected body's cravings – at least this is what her inner daimon "told" her – the way she rationalized her binges.

The cost of these repeated "surrenders," however, was that Mary never got filled up in a way that gave her the "fullness" she was looking for. Quite the contrary; her midnight trysts with the food devil were tantamount to repeated rapes and violations. In the sober light of morning she felt devastated, her hopes crushed, her diet broken, her relationship to therapy and to me threatened with guilt. The pattern, she reiterated, was truly "perverse."

The next session, Mary reported an important dream (reported here in the first person). The dream tells us more about her inner daimon-lover.

I'm checking into a hospital with my friend Patty [Patty was a much younger, very innocent new nurse on her service]. We're there for some kind of procedure, maybe a blood test or something. I'm not sure. It's all very high-tech with many machines, etc. The doctor in his white coat is very nice as he introduces us to the hospital. But as we walk down the hall to the place our blood will be drawn I begin to feel uneasy because there is something wrong with the other patients. They're all in a trance or something – like zombies. Their essence has been removed. I realize that we've been tricked! The doctor has lured us into a trap. The place is like a concentration camp! Instead of testing our blood he is going to inject us with a serum that will make us zombies too. I have this hopeless feeling that there is no way out of this. No-one can hear us. There are no phones. I think "Oh my God, Mommy will die and they won't be able to let me know!" I hear the doctor's footsteps coming down the hall and I wake up in a sweat.

Interpretation and theoretical commentary

So here we have a sequence of historical and psychological "events" that point to an early trauma and its defense. First, we have the early traumatic abandonment that Mary and I were uncovering, then the dream of the terrified motherless baby fading into space that appeared in connection with this exploration, then the "breakthrough" of forbidden dependency feelings in the transference, the violent resistance to this implied in the acting out of the food binge (with its seductive daimonic voice), and finally the dream of the Trickster-doctor who seduces her into the zombie-hospital and the accompanying thought that "Mommy will die and. . . I won't know it." I would ask the reader to hold these themes in mind while I briefly review some literature which illuminates the nature of anxiety and splitting in cases of early trauma.

The nature of Mary's anxiety

The first thing that helps us to understand this case is the nature of Mary's anxiety. Both Winnicott and Kohut have pointed out that a certain level of "unthinkable" anxiety originates at a symbiotic stage of child development where the child is totally dependent on the mother as a kind of external metabolizing organ of psychological experience. The mother's role is to help mediate experience, and this means especially to help metabolize anxiety. It is as though the infant breathes in psychological oxygen through "lungs" supplied by the mother. What happens, then, when suddenly the mother is gone? Winnicott puts it this way:

> [for the baby] the feeling of the mother's existence lasts x minutes. If the mother is away more than x minutes, then the imago fades, and along with this the baby's capacity to use the symbol of the union ceases. The baby is distressed, but this distress is soon *mended* because the mother returns in x + y minutes. In x + y minutes the baby has not become altered. But in x + y + z minutes the baby has become *traumatized*. In x + y + z minutes the mother's return does not mend the baby's altered state. Trauma implies that the baby has experienced a break in life's continuity, so that primitive defences now become organized to defend against a repetition of 'unthinkable anxiety' or a return to the acute confusional state that belongs to disintegration of nascent ego structure.
>
> We must assume that the vast majority of babies never experience the x + y + z quantity of deprivation. This means that the majority of children do not carry around with them for life the knowledge from experience of having been mad. Madness here simply means a *breakup* of whatever may exist at the time of *a personal continuity of existence*. After 'recovery' from x + y + z deprivation a baby has to start again permanently deprived of the root which could provide *continuity with the personal beginning*.
>
> (Winnicott, 1971b: 97; emphases in original)

In the case of Mary, the dream image that emerged of what must have been her long-forgotten x + y + z deprivation was that of a little girl falling into space, with her arms outstretched in a silent scream for her mother, with no supply of oxygen – no connection to the "mother" ship. Anxiety over the lost mother-connection returns in the second dream where she is trapped in the zombie-hospital. Her central anxiety there is that her mother will die and she will not know it. Again, Winnicott has taught us that many *dreads* of this kind are really encoded *memories* of things that have already happened before full ego-formation (see Winnicott, 1963: 87), and if we apply this insight to Mary's dream, we might surmise that her mother's "death" is *something that has already happened emotionally many times*, even though she doesn't "know it" and even though her actual mother is still alive. In other words, the zombie-hospital is a "place" where she will be anesthetized to the loss of the mother – where she will lose all psychic connection to this fact. This will be assured by the Trickster-doctor who will administer his mind-altering serum.

Translated into Jungian language, we might say that an "unthinkable" level of anxiety results when archetypal energies fail to be humanized and the child is left at the mercy of the Terrible Mother as well as the Good Mother archetype. But this language *does not capture the emotional essence of this experience for the child who is now our patient.* Heinz Kohut comes closer when he calls this anxiety "disintegration anxiety." It is, he says, the "deepest anxiety man can experience" (Kohut, 1984: 16). It threatens the total annihilation of one's very humanity – the outright destruction of the human personality. To prevent this destruction, we might say that an archetypal "force" comes to the rescue. This archetypal force represents a self-care defensive system which is far more archaic and devastating than the more common level of ego-defenses. We might think of this figure as "Mr. Dissociation" himself – an emissary from the dark world of the unconscious, a true *diabolos*. We find him in Mary's material in two places – first, as the diabolical "voice" of her food binge, and second, as the Trickster-doctor, seducing her into the zombie-hospital where she will be forever separated from her life and from the mother's "death." We will come back to these appearances in a moment.

Two levels of trauma's inner world

The disintegration anxiety which Mary carried inside her body is the kind of anxiety that we must imagine got its start in her very early life before a coherent ego was formed. So, when this anxiety starts to come up again, it threatens to *fragment* the personality, and the nature of dissociation required to prevent this is more severe and archaic than the more "benign" forms of dissociation we associate with neurotic conflict. For the neurotic, the return of dissociated shadow-material creates anxiety, but this material can be recognized and integrated, leading to an inner *coniunctio oppositorum* and greater wholeness of personality. *This is because the neurotic has a place within his psyche for repressed material.* It is different with the victim of early trauma. For these patients, disowned material is not psychically represented but *has been banished to the body* or relegated to discreet psychical fragments between which amnesia barriers have been erected. It must *never* be allowed to return to consciousness. A *coniunctio oppositorum* is the most terrifying thing of all, and the dissociation necessary to insure the patient against this catastrophe, is a deeper, archetypal split in the psyche.

Attacks on transitional space and its replacement by fantasy

In order to accomplish his necessary dismembering of experience, we might think of our diabolical imago as operating in two areas of experience. The first of these is the transitional space *between the ego and the external world of reality.* The second is the inner symbolic space *between various parts of the internal world.* When operating between ego and world, our diabolical figure tries to encapsulate the personality in a kind of counter-dependent self-sufficient bubble. He (or she) seems to function in that "transitional zone" between inner self and outer world – precisely the interface where Mary's traumatic anxiety was experienced before her ego had formed. Winnicott has helped us to understand that when "un-thinkable" trauma occurs, something dreadful happens to this transitional space. Internally there is a split in the ego (the classic schizoid position) but there is a corresponding split in the "potential space" where the personality is alive between illusion and reality. This "transitional space" is the place where the child learns how to play and use symbols.

Repeated exposure to traumatic anxiety *forecloses transitional space,* kills the symbolic activity of creative imagination, and replaces it with what Winnicott calls "fantasying" (Winnicott, 1971b). Fantasying is a dissociated state, which is neither imagination nor living in external reality, but a kind of melancholic self-soothing compromise which goes on forever – a defensive use of the imagination in the service of anxiety avoidance. My patient Mary was seduced into this "limbo" many times by her wistful self-soothing daimon, sadly fantasying about and idealizing the mother she never really had – rewriting history to deny at all costs her underlying despair and fury.

Following from these considerations, psychotherapists must be very careful, with patients like Mary, to distinguish between genuine imagination and fantasy, which is the self-soothing activity of the daimon. This self-soothing really amounts to a self-hypnotic spell – an unconscious undertow into non-differentiation to escape conscious feeling. Here a retreat into "oneness" replaces the hard work of separation necessary for "wholeness."[1] This is not regression, as we like to think of it in the service of the ego, but "malignant regression"[2] – regression which suspends a part of her in an auto-hypnotic twilight state[3] in order (so our diabolical figure thinks) to assure the survival of herself as a human person.

In the dream material of the trauma victim, this preserved personal spirit is often represented as an innocent "child" or animal appearing in tandem with the caretaking side of our self-care system – like the dying baby calling out for its mother, for example, or the patient and her food daimon in their nightly trysts. Looked at from the standpoint of the patient's survival, even Mary's food daimon is a kind of guardian angel who watches out for the deprived part of herself and cares for it (feeding it with substitutes) as long as the vulnerable creature never wants to leave its comfortable prison and emerge into the world (or come down into the body). Here we have a structure in the psyche which is simultaneously infantile and very grown up, innocent and jaded at the same time.

Psychotherapists who have worked with people like Mary will confirm how utterly vulnerable, uninitiated, needy, and infantile they are, on the one hand, and how haughty, inflated, arrogant, know-it-all, and resistant they are on the other. This inflated inner defensive structure, like a "king-baby" or the "queen-baby," represents the unholy marriage between the caretaking self and its infantile object. It is extremely difficult for patients to give up these omnipotent inner self/object units in the absence of genuinely satisfying early experiences of dependency.[4]

As applied to our case, this would mean that Mary would have to give up her self-care illusions – the fantasy world in which she and her mother existed in a kind of blissful dual union, bathed in goodness and innocent "love," needing no-one else (including her therapist). Into this comforting illusion she would have to let the horrific reality of her actual abandonment by her real mother, in stark contrast to the illusory Good Mother she never had and never would have. She would also have to mourn all the unlived life that her self-care system had cut her off from. This would mean the dual sacrifice of both her God-like self-sufficiency and the innocent demands associated with it. In Melanie Klein's language, she would have to give up her manic defense and begin to mourn the loss of her objects, entering the "depressive position."

We know, however, that this process never happens without the release of much of rage and aggression – and this is exactly what I was beginning to feel in my counter-transference reaction to Mary's food binge. We might say that I was beginning to wrestle with her daimon, our diabolical figure. I could feel his grip on her and his hatred and suspicion of me. I could also "see" him in the diabolical Trickster-doctor of Mary's zombie-hospital dream. I could see how he had lured the dream-ego into an ostensible place of healing, now revealed as a concentration camp enclosure full of bloodless wraiths, their human essence removed, injected with de-humanizing "zombie-serum."[5]

Dissociation and attacks against linking in the inner world

In Mary's dream, the Trickster-doctor lured her into a hospital on the pretense of testing her blood, but his "intention" was to turn her into a zombie – to take away her "essence," to put her into a trance. This is one of the major effects of the dissociative defense and involves a temporary dismemberment of experience – an inner separation of the ego or "de-cathexis" of its reality functions in the interest of psychic numbness. This involves an attack on the very capacity for experience itself, which means "attacking the links" (Bion, 1959) between affect and image, perception and thought, sensation and knowledge. The result is that experience is rendered meaningless, coherent memory is "disintegrated," and individuation is interrupted.

The most interesting current theory about trauma's effects on the psyche takes into account how difficult it is for us humans to *process* certain aspects of our experience (see Eigen,1995). Work by clinicians such as Henry Krystal (1988) on trauma and affect, Joyce McDougall (1989) on psychosomatic disorder, Frances

Tustin (1990) on autism, have combined to help us understand that "whole" experience is a unity of many factors and that *integrated* experience is not always easy. One researcher (Braun, 1988), for example, describes four aspects of experience along which dissociation can occur, namely *behavior, affect, sensation* and *knowledge* – otherwise known as the BASK model of dissociation. In dissociative disorder, any of these aspects can be split within itself or the usual links among them or between them can be severed.

The normally integrated components of experience include both *somatic* and *mental* elements – affects and sensations from the body, thoughts, images and cognitive mechanisms in the mind, as well as a mysterious "meaning" dimension which has to do with whether something can be integrated as a part of one's personal identity and narrative history. Related to this dimension of meaning, and rarely discussed by clinicians, is that animating *spirit* at the center of all healthy living. This spirit, which we have described as the transcendent essence of the self seems to be compromised in severe trauma. It is never annihilated completely because, presumably, this would be the literal death of the person. But it may be "killed" in the sense that it cannot continue living in the embodied ego. Or it may be put in "cold storage" in the unconscious psyche or take bizarre forms in the (mad) mind.

For experience to become *meaningful* requires that bodily excitations, including the archaic affects of infancy, be given mental representation by a transitional parental figure so that eventually they can reach verbal expression in language and be shared with another person. This process of mediation of archaic affects, their eventual symbolization and shared expression in language, is the crucial element in the personalization of all archetypal affects, including those of early trauma. Winnicott describes personalization (the opposite of de-personalization) as being related to the gradual process of "indwelling." Indwelling occurs as the mother repeatedly "introduces and re-introduces the baby's mind and psyche to each other" (Winnicott, 1970: 271). It is interesting that Winnicott does not say what part of the self "indwells" – the personal spirit perhaps?

In trauma, affect-experience is simply too much to bear. Splitting is necessary. Whole experience is dismembered. The links between the BASK elements of experience are attacked by the archaic defense. Events and their meanings are disconnected, or perhaps the diabolical inner tyrant convinces the child's ego that the unbearable events are no longer happening to "me." In severe cases, experience loses all dimensionality. The child no longer attributes meaning to his perception at all. Unbearable infantile affects and sensations from the body are not permitted to acquire symbolic mental representation. The result is an inner world in which archaic affects and their fantastically elaborated archaic objects remain unnamed and disconnected from personal meaning or significance. Primal affects have not been modulated, humanized, and personalized through the usual projective/identificatory processes so well described by Winnicott and others. The result is psychosomatic illness or what Joyce McDougall referred to as "alexithymia" – patients who have no words for feelings and who as a result are "dis-affected" or in the language of the current discussion, "dis-spirited" (cf., McDougall, 1985).

In less severe cases, dissociation is not as severe and the inner world is not as persecutory. Archetypal fantasy takes over and replaces imaginal engagement with the outer world. A rich inner world sometimes develops and access to the positive side of the Self and its numinous energies support a fragile ego, albeit "defensively." This "schizoid" picture is prognostically more favorable for analytic therapy, because it means that the positive side of the archetypal world is embodied in infancy and early childhood. If a safe intermediate "play" space can be found, and if the *sanctum originalis* can be re-contacted in metaphor and symbol, rebuilding can begin and enough trust can be established so that the negative affects can also begin to be tolerated and worked through.

Archetypal defenses, then, allow for survival at the expense of individuation. They assure the survival of the person, but at the expense of personality development. Their "goal" as I have come to understand it, is to keep the personal spirit "safe" but disembodied, encapsulated, or otherwise driven out of the body/mind unity – foreclosed from entering time and space reality. Instead of slowly and painfully incarnating in a cohesive self, the volcanic opposing dynamisms of the inner world become organized around defensive purposes, constituting a "self-care system" for the individual. Instead of individuation and the integration of mental life, the archaic defense engineers dis-incarnation (dis-embodiment) and dis-integration in order to help a weakened anxiety-ridden ego to survive, albeit as a partially "false" self.

The Trickster and archetypal defenses of the self

As we have already seen in Mary's food addiction, her compulsion seemed to be "personalized" in the unconscious in diabolical form as the seductive food daimon, on the one hand, and in the figure of the Trickster-doctor on the other. Jung himself was interested in the psyche's Trickster energies and how they related to compulsive and addictive trends. For example, in his alchemical studies, he compared the possessing "spirit" of compulsion to the alchemical sulphur, a substance associated with hell and the Devil as well as with the poisonous, crafty, and treacherous Trickster figure of Alchemy, Hermes/Mercurius. Like all ambivalent Self-figures, Mercurius, the Trickster-god was ambivalent, a paradox, and the source of healing as well as destruction (see Jung, 1955: para. 148). This fact is symbolically demonstrated in his winged staff, the caduceus, with two opposing serpents twined around it, one containing poison, the other the antidote. So, as Alchemy says, the darkest, vilest of inner figures, the very personification of evil itself "was destined to be the medicina" (Jung, 1955: para. 148). This is the mystery of the ambivalent figure of Mercurius and of all ostensibly "evil" things in the psyche. Jung was impressed all his life by the paradoxical role of evil in delivering people from darkness and from suffering.

The Trickster is a well-known figure in primitive cultures and perhaps the most

38

archaic god-image known in mythology (see Hill, 1970). He is present from the primordial beginning of things and hence is often pictured as an old man. His essential nature is quixotic, ambivalent – like Hermes/Mercury (one of his personifications). On the one hand, he is a killer, amoral and evil, often identified with powerful underworld daimons or animals. He is responsible for bringing pain and death into an Eden-like paradisiacal world. But he is also capable of great good. Not uncommonly, he is a psychopomp, an intermediary between the gods and men, and often his diabolical nature is precisely what is necessary to help initiate a new beginning – like, for example, Satan as the Trickster-snake in the Garden of Eden, tempting Eve into the act of knowing which ended mankind's participation mystique and started (mythologically speaking) the history of human consciousness.

The Trickster's paradoxical nature, combining two opposing aspects, often makes him a *threshold* deity – a god, if you will, of transitional space. This was true, for example of the archaic Roman god Janus, whose name means "door" and who, by facing both ways, was the god of all gateways and passageways (see Palmer, 1970). As patron of all entrances, he is also the protector and promoter of all *beginnings* – hence also our January, the beginning of the year. But he is also the god of exits, celebrated at the year's harvest, and early cults in his name worshipped Mars, god of war. In the Roman Forum, his temple had two sets of swinging doors. When the doors were closed, Rome was at peace. When the doors were open, there was civil war. So Janus, like all Tricksters, embraces a pair of opposites.

We find this same two-facedness in the earliest ambivalent imagery of Yahweh, the Old Testament God who is also a two-faced Trickster. Yahweh's left hand is one of divine wrath, vengeance and jealousy – sending flood, disease, and death to persecute the Israelites. Conversely, his right hand is one of mercy, love and protection. But frequently Yahweh's hands don't seem to be coordinated and Israel suffers more of his wrath than his mercy. Gradually, through the suffering of the people, and especially his chosen servants, Moses, Joshua, Jacob, Noah and Job, Yahweh reaches a kind of "depressive position" and integrates his aggressive and libidinal nature. This is the meaning of the rainbow in the flood myth and of the covenant between Yahweh and the nation of Israel, secured in the Ark and "written upon the hearts" of his people.

The problem of Yahweh's right and left hands being either integrated or dissociated speaks to another interesting aspect of the Trickster figure. This is the fact that the Trickster often dissociates a part of his body which then leads a kind of independent existence. In some tales he dissociates his anus and gives it a task, which it then fails to perform whereupon he foolishly punishes it, thereby causing himself great suffering. In the Winnebago cycle, the Trickster's right arm quarrels and fights with his left and sometimes he sends his penis off to rape the daughter of a neighboring chief. In one story, he stupidly mistakes his enormous penis for a flagpole to no end of hilarity among the assembled tribespeople watching these antics.

All these mythological traditions show the Trickster as both diabolical and symbolical. As a threshold deity, he either dissociates or associates various inner images and affects. He links things together or he tears them apart. Changing his shape at will, he is either creative or destructive, transforming and protective, or negating and persecutory. He is totally amoral, like life itself, instinctual, undeveloped, a stupid blockhead, a practical joker, a hero who aids mankind and changes the world (see Radin, 1976).

In his incarnation as Mary's food daimon, he seduced her ego into addictive eating binges and other aberrant distractive activities and away from any struggle with reality. This inevitably put her into an "altered state." As her Daimon-lover he had access to the inflating archetypal energies of the inner world itself, and like a veritable Phantom of the Opera, he seduced Mary with his "music," drawing her ineluctably into a web of aggrandized, melodramatic fantasy – but out of creative living, with its struggles, frustrations, and disillusionments. In this way, we can imagine that his "intention" is to encapsulate the threatened personal spirit within a world of illusion, in order to prevent it from being dismembered in a too-harsh reality.

Needless to say, the Trickster is a formidable adversary in the working-through process with patients like Mary. Often in this process we must struggle with our own diabolical impulses, developing enough neutralized aggression to confront the Trickster's seductiveness in the patient and in ourselves, while at the same time maintaining "rapport" with the patient's genuine woundedness and need. This struggle constitutes a genuine "moment of urgency" in the therapeutic process and many treatments have been shipwrecked on the Scylla of too much confrontation or the Charybdis of too much compassion and complicity with the undertow of the patient's malignant regression. If the patient's traumatized ego is to be coaxed out of its inner sanctum and inspired to trust the world again, a middle way will have to be found between compassion and confrontation. Finding this "middle way" provides both the daunting challenge and the enormous opportunity of psychotherapeutic work with the victims of early trauma.

2

FURTHER CLINICAL ILLUSTRATIONS OF THE SELF-CARE SYSTEM

The false God changes suffering into violence. The True God changes violence into suffering.

(Simone Weil, 1987: 65)

In the vignettes that follow, other facets of the self-care system are explored, especially its role as Protector, guardian, and sometimes tyrannical imprisoner of an anxiety-ridden child-ego. After each clinical example, there is a brief interpretive comment and in the second case (Gustav) a more extended description of how traumatic memory is recovered through the unfolding of a dream series in psychotherapy. A final case (Patricia) illustrates the "return" of the personal spirit to the body during an advanced stage of grief work in analysis. The chapter concludes with some theoretical speculations about psychosomatic illness and the self-care system's role in the splitting of mind and body.

THE LITTLE GIRL AND THE ANGEL

One of the most moving stories about the spirit-preserving role of the self-care system and its guardian Self was reported by Edward Edinger in the course of his audio-taped lecture series on the Old Testament at the Los Angeles Jung Institute (see Edinger, 1986). The story apparently originated with the New York analyst Esther Harding who knew the person in England to whom it happened. It goes as follows:

A mother sent her young daughter, aged 6 or 7, to her father's study one morning to deliver an important message. Shortly thereafter the daughter came back and said "I'm sorry mother, the angel won't let me go in." Whereupon the mother sent the daughter back a second time, with the same result. At this point the mother became quite annoyed at her young girl's imaginative excess, so she marched the message over to the father herself. Upon entering, she found her husband dead in his study.

This story brings home to us how the psyche seems to handle unbearable emotion. Certain affects simply cannot be processed with the normal resources

41

available to the ego, and "deeper" resources need to be marshalled. These deeper resources are the life-saving defenses of the Self and they block the ego's path at those traumatic times when, as these defenses can apparently "see" in their wisdom, the psychic circuit-breaker needs to be thrown, so to speak, so that lightning does not burn up all the circuits in the house.

One of the effects of the Self's "angel" in this case, was to bring the little girl's mother into the picture. Trauma of this magnitude cannot be encompassed by the psychic "equipment" of a child. The lightning bolt of unbearable affect is simply too much. Defenses of the Self know this and oversee the necessary "disconnection." They cannot, however, provide the missing resources for very long. Ego-mediation by a transitional person is necessary, and this is where the mother comes in. We do not know how the mother handled this moment, although we can imagine that her response would have been critical. She may have been too involved in her own shock and grief to help her daughter. Or perhaps, in the mother's response, the daughter may have found a "model" for her own feelings and permission to feel them.

In any case, much of the trauma that comes to the psychotherapist for mending is early trauma of this kind, now overlaid with years of defense and partial efforts at mediation, more or less successful. One of the most useful models for the handling of such trauma in psychotherapy was elaborated by the late Dr. Elvin Semrad (Semrad and Buskirk, 1969) and further developed in a recent study by David Garfield (1995). While these authors limit their discussion to psychotherapy with psychotic patients, their threefold technique is relevant to dissociative disorders of all kinds. It involves a meticulous attention to the client's *affect*. First, affect must be *found* in the patient's history and (in the case of psychosis) rescued from its delusional, hallucinatory, or neologistic elements; next, the affect must be *acknowledged* ("owned") and experienced in the body; finally, affect must find *verbal expression* in language and be organized into the narrative history of the individual – into his or her life story. The complexities of these three stages are further illustrated in Garfield's book.

LENORE AND THE FAIRY GODMOTHER

A little girl named Lenore, later a client of mine, was born to a wealthy family in Western Europe. Her mother was an alcoholic, and a woman who, because of serious emotional neglect by her own mother, was in no condition to have a baby. A postpartum depression soon followed Lenore's birth. The father, a high-flying diplomat in the foreign service, was usually out of the picture. By the end of the first month of my patient's infancy, she was malnourished, and near death. She spent ten days in a hospital being fed intravenously, then was sent to live with her paternal grandmother. At the age of 9 months, she rejoined her mother, who by then had fixed up a pink playroom and had peopled it with lifelike baby dolls which the mother dressed up and sang to. Lenore fit right into this dolls' room and was dressed up and treated just like the rest of the mother's "family" of dolls –

except that she can never recall her mother touching her, while she touched and "played with" the other dolls.

By the age of 4, Lenore knew there was something seriously wrong with her. She did not feel real, was somehow different from the other children and never fit in. She could not eat with the family without vomiting, and had begun to hide food in her playroom. She concluded that she must have a low IQ, or be crazy, or contain a bad seed or something. By the age of 8 she began to plan her own suicide. Life in heaven, which she heard about in Sunday school, would be better than this, she thought. Besides, that was where her beloved grandfather had gone when she was 4. She decided to throw herself off the balcony of her aunt's apartment building. But the night before the planned suicide, she had the following dream which repeated itself twice.

I'm in my pink bedroom thinking about dying. Suddenly my fairy god-mother [a fantasy figure who had sustained her] came to me and said in a very stern voice, "If you die, that's it! You'll be buried and disintegrate. You'll never be you again, and there'll be nothing left of you but rotting flesh and bones. This is forever. Forever! Do you understand?! Never again in the earth's history. You will not exist anymore!"

Interpretation and theoretical commentary

Lenore woke up in terror from this dream, but she did not commit suicide. However, in order to stay in life, she did have to "kill" (i.e., dissociate) a part of herself that is, she had to split herself in two, very much like Plato's original man got split in two, each half forever longing for its mate. One half of her was this maladapted, skinny, depressed girl with asthma and stomach ulcers who could not stop herself from having temper tantrums and being beaten up by her enraged mother. But another part of her began to have a secret life woven from the scraps of Broadway musicals, books, and her own imagination. Every time she was humiliated or picked on in school, or when her mother would threaten to put her up for adoption, she would lock herself in her playroom and start to sing to herself about an elaborate secret fantasy world, in which she belonged to a loving family with many adoring brothers. She had seen the Broadway musicals *Seven Brides for Seven Brothers* and *South Pacific*, and *Peter Pan*, and these served as the stimulus for her imaginary family and their adventures. This "family" lived on the frontier in hard times but she and her dog had special powers and a deep communion with the wild animals, the trees, and the stars. In her fantasy world she had a very loving mother who had a very mean sister (her wicked "aunt"), a "father" who was often away, and many adoring brothers who loved to listen to her sing.

Lenore's fantasy world became a temporary refuge and sanctuary for her. I say temporary because by the time she entered therapy even her inner world had partly turned persecutory. But it sustained her for about four years while she was a latency-age girl and things were unbearable in her home. Every night in order to fall asleep, she would entertain herself with it. Even in school, which was a traumatic environment, she continued it. She'd sit in the back of the classroom, dissociated from her lessons, imagining she was posing for photographers who were there to document the fifth-grade life of this famous singing star who sang so beautifully and who lived such an enchanted life in this wonderful family with many brothers. At other times, in order to console herself, Lenore would imagine being sung to by the "mother" in this family and would softly sing to herself:

> Nothing's gonna harm you
> Not while I'm around
> Demons are prowling everywhere, nowadays.
> I'll send 'em howling
> No-one's gonna hurt you
> not while I'm around . . .

My experience with this young woman taught me clinically what Jung means by the superordinate personality he calls the "Self." As a larger more encompassing unitary reality deeply in touch with the universe, this Self saw the tortured ego of my patient and how it was rationalizing its own extinction, and intervened with a dream that kept her in life. Then it hypnotized this fractured, desiccated ego, bathing it in stories – immersing it in a sustaining matrix of archetypal imagery. But finally it had to get help. It took this enfeebled terrified young woman against great resistance and brought her into therapy because it could see that despite its valiant efforts to isolate and feed her beleaguered ego, things were getting worse. Like those hydroponic plants grown without earth, this little girl's fragile identify stayed "green" on its rarified diet of illusion, but it never grew. And try as it might, the positive side of the Self could not extinguish the growing presence of the "prowling Demons."

This fact was brought home to me when it became clear that there was another, darker side to Lenore's fantasy life. She had a dog named George and every night after those ghastly meals, she and George would go for a walk. They'd have long conversations about how the two of them were going to get free from this house and live somewhere else. And then sometimes if George misbehaved Lenore would become possessed by rage and kick and brutalize the dog, always feeling terrible about this afterwards and making amends.

This dark side of her inner caretaker often persecuted her with self-hating voices. On one occasion she had been to a high school dance at the insistence of the mother. When she came home later that night she made the mistake of telling her mother what a terrible time she had had. No-one had asked her to dance and she had spent the whole night sitting in the dark. Upon hearing this the drunken mother flew into a rage and attacked her physically – how could Lenore humiliate her like this? What would she say to all the ladies at the club, etc.? As the mother's humiliation escalated, Lenore had one of her many temper tantrums until the mother's blows and kicks had broken her spirit. After this, the patient recalled a severe dressing down she got from an *inner* voice which berated her and said: "you stupid little bitch – I told you never to tell your mother the truth! What is the matter with you! We're never going to make it if you don't use your head more than that!"

This was the same voice that told her she was a "bad seed," that she was crazy – that she should never show what was inside her and most of all never hope or expect anything. The voice was masculine and mean. It negated everything: "I want my momma" – "No! you don't want your Momma, you have me!" "I want to get married" – "No! you don't, you want to be free for your career!" It filled her with dark predictions: "Your husband's gonna leave you... you're gonna end up a drunk like your mother... you're gonna throw up ... you're gonna fail!"

So here we see two sides of the self-care system. On the one hand, she is a guardian angel or "fairy godmother" who preserves the patient's life by scaring her out of suicide and in the process helps her to dissociate a part of her true self, sequestered in fantasy and in her pink playroom. She then appears as the enchantress – the archetypal storyteller who reads bedtime stories to a mortified little girl, sings to her, and soothes her with illusory hope. But when this hope starts to be felt for something real in the world, or suffers disappointment in some genuine effort to link up with reality, the Protector part of the self-care system turns *diabolical* and attacks the ego and its vulnerable inner objects.

The soothing and diabolical figures in Lenore's inner world appeared in her conscious life as two extremely powerful "voices" in her head. They spoke with great authority both for and against her. Later in Lenore's analysis, one of our main tasks was to sensitize her to these voices (with which she was totally identified), i.e., we tried to make these ego-syntonic voices *ego-dystonic* and to cultivate a position for her ego in relation to either the seduction or the tyranny of her Protector/Persecutor. In this situation, the therapist's voice and attitude must not be only "nice and understanding," it must also partake a bit of the tyrant's strength and firmness – i.e., it must not be afraid to injure the patient's inflated ego, and it must speak with authority. Slowly, Lenore's self-care "voices" were replaced by a more realistic, modulated, tolerant voice, but giving up her Protector/Persecutor and its "voice" proved to be much more difficult than I had thought at first. Lenore told me it felt like betraying an old friend – even an old friend that had saved her life. "If I sever that voice," she said, "it's like telling my mother I don't love her... *in fact I love that Voice...* like I love my mother – sick as it sounds. 'She' got me through a lot ... don't you understand? Your voice is puny by comparison! Where are you going to be when I need help? That Voice has saved my life. It sounds crazy, but I don't know how else to explain it."

Appearance of the dream-child

About four years into her psychotherapy, Lenore suffered a circumstantial trauma which opened up the pain of her early childhood. She had been married for a brief time to a narcissistic man who treated her very much like her mother had treated her in the pink playroom of her childhood – like an object, like a doll. Early in their courtship he had even called her his "living doll." On the eve of the session I will report here, this man had told her coldly and without feeling that he no longer loved her and wanted a divorce. Lenore was naturally in despair about this, even though for years she had not felt close to this man.

By this time she had a solid relationship with me in the transference and one of the very interesting things that had happened the prior year in our work together is that she had started to remember dreams for the first time in her life. One of the regular figures in her dreams turned out to be the image of an innocent, angry, neglected little girl. This dream-child had become very important to this patient (and to me), because each time the little girl appeared and we talked about her, Lenore would start to cry; this was grief she had never experienced before – grief for the neglect and abuse she had experienced as a little girl who had split herself in two. With the aid of this dream-child she could also start to grieve the loss of those childhood years that had followed this split, years during which she had lived without an animated soul or psyche. *This grief work was her "psychotherapy."*

In the session following the husband's cruel announcement, she started complaining about a terrible knot of tension in her stomach. She was afraid her childhood ulcer was coming back. Otherwise, she felt numb and out of contact. I asked her simply focus on this feeling in her stomach by closing her eyes and breathing into it – telling me any images she might have of her physical pain. I asked her to let her stomach speak and tell us what it had to say. It took her a few minutes to relax enough to engage this process, but suddenly she gasped, eyes wide open in a mixture of fear and excitement. She had suddenly "seen" her "little girl," tears in her eyes from deep suffering, giving only a shy despairing glance at the patient. At this image Lenore burst into tears – an unusual occurrence for this very self-sufficient woman.

For the rest of this very significant session, she simply held her head in her hands and, with my support and encouragement not to split from the feeling, sobbed over this lost, heartbroken little girl. As she did this her numbness went away, the tension in her stomach relaxed, and what we might call her personal spirit "re-entered" her body. In this process, the measure of her growing embodiment was the strength of her spontaneous affect. When she left the session she was exhausted but fundamentally changed. Something long-since dissociated from her life had been linked up again, integrated, incarnated. She had also gained the important insight that her current trauma with the husband was only the most recent edition of a much earlier trauma – one that she had not been able to experience as a little girl but which she was able to experience now in the husband's abandonment and with the help of her positive relationship with me. This did not make her "feel" any better but it gave her devastating pain a new sense of meaning. By way of summary, we could say that in the healing of the split between her mind and body at this moment, an animating spirit returned, the cramp in her body and in her mind relaxed, and she recovered her soul or psyche. This is not a permanent resolution of the problem, but experiences like this are encouraging to the patient and support the work of mourning which is otherwise so humiliating to the trauma victim.

GUSTAV AND HIS HEAVENLY PARENTS

This is the story of a lost little boy who I will call Gustav – later my patient – born in a large German city on the eve of World War II. His father was a Nazi soldier and an alcoholic. Gustav remembered him as a brutal, tyrannical man who, when home from the front, would grab his son by the ear and twist until he cried and begged for him to stop. His mother was a pretty peasant woman who worked in a bakery and tried half-heartedly to protect Gustav from the father, although she herself was also frequently beaten up. When he was 6 years old the Allied bombing of Germany began. He remembered the first bombings, hiding in the basement and walking outside into the rubble afterwards. He remembered feeling no fear while with his mother. Then, as the bombings intensified, he was sent away to his aunt's house in the country where they lived on the grounds of a "mental asylum." His uncle was the butcher for the institution and a terrifying man whose butcher's apron was often spattered with blood. He remembered very little about his four years there except constant bewilderment and fear, a nameless terror he felt about the asylum, the humiliation of going to the bathroom on newspapers under his bed for fear of crossing the dark hallway past his uncle's room, the continual crying for his mother and the scoldings she gave him on her visits for being such a crybaby.

Five years later, with the war over and his father in a P.O.W. camp, he returned with his mother to the bombed-out apartment where he'd spent the first six years of his life. There was nothing left of their home except four walls and an old desk that had belonged to his father. The streets were full of rubble and marauding gangs of teenagers who beat him up, stole his food, or sexually molested him. His mother was humiliated and chased out of farmers' fields for stealing potatoes. He lived in fear of unexploded bombs. Shortly after his father came home, his mother, now pregnant, induced an abortion with a knitting needle, bled profusely and ended up in the hospital, leaving Gustav at home with his drunken father for a week.

That is all he remembered. Something terrible happened to him with his father on that occasion – he did not know what. With an axe, he chopped up the old desk in a rage – or so he was told. He remembered that his mother had to leave her hospital bed to "save him." Vaguely he recalled the mental hospital where he was taken in a delirious state, speaking in tongues. He remembered how after this event nothing was the same. "Something broke in me then," he reported to me forty years later. "I died to my real life and was resurrected as a shell. From then on I could never get up in the morning. I lost all interest in everything – until I came to America . . ."

And yet, through all these terrible years, this little boy was not without hope. Every day, he waited excitedly for bedtime, because at night, in the darkness of his room at the butcher's house, he played an imaginal game with himself. He had once read in a German magazine about the discovery of King Tut's tomb, and had seen pictures of all the beautiful artefacts and treasures of gold, and in his fantasy he himself was the boy-king who reigned over an enormous Egyptian kingdom stretching all the way south into Africa. In this fantasy he was provided with everything he needed. He was pampered and fed and provided for in lavish style. Most important, he had a special mentor – the high Priest who he loved and who loved him. This man – who had superhuman powers and was really a kind of god – would teach him all that he needed to know about the world – about astronomy, the world of nature, the mysterious powers of the gods, how to be a soldier. The priest would also play games with him – complicated games with strange hieroglyphs defining the rules. And paired with his priest/father there was a high priestess/mother – a beautiful woman/goddess who taught him all the women's arts, including music and sexuality.

He thought of these two as his "heavenly parents" and their reassuring presence in his life was not limited to the King Tut fantasy. They also appeared in his room when he fell asleep – in his dreams. In his dreams, however, they were different. They never interacted with him as they did in his fantasy – they were just "there" – in their long blue robes. They would appear in all those dreams in which Gustav was terrified or upset beyond what he could usually handle. Just their presence was enough to calm him inwardly. Sometimes they would also say things in a reassuring tone – he never remembered what they told him, just that whatever it was, it calmed him and made him feel safe.

Interpretation and theoretical commentary

With this imaginative fantasy, Gustav was able to keep hope alive, and in this way he kept himself apart from the suicidal despair that haunted him daily. Classical psychoanalysis might see this as the beginning of this child's serious psychopathology – the first signs of a major split in his self-experience between a distorted, fantastically elaborated, inner world, and an outer world that had become intolerable. Classical analysis would want to analyze this fantasy as a defense, and reduce its content to this boy's regressively hallucinated relationship with the missing father and mother. All this would be true, and indeed, when this little boy grew up and I had the privilege of working with him as a patient, much of our work together centered around the imagos of his personal parents. But a Jungian approach would not be content to let the matter rest with the purely personal drama and would want to look beyond the reductive interpretation at the *telos* of this fantasy – its purpose – and also at its archetypal content.

A Jungian approach to this material would want it acknowledged that – given the circumstances of this boy's life – the psyche's capacity to invent such a fantasy was a kind of a miracle in its own right and it had a miraculous effect – it kept him alive, both physically and psychically. To be more precise, it kept his spirit alive, even though entombed in his fantasy, like the boy-king, to be resurrected later. So we see that one of the "purposes" of the archetypal psyche and its central organizing archetype which we call the Self, is to keep the ego-germ alive and in life, to support the personal spirit when otherwise life has forsaken it; in this case, to keep it alive by telling it stories – stories that give it a meaningful (albeit magical) "place" in life and, therefore, hope. We might add, parenthetically, that the archetypal psyche cannot do this indefinitely without help from reality, and that usually there is a high price to be paid in the person's adaptation to reality when the inner world must come to the rescue of a beleaguered ego in this way. Sandor Ferenczi describes this process beautifully in relation to a case much like Gustav's:

> A surprising but apparently generally valid feature of this process of self-splitting is the sudden change of the object-relation that has become intolerable, into narcissism. The man abandoned by all gods escapes completely from reality and creates for himself another world in which he, unimpeded by earthly gravity, can achieve anything he wants. Has he been unloved, even tormented, he now splits off from himself a part which in the form of a helpful loving, often motherly, minder commiserates with the tormented reminder of the self, nurses him and decides for him; and all this is done with deepest wisdom and most penetrating intelligence. He is intelligence and kindness itself, so to speak a guardian angel. This angel sees the suffering or murdered child from the outside, he wanders through the whole Universe seeking help, invents fantasies for the child that cannot be saved in any other way, etc. But in the moment of a very strong, repeated trauma even this guardian angel must confess his own helplessness and well-meaning deceptive swindles to the tortured child and then nothing else remains but suicide, unless at the last moment some favourable change in the reality occurs. This favourable event to which we can point against the suicidal impulse is the fact that in this new traumatic struggle the patient is no longer alone.
>
> (Ferenczi, 1933: 237)

Also, in approaching this material from a Jungian perspective, we would at least like to note that this little boy's fantasy contains universal motifs – archetypal images that we find, for example, in the common motif among primitive peoples of "dual parents," one earthly, one heavenly. The idea that behind the personal parents there stand their spiritual equivalents is a widespread belief that follows us into the present time in the custom of "godparents" who are present at a child's baptism and oversee the child's spiritual life. This custom, in turn, embodies the psychological fact that for a child the personal father "carries" the archetype of the "Father," i.e., the Self, with all its spiritual implications world-wide.

49

Here we have an example of how the traumatized ego, missing a warm and approachable personal father with whom to grow itself up, is sustained by the background object from the collective psyche which "steps in," so to speak, to sustain the ego in fantasy (the self-care system). It would not be satisfactory to say simply that Gustav "made up" his heavenly parents out of wish-fulfillment – a classically Freudian view. Rather, when his broken ego fell into the abyss of trauma, it discovered something there to "catch it" – the archetypal psyche – a level of structured "being" in the psyche that is not of the ego's making.

Finally, by being compellingly drawn to the unearthing of the boy-king Tut's grave, we have to imagine that Gustav found an archeological reality which externalized his own premature "death," i.e., the loss of his "spirit" in the combined traumas of his life. Egyptian entombment, with its elaborate preparations of the mummified body, its multiple nested coffins, and its provisions of victuals for the deceased, all was carefully designed to assure a house for the *Ba* and *Ka*, the spirit and soul of the deceased. And it was the priests, i.e., the "godmen," carriers of the Self, who prepared this place for the safe-keeping of the personal spirit. In the following brief description of his therapy process we will see how fiercely "they" (members of the self-care system) refused to give it up as work with his traumatized feelings began.

Gustav's therapy: recovery of traumatic memory

The first weeks of Gustav's therapy were an elaborate to-and-fro wrangle designed to test the reliability of the analytic container and to assure himself that he could trust me. As soon as he started to "give in" to the support he felt, long-buried feelings began to emerge, like flickering flames around the wick of dreams. Here is the first dream he presented – one which reveals the unbearable sadness at the core of his childhood self and also the archetypal Self-figure protecting his vulnerable spirit.

> I'm in a big building on the second floor. There is fear of World War III starting. I go to the bathroom. There is a panorama window and stalls. A 12-year-old boy leans against the wall between the stalls, sick, with his eyes closed in fear, pain, and despair. He has vomited all over. Through the huge window I can see explosions far away, and with my feet I feel tremors transmitted through the ground. The war has begun. I run out of the bathroom to get lower in the house and to a basement if possible to find shelter. The inside of the building is huge and open like a church. There is a crowd standing on the ground level floor. In the air above the crowd is an explosion. I expect a mushroom cloud but there instead unfolds a colorful, awe-inspiring apparition: a joker, or a clown – actually a FOOL in a garment of radiantly colorful luminescent pieces of fabric. I am terrified. I know that this must be the Devil.

Gustav was very worried about this dream. Did it mean he was about to die?

Or go crazy? Was his world about to end? (In fact he had already suffered both a "death" and a breakdown, but I didn't know it then.) I told him I thought the image of the 12-year-old boy in despair (combined with the outbreak of World War III) suggested that something of catastrophic proportions had befallen him at that age – something that "ended his world." I asked him for his recollections of that age, and then began the slow, painful uncovering of the unknown horror that had occurred during that fateful week when his mother was hospitalized. At each session we excavated a little more of the repression that covered this trauma – unwrapped, as it were, one more layer of his mummified spirit. Along with expressions of a bottomless pain and sadness, great resistance was encountered at each step of the way. Before I describe these resistances and the eventual uncovering of the trauma, a word needs to be said about the Fool/Devil.

Here we have an image to which he had no personal associations, which is often true of archetypal imagery. If we wish to understand what the psyche intends by such an image, it is therefore necessary to *amplify* it, i.e., to find out what it has meant in the collective psyche over many generations. Hence, if we look up "Fool" in any one of several symbol dictionaries, we find material such as the following: the Fool often played a therapeutic role in society as a link to the unconscious and to madness. By provoking laughter and liberating suppressed anxieties, he turned the usual order on its head and therefore served as a corrective to the rigidities of conscious life. Hence, his frequent appearance at the medieval court, where in tattered or multi-colored clothing, his antics poked fun at the King and his rule. He was usually a skilled acrobat, sometimes a magician, and in the miracle plays and carnivals of the medieval period his clowning often climaxed in a symbolic death and resurrection. Frequently he appeared as the Devil and was often ushered in by fireworks, smoke, and a sulphurous stench. If you get the Fool in a tarot deck, it is said to mean an immanent plunge into the unconscious (which is exactly what Gustav was in for, but not in the form of a literal death, as he feared).

The Fool personifies what Jung called the Trickster archetype – that shape-shifting quixotic figure who crosses all boundaries – even those established to separate the gods from men. One such Trickster, very popular with Jung, was even described as wearing "omnes colores" – all colors. He was Hermes/Mercurius, the great messenger/mediator, god of Alchemy who alone could cross the threshold between the divine and human realms. His "colors" signified his role in the alchemical process of redeeming the "blackness" of the early stages of the alchemical opus. Jung says of Alchemy:

> The opus magnum had two aims: the rescue of the human soul (its integration) and the salvation of the cosmos. . . . This work is difficult and strewn with obstacles; Right at the beginning you meet the "dragon," the chthonic spirit, the "devil" or, as the alchemists called it, the "blackness," the nigredo, and this encounter produces suffering. In the language of the alchemists, matter suffers until the nigredo disappears, when the "dawn"

(aurora) will be announced by the "peacock's tail" (cauda pavonis) and a new day will break.

(Jung, 1977: 228f)

So we see that the Fool/Devil combines these opposites and pops in at the explosion of nuclear fireworks at the very moment Gustav starts his descent into a traumatic past – still unconscious. Clearly, here is a prime example of our self-care system, i.e., the primal ambivalent Self in its dual role as Protector/Persecutor. We might imagine that this fierce caretaker will be the source of all the resistance to follow.

Three weeks later, Gustav had the following dream:

> A 12-year-old boy has been kidnapped and is being driven away in a bus. I fear that I will never see him again. I have a handgun and I keep firing at the bus driver and must have hit him several times, but he keeps driving the bus away. As the rear of the bus passes me, I can see two guards in the back of the bus. They have bigger guns than mine and I must stop shooting or they will surely kill me. I feel a terrible anguish over the existence of evil. How can life be like this? Is there no God? Will no-one stop this? I awake full of fear.

This dream tells us that some part of his psyche has been threatened by the beginning of the exploration of his history and is trying to encapsulate it in a metal container (the bus) and take it away for ever (i.e., ensure its dissociation from consciousness). This time, however, he seems to have a relationship with the 12-year-old boy. He "fears that he will never see him again," feels terrible anguish at his capture, and he tries to liberate the boy by killing the abductors.

As his therapy continued and Gustav got closer to the unbearable affect of his traumatic experience, he began to dream that he now *was* the 12-year-old boy. For example:

> I am about 12 years old. The mad doctor pushed me through the door into the basement and threw a hand grenade after me. Having thus taken care of me, without any excitement or emotion he went into another part of the house to go about his usual leisure activities. But I had hidden behind the basement door, am unhurt, and now come out. I escape through a steel door through a small opening where I almost get stuck. I run along a road paralleling a beach going north. I realize how easily the doctor, once he misses me . . . could come after me in his car claiming me as his crazy patient, so I will have to be very careful to only go where he is not likely to come.

The trauma

Shortly after this dream, we were able to piece together his traumatic experience. It was not, as I expected, simple physical abuse by the father, but involved his mother also. Again, the clues to this came through a dream:

> I am awakened by my mother who tells me something that hurts me terribly. I am still mostly asleep but begin to scream at her and after her, but she just walks away. I follow still screaming ... "How will I ever be anybody, how will I live my life?" Following her I enter another room, where a big formless shape like a mummy lies on a bed.

As he meditated on this dream, it was as though a poisonous cyst broke inside his mind, and he remembered how, at age 12, he had accidentally barged into the bathroom where his mother was aborting her pregnancy in the toilet. He remembered that she had told him a month earlier that she was pregnant and that he was excited to imagine a new brother or sister and an end to his abyssmal loneliness. Then he found her doing something terrible to herself, with blood on her hands. She had screamed at him and told him to get out, and in his bewilderment and shame he had begged her to take the needle out of herself but she had screamed that she didn't want the baby, and as his hysteria mounted and he banged on the door, she screamed that she *would have aborted him too if she could have.*

That night, sobbing in his bedroom with his mother in the hospital, his father had come into his room and told him to be quiet. A conversation started and Gustav found out that his father didn't want the baby either – that he hated babies; that he hated cry-babies like Gustav – and that he wished Gustav had never been born. And then there was the familiar red rage in his father's face, and the hate in his eyes, and the twisted ear, the screaming ... and that is all Gustav remembered, until he was let out of the mental hospital.

As Gustav abreacted all the deeply repressed sadness and rage associated with this dissociated memory he felt enormous relief. His depression lifted considerably and he even considered leaving therapy. However, no sooner had we consolidated the gains made from this work, preparing to rest a while on our laurels, than his dreams began to "work on" a still earlier trauma. Now it was a 6-year-old boy who appeared, as in the following dream:

> I am being driven in a car by a terrorist/kidnapper. I am sitting in the back. Also in the car is my 5–6-year-old son. The terrorist wants to take us hostage, but I refuse and get out of the car. My son stays inside. I beg and plead with the terrorist to let my son go, too, but he drives around with him in the car in a circle or two, while I must watch powerlessly.

Here we have another example of the child self-representation under the tyrannical control of the Persecutor/Protector. (Gustav's real son was a grown man and so this 5-year-old "dream-son" we took as an aspect of himself.) As we got closer to his experience during this time through a continual review of his early memories, dreams such as the following emerged, as if to tell us we were on the right track:

> The son (about 5 or 6) of a factory owner (a kind of hovering presence, not a person) has been found outside, where he has been lying on the ground,

covered with a layer of snow, for a long time. Now that we have dug him up we express to him our expectation that he might be angry, disappointed, and even enraged about his fate, i.e., about having been outside there and forgotten for so long. Our assumption must be that his father did not miss him much altogether and gave up searching for him all too easily, if indeed he ever was missed and searched for. But he seems to be too weak and afraid for such feelings. He can hardly speak and he stutters, and I believe that this must be from him suffering brain damage when he was deprived of oxygen for so long when covered with snow.

This dream helped us get closer to his feelings as a child of having been abandoned by his father (he was aware of missing his mother). This, in turn, opened up the love he had initially felt for his uncle, the butcher, and how his terror of this man did not have to do with the blood-spattered apron, but with an event that occurred shortly after his arrival at the country house. Late one night, his uncle had come into his bedroom. . . . the details all spilled out as we discussed the following, final dream in this series:

It seems to start with a man's hands around a child's neck. I am about 6 years old and living in a small town in the country. An invisible cloud that swallows up people has come into the world. Every now and then, on its wanderings, it contacts someone, usually a man, and usually at the legs, and they begin to disappear into the invisible cloud.

I go by train to the city. I am glad to escape from the hunting grounds of the cloud, but think that it might follow me to the city and begin to eat people there. Then I am in the main train station when I begin to feel cold and tingling, and realize that I am about to run into the cloud. I try to pull back, but it comes with me. I move towards other people in the hope that it will latch onto them and let me go, but it stays with me. There are some workers close to me. I am desperate to have anyone touch me, so they will draw the cloud away from me. I gesture at the workers to touch me; only one comes and touches my penis, then another, while they are making fun of me. I have them hold on. Their touch takes away some of the feeling of the cloud touching me, but some remains with me. My lower abdomen and sex organs feel cold and tight, as if bewitched or possessed.

Gustav remembered then that his Uncle had lain on top of him and touched his penis and, as he had resisted, his Uncle had muffled his cries and put his hands around his neck to frighten him.

We must interrupt Gustav's story at this point. Not unexpectedly, the uncovering and abreaction of this 6-year-old's trauma, with its accompanying feelings of de-personalization and de-realization, led us still earlier into the second and third year of his childhood. Both Gustav and I were amazed, during this process, at how his dreams eventually led us to the necessary details within which his dissociated affects were hiding – if Gustav felt safe enough in the transference. During this process, he was extremely "touchy" and irritable about the work and at times became positively convinced that this retrospective stuff was a waste of our time! It was as though much shape-shifting *resistance* was being thrown up by the caretaking figure (Fool/Devil, bus driver, mad doctor, terrorist/kidnapper, factory owner, cloud). Only slowly and with great objections did the figure(s) relinquish their control over the "child" in the dream, until the affect associated with the early trauma could be recovered.

This personified *resistance*, engineered by the self-care system, is a common finding in psychotherapy with individuals who have experienced life-rupturing trauma. In object-relations language, these people show what we might call a deep attachment to their persecutory inner "objects." Freud (1923: 4a) was the first to notice this. He called it the "negative therapeutic reaction," so named because when he spoke hopefully to certain patients, they invariably became worse. Freud believed this resulted from an inner attack by a "sadistic superego" on the "masochistic ego" of the patient. However, Freud left something out here. The resistance of trauma patients to change and growth is only partly explained as intimidation by a sadistic superego. Complicating this simple explanation is the fact that the sadistic superego is also a caretaking superego, i.e. a "superior" inner figure who has virtually saved the patient's psychological life, and this is a kind of miracle for which the patient, unconsciously, may be very grateful. Through the ministrations of this inner figure the patient has access to altered states of consciousness (and, we might imagine, altered psycho-physiological states) which have a soothing effect and which are not easily relinquished precisely because they have worked in the past to preserve something which the patient "knows" is precious cargo, i.e., the inviolable spirit of the personality.

KAYE AND HER DOLPHINS

Those of us who work as psychotherapists with people who have suffered early trauma are frequently blessed with glimpses into the psyche's miraculous life-saving powers or, to put it more precisely, with the ways in which numinous psychic reality seems to come to the aid of the traumatized ego. The following clinical example is one of those "glimpses."

A woman whom we shall call Kaye consulted me for psychotherapy following a serious automobile accident which left her hospitalized for several weeks and her hands crippled and disfigured. While recuperating from the acute injuries of her accident, her fiancé "lost his feeling" for her and broke the engagement, and her closest friend in the world unexpectedly died. To make matters worse, her active outdoor job was now threatened, because she could no longer do her work with crippled hands. Many painful reconstructive surgical operations were in store for her if she ever expected full use of her hands, and the financial resources for these operations were questionable. Needless to say, following these multiple traumas, Kaye was depressed and anxious about the future.

As I slowly got to know her, it turned out that traumatic levels of fear were nothing new to Kaye. In fact, because of her exquisitely sensitive disposition as a child, the hard edges of life itself had often seemed devastatingly sharp to her. She spent her first month of life in an incubator because of difficulty breathing after a premature birth. Then, as an otherwise happy and well-adjusted little girl, she had continual fears of dying and night-terrors about death or other frightening things she heard on the news – like possible nuclear war or the horrors of the concentration camps in Germany. Most of all it was death itself that preoccupied her. How could you "be" and then "not be"? How could death just be "it"? She would lie awake all night thinking about such questions. When she asked her parents these questions over and over again, she got the message that she was just "too sensitive." She began to think something was wrong with her. When she was three, her older brother, whom she adored, went to school and she cried for days – too sensitive! Her puppy died and she was devastated – again, the judgment was "too sensitive."

Kaye's vulnerable emotional sensitivities did not fit very well into a family where there was a great emphasis on stoic self-control and religious sacrifice. Kaye's questions, if too far "out of line", would get her mouth washed out with soap by her mother, or her father, who liked his alcohol, would shame her with insulting remarks before he spanked her regularly. This was all exacerbated by a learning disability (how could she be so stupid!) and then in high school she was slow to develop, was a little overweight (her mother was always weighing her), felt ugly, and did not fit in. An insidious form of self-judgment began to set in. Kaye began to blame herself for all her troubles. One of her first dreams in therapy showed the persecutory side of her growing self-care system:

> I was in a concentration camp. We were watching people being led away to be killed. A woman grabbed me by the arm and led me away from our group. She told me to keep my back to the guards at all times. She said that my hands would make me a definite target for the crematorium because I wasn't perfect and they only kept people without flaws.

As her perfectionistic Nazi-like self-care system set in during her adolescence, Kaye retired more and more into her own world. She spent more and more time in her room or on long lonely walks. She began to write reams of sad poetry, kept a journal of her fantasies and stories, and developed an ability she called "popping out." When things got overwhelmingly sad, she could "pop out" of her body and "float" above herself. Floating helped her into free-form imaginal play with images. It was like a waking dream, but one she could enter more or less at will. In this world she was in a state of special communication with herself and with the natural mysteries of the outdoors. It was like swimming, which she loved, and at which she excelled, and so sometimes she imagined her private "floating world" as an underwater world. In this aquatic wonderland, she had a special feeling for and rapport with dolphins.

About eight weeks into our work together, Kaye confronted another trauma.

Her outdoor job, upon which she was dependent for medical coverage for her future surgery, was threatened by "staff cutbacks" arbitrarily administered by an executive at her company who saw her as an insurance risk. Kaye was beside herself with fear over this situation. She felt completely dependent on this work and its insurance benefits and therefore unable to confront the situation as she might have, had she been more independent. The more she tried to please the boss, the worse the situation became, until finally her humiliation reached a breaking point. At this point she had a dream in which dolphins appeared.

We're having a staff meeting. My boss growls something at me and turns his back. I'm upset and ask him what he meant. He rolls his eyes sarcastically. I follow him out onto the street. He turns and says, "What's your problem?" Again I don't understand. Suddenly he looks like a Latino street kid – tough and mean. He leaves me at the corner and tells me to wait. I'm devastated. Suddenly fish started to swim by – I thought it was a big circular aquarium. Kids were pointing at the fish as they stood on the corner. Then two bottle-nosed dolphins swam around the corner and slipped right past me. I was excited to see them. They watched me carefully as they passed. I wanted to swim with them, but I had to wait for my boss. They came around again – this time there were nine. They all watched me. They looked serious; not happy the way dolphins usually look. My boss came back. He said that reviews were up. He said he couldn't work with me any more. I asked why. I was scared and started to shake. He said I embarrassed him – that I should never talk at meetings and complained about other things. The dolphin swam by. I asked him if I was fired. I was crying, but had to hold it back. My boss said he was letting me go. The dolphin came by and slowed down. A voice in my head kept saying, "The dolphins, the dolphins!" I couldn't hold back the tears. I felt like I was choking. I woke up crying.

In associating to this dream, Kaye said that she had had many dolphin dreams over the years. They usually came at times when she was confronting over-whelming difficulties. "I have always felt protected," she said. "I've always felt too vulnerable – but also strangely protected, as if another reality is very close at hand." Two weeks later, Kaye was indeed fired from her job by this boss, and that night the dolphins returned in her dream again, only this time they took her with them.

I am working in an aquatic park with the manager, Dennis [a man who in reality had an explosive temper and frightened her]. We are doing some work in waist-deep water and there are dolphins everywhere. I recognize some of them. I wanted to swim with them, but I had to help Dennis, who just realized he had forgotten something. He was very angry and started blaming me. He was pacing and shouting. The dolphins surfaced again, motioning for me to come with them. I wanted to go with them but I didn't think I'd be able to swim as deep as they could. I was afraid I'd run out of oxygen. Dennis was getting more and more angry and stormed up the bank. The dolphin I knew swam right to me, turned on its side, got under me, and took off really fast so that I had to grab its fin. We dove deeper and deeper. All the other dolphins were swimming with us. I panicked because I didn't think I could breathe and just then we resurfaced. The dolphin showed me how to breathe through the airhole in the back of my neck. I hadn't known it was there. We dove very deep again and as we swam along the dolphin told me to keep touching it.

Dennis had come back down. He was calling for me angrily. We were swimming away from him. I couldn't see where we were going. The dolphin told me to hold on and I would be fine. It was time and I held its fin and we soared through the water.

Interpretation and theoretical commentary

In Kaye's dreams, we see how the transpersonal emissaries of her self-care system in its positive form (the dolphins) come to the rescue of the dream-ego which is experiencing overwhelming anxiety in the face of the rejection and/or raging anger of the negative side of this same "system," (the boss and Dennis). In other words, it is not just the outer events that are traumatizing Kaye. It is the outer events – difficult enough for anyone, to be sure – amplified by her archetypal inner self-critic that makes the situation traumatic. With the concentration camp dream as a backdrop, we know that Kaye's fear is not just a response to outer threat, but that the "Nazis" exist as a part of her punitive inner "perfectionistic" self, taken over from the parental environment. The outer events are not in themselves determinative of trauma. The problem comes from the fact that to her ego, these outer events seem like *proof* that the devastating conclusions she has drawn about her own loathesomeness and "abnormality" are true. This is what Henry Krystal means when he says that trauma is not just overloading the circuits. It is related to *meaning* (Krystal, 1988) – in this case the negative and distorted meaning that Kaye made, as a little girl out of her suffering – that she was somehow at fault for the "bad" things that happened to her.

The dolphin in mythology

It is interesting that Kaye's self-care system comes to her rescue in the form of dolphins. As avatars of the Self's positive healing energies and carriers of the personal spirit at times of dire threat, dolphins are especially apt images mythologically and often appear to rescue persons who are about to die (cf., Graves, 1955). For example, Arion, son of Poseidon and master of the lyre, is condemned to death by a group of sailors who are covetous of his wealth. After singing his last song, Arion jumps overboard and is presumed dead. But a dolphin carries him ahead of the ship to Corinth where – after a royal welcome – he confronts his would-be executioners who are put to death themselves. Similar stories abound. A dolphin reportedly rescued Enalus when, in despair, he jumped overboard to join his sweetheart in the depths. The dolphin's mate rescued his sweetheart. Another dolphin saved Phalanthus from drowning on his way to Italy, and finally, no less than the great Apollo, looking for a likely spot to establish his oracle, jumped on board a Cretan ship disguised as a huge dolphin and led the astounded sailors to Delphi. There he revealed himself and commanded them to establish a shrine of Apollo Delphinius (he of the dolphin), appointing them keepers of his oracle (see Tripp, 1970: 62).

Further association between the dolphin and rebirth of the spirit is found in Pausanius, who reports that Taras, a son of Poseidon by Minos' daughter Satyraea (of the satyrs) was the dolphin-riding New Year Child of the Dorian city Tarentum. From other evidence in Pausanias, Graves finds it likely that the ritual advent of the New Year Child was dramatically presented at Corinth with the aid of a tame dolphin trained by the Sun priests.

These mythic images cement the symbolic relationship between that intelligent "center" in the unconscious psyche which Jung called the Self and the miraculous, intelligent, playful and uniquely human-related denizen of the underwater world, the dolphin. This connection, and its primal guardianship of the personal spirit, are seemingly as old as mankind.

PATRICIA AND THE GHOST-CHILD: WHEN THE SPIRIT RETURNS TO THE BODY

Patricia was a middle-aged woman who had grown up in poverty for most of her younger years, living in trailer parks and motels – the family always evicted from each place of residence, her mother being drunk most of the time. Her father was off at war until she was 2 and when he returned he brought warfare into the house in the form of alcoholic rages and beatings of the mother. Once the father strangled the mother to near death in front of my patient who then was forced to sleep with her mother for the mother's protection. Patricia's whole childhood was spent in fear. She tried as best she could to hold things together – to care for the other children – to give them the childhood she was slowly losing as the years went by. She became the little mother of the family – cooking the meals, making the beds, dragging the mother out of bars, and so on. At some point in this process, around the age of 4 or 5, this valiant little girl who was later my patient, simply gave up. Her spirit just left. All the color went out of her life. The rest of her childhood, she said, was literally in black and white.

Prior to her therapy with me, this patient had gone to a workshop and did a kind of active imagination work, and the image she had imagined was part of her motivation for therapy. In her vision, a male guide came and took her into a temple. Deep inside this stone sanctuary in a darkened room was a female child lying on a kind of altar. But the child was made of stone. Slowly, as Patricia stayed with this child, it came to life. The child opened its hand and inside was a star. The star sparkled and was beautiful and golden, but then slowly it took the shape of a sheriff's badge and the vision ended.

My patient's association to the sheriff's badge was an important link to the dream I will report below. During her earlier career, she had worked at a home for neglected and dependent children and was frequently involved in adoption procedings. At her agency, whenever a birth-mother gave up her child for adoption, the local sheriff would serve papers making it official that the mother was giving up all rights to the child. My patient always hated this procedure and felt it was adding insult to injury for the birth-mother.

This all came out later. At the time she had the vision, Patricia knew that this girl child in the temple was also her, and it made sense to her that the child was made of stone, because she herself felt frozen in her body, split off from her emotions, her sexuality, and she was depressed.

In her subsequent therapy with me, after many sessions spent exploring her early life and trauma history, there emerged the actual experience of trauma in the transference. This had to do with her rage and grief that the "love" she felt for her analyst could not be lived out in the "real" world, and that some of the total mutuality she had imagined in our relationship was illusory. This led to a back-and-forth, withdrawal and reconnection cycle in the sessions which, in retrospect, I see as the gradual transformation of her self-care defense. Her daimon would whisper, "See, I told you so – he doesn't care – you're just another case!" – and he would pull her out of relationship to me. Then, after her withdrawal, we would somehow restore the feeling connection and the work could proceed. Each time she opened up her feeling in this way she betrayed her daimon and released herself into the relationship and into her true self.

This is more or less the process of "grief work" that I was involved in with Patricia and it is important to note that it also involved "grief work" for myself. To do the work necessary for "phase-appropriate" disillusionment of a trauma defense, it is necessary to challenge the mutually enjoyable positive transference/counter-transference connection that both parties are all too likely to enjoy and to indulge *ad infinitum*. Often, the diabolical "voice" of the self-care system so demoralizes the patient that the sympathetic therapist is easily seduced into simply providing a positive "counter" voice in an effort to reassure the patient and provide some encouragement. Indeed, this is necessary in the beginning phases of therapy, but encouragement alone leaves the patient at the mercy of her daimons and it is necessary to constellate a bit of the original "trauma" in the transference, in other words, to constellate a *conflict* with the patient. Extreme delicacy is called for here, because the inner daimon exploits the impersonal nature of therapy in an effort to convince the patient from within that it is futile to hope for a "real relationship" with the therapist, and that without this everything is hopeless. Indeed, sometimes one wonders whether psychotherapy can ever provide enough of the missing mutuality of experience that is at the core of most trauma victims' early deprivation, and there are, of course, certain people who are so badly damaged in infancy that they cannot benefit from psychotherapy precisely because of its paradoxical combination of intimacy and separation.

In any case, this was not Patricia's problem. She bravely confronted each increment of disappointment in me and the situation, knowing that this was somehow part of recovering her true life in the world and she wanted this desperately. Each time, as we honestly struggled with the limitations inherent in our therapy relationship, what was sacrificed on one level (illusion), was restored on another (relationship) – which is why *sacrifice* means to "make sacred." During this difficult time, something began to happen which I can only describe as her spirit returning to her body. It is a dream about this I want to report because the dream gave us both an image of when, in childhood, her spirit had left. Ironically, this dream, about her spirit's departure was only "possible to be dreamed," so to speak, when it was safe for it to return.

Her dream was set in the context of her early agency work. I will tell it in the first person as she told it to me.

> I am in a house where a little girl apparently lives and all kinds of lawyers are present. A case is being developed to get this little girl out of a traumatic environment with her parents ... terminating parental rights. The head lawyer is drawing a chart on the wall showing how the child gets anxious whenever the father or mother are present. Nearby is the child's grandmother and she loves the child incredibly and is there for its protection from the mother and father. I'm the case-worker in this situation. I see that the grandmother will give the child up. She's not letting on how terrible she feels. She has to be tough and unfeeling to create the appearance that there is no feeling for this child in this family, because she wants the head lawyer to get this child out. I take the grandmother outside and hold her very tightly in a full body hug, in order to draw out her feelings. We both start to cry. I know she must feel all of her grief. She's willing to lose this little girl because she knows it's the only way to save the child.
>
> Then I look up and I see the little girl looking down from an upper window and at this point I realize the child is also me. I/she am about 4 or 5 years old. I motion for her to come down and as she does this I realize she's not a real child, but a kind of ghost-child. She's all ethereal and sort of floats down to us. I put her in her grandmother's arms so she can feel all the love we have for her as she is released into safety.

As the adult Patricia reported this dream she felt an enormous sadness but she didn't know why. She wondered if it had to do with a case at work. Following a long silence, I said to her simply that I thought this dream was about what happened to her when she was 5 years old. . . that she could no longer live as a whole person then and that a part of her had to be "released" into safety. I said that this had been a terrible loss – one she had been unable to grieve until now, and that she could have this dream now because, paradoxically, after our work together, this child was returning to her body. She was now strong enough to feel her loss and let it "mean" something.

This made sense to her and brought up still more affect, which continued for the rest of the hour. This is an example of how, when the psyche is ready, a dream can bring together affect and image to create *meaning*, which in turn makes further suffering possible – this time meaningful suffering – suffering that can be incorporated in the deep narrative history of an individual's life. Here is the transcendent function, the capacity for imagination restored, the renewed possibility of a symbolic life.

The way I understand this dream and the prior vision of the stone child is that at the age of 4 or 5, when the little girl who was later my patient had her hopes for life broken and gave up her spirit, something in the psyche I have described as the archetypal defense of the Self was there to catch it. This figure, I would propose, turned this spirit into stone and put a star in its hand – a star which symbolized both its imperishable, irreplaceable essence and, as sheriff's badge, the "sign" that this child's spirit had been given up "officially."

The dream pictures the moment of her spirit's release. The head lawyer and the grandmother I would interpret as differing aspects of her Trickster-guardian self-care system. Together, they are "tricking" the family. The head lawyer and grandmother are collaborating to make sure the spirit-child will be released into safety and the patient, now having descended into her body, makes sure this child feels loved as it is "released." The "full-body hug" bespeaks the patient's new-found embodiment.

We might think of this moment also as the release of the Self from its defensive functions, for its real work as a psychopomp and mediator of the individuation process. At least this is one way to envision what Patricia and I experienced as an enormous deepening of the work at this time. Over the following weeks, her dreams started to cohere around a particular telos or direction, the sessions felt more mutual and collaborative, everything slowed down, and there was a sense of gratitude for the meaning of the work.

We encounter here a supreme irony in our work with the psyche. The self-same powers that seemed so set on undermining our therapeutic efforts – so ostensibly devoted to death, dismemberment, and annihilation of consciousness – are the very reservoir from which new life, fuller integration, and true enlightenment derive – if they are humanized through the transformative process of "good enough" psychoanalysis. We come closer here to understanding the Devil's self-description in Faust (Goethe, 1941). When asked "Who are you then?" the Devil responds:

> Part of that Power which would
> the Evil ever do, and ever does the Good.

PSYCHOSOMATIC ILLNESS AND THE SELF-CARE SYSTEM

In the following remarks, I want to use the case examples of Lenore and Patricia to illustrate the relationship between mind, body, psyche, and spirit in both

62

psychological health and trauma-related psychological disturbance. We know our trauma patients have been forced to dissociate mind and body and, as a result, they are psychologically depressed and have lost their spirit. How do we understand the loss of this spirit and how does it relate to mind, body, psyche, and soul? How can we help these people get their spirit back? What is the work necessary to prepare for its return?

Mind

D. W. Winnicott suggests that when maternal environmental care is inadequate, the mind, which under optimal conditions is completely integrated with the psychosomatic experience, *becomes a "thing in itself"* (Winnicott, 1949: 246). This constitutes a "usurpation of environmental functions by the mind (which has developed precociously) and the result is a "mind-psyche, which is pathological" (ibid.: 247) This pathological "mind-psyche" or "mind-object" (see Corrigan and Gordon, 1995) is equivalent to our self-care system. Instead of the mind being used to make meaning out of sensate experience, the mind *imposes the meaning it has made in the initial traumatic situation.* As we have seen, this is usually equivalent to a condemnation of an inner child-self by a tyrannical Protector/ Persecutor.

Ordinarily, by "mind" we mean the mental, rational capacities of thought associated mostly with the left brain and its tendencies toward abstraction, conceptual formulation, and logic. This would include the capacity for reflection and transcendence of immediacy through a process in which neural and hormonal signals from the body are transmuted into representations such as words and concepts. In Jungian parlance, this is the logos function – the way in which our minds give form and representation to otherwise undifferentiated input from the body and its senses. Language is a crucial part of this logos function and the evolution of a representational language makes experience comprehensible both to the self and to others. If we include right-brain function in our notion of mind, then representation will not just be in desiccated words, but in moving images, in words that connect to the body – in poetry, for example.

Spirit

Earlier, we said that when Lenore's and Patricia's early trauma became un-bearable, their psyches split and with this split, their personal spirits escaped the mind/body unity and went into the unconscious, where they later informed a particular kind of melancholy fantasy. Such fantasy is an ethereal place and, as Winnicott makes clear, is not equivalent to imagination. These clinical facts are reflected in the ancient energy system of Alchemy which interested Jung a great deal. An old alchemical dictum says: "There is in the human body a certain aethereal substance . . . of heavenly nature, known to very few, which needeth no medicament, being itself the incorrupt medicament" (Jung, 1955: para.114n).

This "animating principle," according to Alchemy was a *natura abscondita* (hidden nature) perceived only by the inward man. In Alchemy the body's "animating" spirit had two aspects – an earthly one and a celestial one. In its celestial aspect, it had wings and could ascend the ethereal heights of Olympus to commune with the Gods and then deliver their messages to man. Alchemy's name for this twofold spirit was Hermes or Mercurius, and Mercurius was duplex – himself a union of opposites, both body and mind, dark and light, feminine and masculine. As the embodied spirit, Mercurius represented what Paracelsus called the *"lumen naturae"* (light of nature); as a rarified heavenly spirit, on the other hand, he represented the celestial, radiant "numen" or heavenly light. And as Paracelsus reminds us:

> as little as aught can exist in man without the divine numen, so little can aught exist in man without the natural lumen. A man is made perfect by numen and lumen and these two alone. Everything springs from these two and these two are in man, but without them man is nothing.
>
> (Jung, 1954: para. 388).

What Paracelsus calls the "luminous" vehicle or "lumen naturae," neo-Platonic philosophers called the "subtle body." It was seen as composed of a finer order of matter than that known to the physical disciplines, and yet it was not quite spiritual stuff either. The word for spirit among these philosophers was "pneuma" and so their word for this intermediate realm was "soma pneumatikon," ethereal or spirit-body, which of course is a paradox. This subtle or spirit-body, represented to these philosophers the vital inner formative principle of any person. Its perfection was a preoccupation of Alchemy (see Mead, 1967: 34ff.). It corresponds with what we know as the psyche.

Psyche

The subtle body or spirit-body is very close to what Jung meant by the psyche, and sometimes he even equated the two. A clinical example given by Jung shows how someone could be sick in this place – in his psyche – while not being sick in either his body or his mind.

Jung's patient was a very intelligent, successful man who was obsessed with the idea that he had intestinal cancer even though all actual tests were negative. Doctors had often reassured the patient that there was nothing physically wrong with him, i.e., he did not suffer from a "real" cancer. But his morbid idea persisted and obsessed him to the point where his whole life had become absorbed by it – all this despite the fact that he "knew" rationally, in his mind, that the cancer was a purely imaginary affair (Jung, 1937b: para. 12). Jung further comments:

> Our usual materialistic conception of the psyche is, I am afraid, not particularly helpful in [such cases]. If only the soul were endowed with a subtle body, then one could at least say that this breath- or vapour-body was

suffering from a real though somewhat ethereal cancer, in the same way as the gross material body succumb to a cancerous disease.

(ibid.: para. 13)

Jung goes on to talk about how ill this man was, *not in his body and not in his mind* – he knew he had no cancer – but he was ill in his *psyche*, a kind of intermediate third area. Jung is emphasizing the reality of the psyche here. Illness in the psyche, he says, is just as "real" as illness in the body or the mind, even though psychological reality is subtle and hard to hold onto. Of the psyche, Jung once said:

the underlying idea of the psyche proves it to be a half bodily, half spiritual substance, an *anima media natura*, as the alchemists call it, an hermaphroditic being capable of uniting the opposites, but who is never complete in the individual unless related to another individual. The unrelated human being lacks wholeness, for he can achieve wholeness only through the soul, and the soul cannot exist without its other side, which is always found in a "You;" Wholeness is a combination of I and You, and these show themselves to be parts of a transcendent unity whose nature can only be grasped symbolically, as in the symbols of the *rotundum*, the rose, the wheel, or the *conjiunctio Solis et Lunai*.

(Jung, 1946: para. 454)

So we locate the psyche in what Winnicott (1951) called "transitional space." The person who suffers a mind/body split after trauma is ill in this third place – in his or her psyche – not necessarily in the mind or in the body. The post-traumatic individual may have an excellent "mind." He or she may be highly gifted and effective intellectually (even though usually these individuals are more at home in abstractions or rarified aesthetic pursuits than they are in personally grounded thinking). Similarly, the post-traumatic individual may have a healthy body. Such a person may push his or her body to extraordinary feats – undertaking marathons, decathalons, body-building, and so on. But closer examination reveals that there is something missing in these people's body-experience, and this we can only vaguely describe as a missing personal spirit, a sense of animation, intimacy, and vulnerability that leaves them compulsively unsatisfied and wanting more and more stimulation. What these individuals are really looking for is psyche, or soul – the place where body meets mind and the two fall in love. If this tension could be held, a true birth of the personal spirit would be possible, but psyche, or soul, is necessary first. For this reason we speak of psychopathology and of psychotherapy.

Understanding the psyche as a half-bodily – half spiritual (or mental) entity has some important implications. One danger of psychotherapy is that it becomes too "mental" (wordy) and loses the link with the body. When this happens, psychotherapy loses the psyche also. Correspondingly, a danger of pure bodywork is that it may release much somatized energy without this raw affect becoming available to the mind in the form of images or words that would enable it to be understood. If affect from the body cannot be expressed in verbal or symbolic language between people, it cannot reach the level of "meaning" which is where the psyche is. So body-workers can also lose the psyche and if this happens, the possibility of truly transformative work is also lost.

The split-up of mind, body, and spirit in trauma

In the previous chapter, we discussed how the self-care system of early trauma cannot allow all the elements of whole experience to be present at once and how this results in an attack against links between somatic and mental components of experience. Because somatic and mental elements are "different," we might say that the self-care defense exploits the incommensurability between the mind and the body and divides up experience accordingly. The affect and sensation aspects of experience stay with the body and the mental representation aspect is split off into the "mind." Such a person will not be able to let somatic sensations and excited bodily states into mental awareness, i.e., will not be able to let his or her mind give shape to bodily impulses in words or images. Instead, messages from the body will have to be discharged in some other way and will therefore remain pre-symbolic. Such an individual will have no words for feelings, and this will put him or her at a terrible disadvantage. This person will not be able to work through sensate experience psychically – to play with symbolic meanings – and this will rob him or her of the experience of feeling real and fully alive, a tragic condition we know as de-personalization.

For example, Lenore's repeated early abandonment by her mother could not be "retained" as a memory except in a terrible tension in her stomach that had given rise to her earlier ulcer. Only when she relived this abandonment in her marriage did she recover the "state-dependent" memory of the earlier trauma – and only then when she had an image of her childhood self and a supportive therapeutic relationship to help her. Jung once said that the abreaction of trauma was not the healing factor: "the experience must be rehearsed in the presence of the doctor" (Jung, 1928a: para. 269). The presence of a witness to experience seems to be necessary to constellate that "otherness" which brings the *psyche* into being as a "third" factor.

Usually, the psyche is that organ of experience which creates links and associations among elements of the personality in the interest of integration, wholeness, and personal integrity. In trauma, however, we see the psyche operating not to link but to de-link – to split or to dissociate. We might think of the psyche's dissociative defenses as a little person who controls that circuit-breaker in the house, who throws the breaker if lightning strikes. This assures the personality's survival – in trauma, the psyche's goal is survival, not individuation. So the defense is life-saving, but then later mistakes every "flash of light" for the original catastrophe and breaks the connection compulsively. This entails a terrible cost –

the loss of the spirit. When mind and body split, the animating principle of psychological life, or what we would call the spirit leaves.

At this point things get more complicated, because the question then becomes, "Where does the spirit go when it leaves?" From our case examples we have seen that one "place" the spirit seems to go is into those knots in the stomach as state-dependent "memories." In other words, it is encapsulated in a kind of "somatic" unconscious state. However, with my patient Lenore, we also saw that her spirit seemed to be encapsulated in her "mind" – in that disturbed and disturbing inner world which was woven out of archetypal fantasy – what Winnicott (1971a: 32) calls "fantasying" instead of imagination. We might call this the "mental" or "spiritual" unconscious. In her case, it was as though there was one "place" of encapsulated energy in her body and another "place" of encapsulated energy in her mind. Both were "unconscious." Instead of speaking of two "uncon-sciouses", however, it would be better to say, along with Jung, that the unconscious has two aspects or "poles" – one closely related to instinct and the body, one associated with the spiritual dimension of being.

In Jung's analogy, the psyche can be thought of as the visible spectrum of light. In this spectrum, the human eye can only see from red on one end to violet on the other. On either side of this spectrum there exist "colors" which are "un-conscious", as it were – forever out of awareness. On one side is the infra-red, on the other, the ultra-violet. We might think of the infra-red as the chthonic or "psychoid" level – the instinctual body-side of the unconscious and the ultra-violet side as the spiritual or "higher" mental dimension of the unconscious. The psyche seems to use the extremes on the body/mind spectrum as "places" in which to deposit the personal spirit – places for it to hide in. When the spirit is split out of the body/mind unity, it seems to go to both places simultaneously. When it "returns," it does so from both places at once. It does not just descend from the heavens like the dove of the Holy Spirit in medieval images of inspiration or annunciation. It also comes up from below – from the underworld of the body like the uncoiling of the Kundalini snake. When these two aspects of the spirit meet, we have what we might call the birth of the soul or psyche and the incarnation of its spirit or divine child, "*numen*" and "*lumen*" together (see Jung, 1949: paras 259–305).

3

FREUD AND JUNG'S DIALOGUE ABOUT TRAUMA'S INNER WORLD

The awful thing is that beauty is mysterious as well as terrible.
God and the devil are fighting there and the battlefield
is the heart of man.

(Dostoyevsky, *The Brothers Karamazov*, 1950: 127)

JANET AND THE INNER DAIMONS

Depth psychology had its beginnings in the discovery that the human personality contained not one but two (or more) centers of organization and identity. By the mid-nineteenth century, a series of remarkable case studies by practitioners of "animal magnetism" and hypnosis had appeared describing in vivid detail double or multiple personality, somnambulistic possession, catalepsy, and other forms of "Dipsychism" (see Ellenberger, 1970: 112–47). These studies dramatically showed how a secondary ego-state with a whole life of its own could take over the subject's customary personality during altered states of consciousness.

The secondary personality uncovered in these early investigations was understood to be "daimonic," i.e., consisting of a "spirit" (usually evil) possessing the personality from within. In hypnotic trance, this possessing spirit would often identify itself as a daimon. Long before Freud and Jung appeared on the scene, it was known that the daimon's powers of possession originated in severe trauma and that somehow the daimonic "trance" made the traumatic experience inaccessible as a memory. In the early work of Charcot and Janet, for example, daimons were named, flattered, and their cooperation enlisted in the treatment so that their hypnotic powers over the patient's ego could be "transferred" to the physician, and the traumatic memories thus recovered.

Janet in particular was fond of tricking the inner daimons. One of his male patients named Achilles was "possessed" by the Devil and spoke compulsively in profanities and blasphemies until Janet tricked the inner daimon (through automatic writing) into cooperating with the treatment and taking over the actual hypnosis of the patient from within! Soon thereafter, the traumatic story emerged of how the patient, on a business trip, had been unfaithful to his wife. He had then begun to dream of the Devil and suddenly found himself possessed. It was not until this deeply conflictual story had been wrested from the patient by Janet that the patient lost his delusion. There was great resistance to this thrown up by the patient's inner daimon, until finally its cooperation was enlisted. Janet summarizes the case by saying that the true illness of the patient did not lie in the daimon; instead, the true illness was remorse (see Ellenberger, 1970: 370).

In this case, Janet showed his truly "modern" understanding that the "true illness" is an intra-psychic conflict (unconscious guilt/remorse) that cannot be borne by the patient's ego; it is too painful. The psyche's defense against this unbearable pain is to send an archetypal daimon – a representative of the psyche's self-care system, to help dissociate the patient from his intolerable shame/anxiety. The daimon, "thinks" and "speaks" with a voice which constitutes the patient's *interpretation* of his unconscious pain. "To interpret" is from the Greek *hermenuenein*, itself from Hermes, god of communication and hermeneutics, and wise mediator between the divine and human realms. As god of boundaries and crossroads (what Winnicott (1951) called "transitional space") Hermes is also patron saint of depth psychology. So we see how the inner world of trauma is filled with the creations of Hermes who is also a Trickster. His communications are often lies and deceptions (see Radin, 1976). He is perhaps as close as we can come to finding a single personification for what I have described as the psyche's archetypal self-care system, and in the second half of the book we will see much of him in various disguises.

TRAUMA AND FREUD'S DISCOVERY OF PSYCHICAL REALITY

By the time of Freud's early work, case reports such as Janet's of Achilles showed that by hypnotically inducing the "second," altered state of consciousness controlled by the "daimon," healing results could be obtained. But the dynamic mechanism for these cures was not understood. Usually, the double ego of psychiatric patients was thought to arise from some hereditary "lesion" in the brain or some pathological mental weakness in the patient, so no meaning could be made of the fact that evoking (and exorcising) the daimon often cured the patient.

As Freud applied Charcot's hypnotic techniques to his own hysterical patients, and began to elicit their stories in detail, he started to make discoveries that led to the first psychoanalytic theory of trauma and, more importantly, to the discovery of psychical reality *per se*. Freud found that behind the hysterical symptoms of his patients lay some painful affect that remained in a "strangulated" state and that this affect was attached to a memory that was cut off from consciousness. The strangulated affect-memory became the nucleus of what Freud called a "second psychical group" (Freud, 1894: 49) or a "sub-conscious complex of ideas" (Freud, 1893: 69n). Once this nucleus was formed "at a traumatic moment" (Freud, 1894: 50) it established a vulnerability to later recurrences of _uma if impressions of a similar sort occurred. Hence treatment was usually successful unless the original moment was reached _along with the affect_ _sociated with this moment. In the now-famous language of the authors, "Hysterics suffer mainly from reminiscences" (Freud, 1893: 7).

The question then became, "Reminiscences of what?" What were the traumatic moments and their associated "strangulated affects?" Here, Freud left no doubt about which moments he considered traumatic. "In all the cases I have analysed," he said, "it was the subject's sexual life that [gave] rise to the distressing affect" (Freud, 1894: 52). In 1896 Freud set forth an even more sweeping claim:

> I therefore put forward the thesis that at the bottom of every case of hysteria there are one or more occurrences of premature sexual experience . . . I believe that this is an important finding, the discovery of a _caput Nili_ [source of the Nile] in neuropathology.
>
> (Freud, 1896: 203)

In summary then, instead of a lesion in the brain, Freud proposed that trauma created a lesion in the _psyche_ (a splitting of the ego) and that this led to a "second psychical group" which became a source of resistance to healing.

THE SEDUCTION THEORY

Freud's early investigations soon ran into various obstacles, calling for further revisions in theory and practice. First, many traumatized patients refused to be hypnotized and in many other ways resisted the efforts of the analyst to gain access to their dissociated material. Second, Freud found that some of his patients were abreacting _fantasies_ of traumatic sexual abuse rather than actual traumatic seductions. Writing to Fliess in 1898, Freud complained, "initially I defined the aetiology [of neurosis] too narrowly; the share of fantasy in it is far greater than I had thought in the beginning" (Freud, 1954).

This did not represent an "abandonment" of the seduction theory as Masson (1984) asserted in various writings (see Kugler, 1986). Instead, it expressed Freud's growing doubt about whether objective trauma alone could give rise to neurosis without the participation of deeper layers of the mind, in particular, the participation of _unconscious fantasy_, and associated levels of unconscious _anxiety_. Freud was searching here for a psychological factor that would honor the fact that it is not trauma that splits the psyche, but a feared _meaning_ of trauma to the individual that leads to this result. This meaning must be found, reasoned Freud, in a universal unconscious fantasy – a kind of nuclear or "_Kerncomplex_" that underlies all neurosis (see Kerr, 1993: 247ff.).

Freud's case of Little Hans provided the clearest evidence. He found in this young patient sexually explicit feelings of jealousy toward the mother and anger against the father as "rival" – themes which found their mythological expression in the myth of Oedipus, which Freud enshrined as a sort of universal trauma. In light of this myth, the father's scolding of the little boy for playing with his penis

70

did not constitute a trauma as such; rather, this scolding *meant* a threat of castration, and this meaning in turn created traumatic anxiety. It was anxiety based on unconscious fantasy that split the psyche. The emphasis was on psychical reality. The external traumatic event was no longer in itself seen as pathogenic – rather its internal representation, affect, or amplified *meaning* was seen as the source of the psychopathology.

JUNG'S COMPLEX THEORY AND TRAUMA

Jung was entirely in agreement with Freud's effort to include the dimension of meaning, unconscious fantasy, and unconscious anxiety in the discussion of trauma. Precisely *what* meaning and *what* unconscious fantasy was another matter – one that would ultimately become the watershed dividing their respective theories of trauma – but the idea that trauma was more than just "overloading the circuits" and was related to unconscious *meaning* was very important to Jung. Even on the threshold of his major break with Freud in 1912, Jung asserted this agreement at his Fordham University Lectures:

> there are a great many ... people who experience traumata in childhood or adult life without getting a neurosis... [whereas others clearly do.] With this discovery, somewhat bewildering at first sight, the aetiological significance of the sexual trauma in childhood falls to the ground, as it now appears totally irrelevant whether the trauma really occurred or not. *Experience shows us that fantasies can be just as traumatic in their effects as real traumata.*
>
> (Jung, 1912a: paras 216–17; emphasis added)

One can imagine that Jung is exaggerating his point (this was characteristic of him) when he says "it now appears *totally irrelevant* whether the trauma really occurred or not." Clearly, this is not the case clinically and Jung himself did not believe it. For example, in other writings, Jung is eloquent in his grasp of how important the actual historical event and story of the trauma are for psychotherapy (see Jung, 1963: 117).

At this time in psychoanalytic history, both Freud and Jung were emphasizing – against the more popular "brain lesion" theory – the potentially *traumatogenic effect of unconscious fantasy*. Both men saw in their patients how the memory of traumatic events was often confabulated with unconscious fantasies, making it difficult to distinguish fact from fiction and making the trauma worse. Both agreed that these fantasies could be just as traumatic in their effects as outer traumata, often continuing the trauma internally far after the outer event (Freud's later "repetition compulsion"). In other words, for both men, outer trauma alone (usually) does not account for the profound effects in the psyche that it triggers. For this effect to be understood the fantasy component must be added. But what fantasy? This is where Freud and Jung could not agree, and where, over eighty years later, we are still suffering from the confusion left by their tragic split.

Independently of Freud, and before the two men met in 1907, Jung had explored his own version of Freud's "second psychical group" of ideas based on "strangulated affects." Jung's methodology was the word association test and his search was for the internal factors that led to disturbances in normal ego-function, measured as an unrestricted flow of associations to a list of stimulus words. Jung discovered that the subject's normal flow of associations was usually impeded by various affects – hence the term "feeling toned complex." When Jung further grouped these affect words together, they seemed to betray a common theme, but *this theme was by no means always sexuality.* Indeed, there were erotic complexes where all words with prolonged reaction time described erotic activities, but there were many other complexes as well, including inferiority complexes, power complexes, parental complexes, or a complex surrounding some specific guilty act, like Janet's patient's extra-marital affair.

For Jung, then, the secondary ego-states embodied in complexes are not precipitated by sexual trauma alone – but by the full range of human tragedy and misfortune, each one uniquely personal. He was no less interested than Freud in finding a "universal" core complex behind traumatic neuroses. But his exploration of the "strangulated affects" in dissociated states led him to *many* traumas and many different personal stories and fantasies (complexes) about these traumas. Not surprisingly, his later libido theory was pluralistic and multiple, not attributable to one instinct such as the Oedipal drama with its (universal) castration trauma forcing renunciation of an incestuous sexual wish. Deeply immersed in the study of mythology himself, Jung was convinced that human sexuality was only one of the avenues through which universal unconscious fantasy becomes problematical (traumatic) for the developing ego.

From these discoveries, Jung eventually elaborated a pluralistic model of the psyche's dissociability into many different complexes, each containing an archetypal set of motifs or images at its core. These archetypal images defined a deeper "strata" of the unconscious which gave them a "numinous" character. As carriers of the numinosum, they participated in aboriginal man's experience of the sacred, at once both awe-inspiring and terrifying, i.e., potentially traumatic. For Jung, it was among these numinous ambivalent archetypal images and their associated complexes that the search for a universal trauma-related unconscious fantasy in neurosis would have to proceed. In other words, Oedipus and sexuality were not the only "daimons" for Jung. Many other "gods" were also traumatic for the developing ego and especially the dark side of daimonic reality that Jung encountered in the following case.

THE LADY WHO LIVED ON THE MOON

Jung's discovery of the religious dimension of unconscious fantasy and its relation to trauma is an interesting part of psychoanalytic history. Jung was especially intrigued by a fantasy one traumatized female patient reported of a whole secret drama where she lived on the moon and there tried to save the children from a winged vampire who menaced the land. Jung completely cured this patient of her psychosis and this cure required him to carry an archetypal image in the transference – an image of her diabolical "daimon-lover" who was the principal figure in her fairy-tale-like fantasy. In the projection of this figure, Jung saw a redemptive "intention" in the psyche which didn't seem to fit the Freudian reduction of such material to sexual wishes or "daydreams."

The young woman was 17 years old and catatonic when Jung first saw her. She had had only a rudimentary education, had grown up in a small town nearby, and had no trace of mythological knowledge. Two years earlier she had been seduced by her older brother, a doctor, and further abused by a schoolmate. These traumatic events had fragmented her psyche and she had withdrawn into complete isolation – her only relationship being with a vicious watchdog which belonged to a neighboring family. The brother, in desperation, brought her to Jung and gave him *carte blanche* to do everything that was humanly possible to help her – despite the obvious risks of suicide. By the time Jung first saw her she was completely mute, refused food, and heard voices. Jung describes her first appearance:

> her hands were cold and bluish, she had livid patches on her face and dilated, feebly reacting pupils. I lodged her in a sanatorium nearby, and from there she was brought to me every day for an hour's consultation. After weeks of effort I succeeded by dint of constantly repeated questions, in getting her to whisper a few words at the end of every session. The moment she started to speak, her pupils contracted, the livid patches on her face disappeared, soon her hands grew warm and assumed their normal colour. Finally she began – with endless blockings at first – to talk and to tell me the content of her psychosis. She now related to me a long and elaborate myth, a description of her life on the moon, where she played the role of a female saviour for the moon people. The classical connection of the moon with "lunacy" was as unknown to her as the numerous other mythological motifs in her story.

> (Jung, 1958: para. 571)

Here is the fantasy that she finally told Jung:

> she had lived on the moon. The moon, it seemed, was inhabited, but at first she had seen only men. They had once taken her with them and deposited her in a sublunar dwelling where their children and wives were kept. For on the high mountains of the moon there lived a vampire who kidnapped and killed the women and children, so that the moon people were threatened with extinction. That was the reason for the sublunar existence of the feminine half of the population.

> My patient made up her mind to do something for the moon people, and planned to destroy the vampire. After long preparations, she waited for the vampire on the platform of a tower which had been erected for this purpose. After a number of nights she at last saw the monster approaching from afar,

winging his way toward her like a great black bird. She took her long sacrificial knife, concealed it in her gown, and waited for the vampire's arrival. Suddenly he stood before her. He had several pairs of wings. His face and entire figure were covered by them, so that she could see nothing but his feathers. Wonder-struck, she was seized by curiosity to find out what he really looked like. She approached, hand on the knife. Suddenly the wings opened and a man of unearthly beauty stood before her. He enclosed her in his winged arms with an iron grip, so that she could no longer wield the knife. In any case she was so spellbound by the vampire's look that she would not have been capable of striking. He raised her from the platform and flew off with her.

(Jung, 1963: 129)

After telling Jung her story, the patient was able to speak again without inhibition, but having betrayed her secret, she suddenly realized that she could no longer go back to the moon, whereupon she became violently insane again and had to be re-hospitalized until her catatonia abated. After a two-month interval, she could be moved back to the sanatorium and was able to resume her sessions. Slowly, reported Jung, she began to see that life on earth was unavoidable. She could not return to the moon. "Desperately, she fought against this conclusion and its consequences," once again giving in to her daimon and being sent back to the sanatorium. "'Why should I return to earth', she wondered, 'this world is not beautiful, but the moon is beautiful and life there is rich in meaning. . .'" (Jung, 1963:12a).

Once this patient had resigned herself to her fate of entering this world for good, so to speak, she took a job as a nurse in a sanatorium where it turned out that she carried around a concealed revolver. A young doctor there made a pass at her and she shot him. In her last interview with Jung, she handed him the loaded gun, telling him, to his amazement "I would have shot *you* down if you had failed me!" After the excitement about the shooting had subsided (the doctor survived), she returned to her native town, married, had several children, and for more than thirty years thereafter kept Jung informed by letter about the state of her health, which continued to be excellent (see Jung, 1963: 130 and 1958: paras 571–3).

Jung gives the following interpretation of the Moon-lady's fantasies:

As a result of the incest to which she had been subjected as a girl, she felt humiliated in the eyes of the world, but elevated in the realm of fantasy. She had been transported into a mythic realm; for incest is traditionally a prerogative of royalty and divinities. The consequence was complete alienation from the world, a state of psychosis. She became "extra-mundane," as it were, and lost contact with humanity. She plunged into cosmic distances, into outer space, where she met with the winged daimon. As a rule with such things, *she projected his figure onto me during the treatment.* Thus I was automatically threatened with death, as was everyone who might have persuaded her to return to normal human life. By telling

me her story she had in a sense betrayed the daimon and attached herself to
an earthly human being. Hence she was able to return to life and even
to marry.

(Jung, 1963: 130; emphasis added)

Jung's interpretation of his case needs to be taken a little further in order to
bring it into line with the present investigation. We would want to say "yes,"
Jung's patient did indeed project the vampire-daimon onto Jung, but not just his
dangerous, destructive side. She also projected his "beautiful" awe-inspiring
aspect, i.e., that positive side of the daimon that gave him the power to enchant
her. Only if she had loved Jung in the transference and found her curiosity aroused
by a real object and by what he held out to her as a real possibility would she have
told her story and betrayed the daimon. This process, we know from the case
report, was fiercely resisted by the daimon itself. It was Jung's incredible interest
as a young psychiatrist in her situation that allowed her self-care system to
relinquish its control over her inner world.

Throughout the time during which Jung was treating this case, he was writing
to Freud. A sense of how crucial this case was to the evolution of his thinking can
be gained from this correspondence. For example, in September, 1910, Jung wrote
to Freud:

I am working like a horse and am at present immersed in Iranian
archaeology. I think my conjecture that the Miller fantasies really add up to
a redemption mystery can be proved to the hilt. Only the other day a so-
called Dem. praec. patient, whom I have almost set on her feet again, came
out with a really grand, hitherto anxiously guarded, moon-fantasy which is
a redemption mystery composed entirely of liturgical imagery. A thing of
marvellous beauty but very difficult, built on incest with her brother. . . .
The interesting thing . . . is that prior knowledge is entirely lacking; the
fantasy originated in early childhood (about the 7th year). She is now 18 ½
years old, Jewish. – As I said, I wallow in wonders.

(McGuire, 1974: 356)

And in March of the following year, Jung complained:

For more than a year now, amid unspeakable difficulties, I have been
analysing a Dem. praec. case, which has yielded very strange fruits; I am
trying to make them comprehensible to myself by a parallel investigation
of incestuous fantasy in relation to "creative" fantasy. Once my thoughts
have matured I must seek your advice. I am still brooding on it.

(ibid.: 407)

And in June of 1911:

Everything I am doing now revolves round the contents and forms of
unconscious fantasies. I think I've already got some really fine results. . . .
Often I longed for you to be here so that I could discuss an extremely difficult

case: Dem. praec. with, one can well say, a tremendous unconscious fantasy system which I have to drag into the light of day with unspeakable effort and patience. On top of that, constant danger of suicide. A really devilish case, but extraordinarily interesting and instructive. . . . It seems that in Dem. praec. you have at all costs to bring to light the inner world produced by the introversion of libido. . . [this] introversion leads not only, as in hysteria, to a recrudescence of infantile memories but also to a loosening up of the historical layers of the unconscious, thus giving rise to perilous formations which come to light only in exceptional cases.

(ibid.: 426–7)

Freud did not like this allusion to an archetypal layer of the unconscious. He hastily replied to Jung:

I am very much interested in what you tell me about the system of unc. fantasies in a case of D. pr. These constructions are known to me from hysteria and obsessional neurosis; *they are nothing other than carefully cultivated daydreams.* I took them into account by saying that the symptoms spring not directly from the memories but from the fantasies built on them. . . . Where I have found [such a system of fantasies], its production was no more important than were the aetiology and the motives and the rewards held out by real life.

(ibid.: 429–30; emphasis added)

Here Freud was attacking the very core of Jung's excitement over the seemingly mythopoetic aspect of the unconscious – that aspect he was later to call the archetypal or "collective" layer. Jung shot back:

That it is not of great therapeutic importance to get patients to produce their latent fantasies seems to me a very dubious proposition. The unconscious fantasies contain a whole lot of relevant material, and bring the inside to the outside as nothing else can, so that I see a faint hope of getting at even the "inaccessible" cases by this means. These days my interest turns more and more to ucs. fantasy, and it is quite possible that I'm attaching too great hopes to these excavations. Ucs. fantasy is an amazing witches' cauldron: "Formation, transformation, Eternal Mind's eternal recreation . . ."

(ibid.: 430–1)

TRAUMA AND THE TRANSPERSONAL IN UNCONSCIOUS FANTASY

In the Moon-lady's "redemptive" fantasy, then, Jung thought he had glimpsed a deeper understanding of how the psyche tries to heal itself after unbearable trauma. Could it be, Jung wondered, that this truly mythic story was simply a disguised "sexual daydream," as Freud thought? Was the feathered body of the winged daimon, for example, a possible stand-in for the brother whose naked body had perhaps been revealed for the first time to the patient on the occasion of her violation? Or did this figure with its "numinous" power stand for something more? Did it perhaps represent a part of the patient's self-care system that had come to the rescue here – that had cast a spell over her, encased her in a world of "lunacy" in order to protect her from being injured again, i.e., in order to keep her from ever trusting anyone again? These were the kinds of teleological intuitions that Jung had about such material. The psyche seemed to be making use of "historical layers" of the unconscious in order to give form to, or "outpicture," otherwise unbearable suffering – suffering that had no expression except in mythopoetic form.

The wisdom of Jung's intuition here can be apprehended from a slightly different angle if we consider the frequent relationship between religion and trauma. In a book called *God is a Trauma* (1989), Greg Mogenson makes the interesting point that we tend to experience and propitiate traumatic events as if they were divine, and that we do this, to use Winnicott's language, because a trauma is an event whose overwhelming pain cannot be experienced within the area of omnipotence, i.e., cannot be symbolized (see Winnicott, 1960b: 37). Says Mogenson:

> Whatever we cannot inhabit psychologically, we propitiate with religious responses. It is not just that God is unknowable and unimaginable; it is that we reach for "God" most earnestly when imagination fails us. . . to stand before an event for which we have no metaphors is to stand in the tabernacle of the Lord.
>
> (Mogenson, 1989: 7)

And yet, says Mogenson, the slow evolution of symbolic metaphors seems to be the only way severe trauma can be healed.

> Overwhelming events, events which cannot be incorporated into the life we have imagined for ourselves, cause the soul to bend back on itself, to commit "incest" with itself, and to revert to the heretical modes of the *primary principle*. Like the festering process which removes the sliver from a wound, the traumatized imagination works and re-works its metaphors until the events which have "pierced" it can be viewed in a more benign fashion. The traumatized soul is a theologizing soul.
>
> (ibid.: 156 and 159; emphasis added)

It was just this "primary principle" that Jung thought he had glimpsed through the trauma that befell his patient. The winged daimon, he felt, was a "religious" figure from the mythopoetic strata of the unconscious, "deeper" than the self-serving illusions that disguised sexual desires toward the parents, or in this case toward the older brother. This level of the unconscious is where our internal object-relations shade over into what Jung described as the mythical or "imago" level (Jung, 1912a: para. 305). At this level the personal father imago shades off into a more archaic, Janus-faced "Father-God" – both terrible and benign. Hence the winged daimon both protects the patient's fragile ego, sweeping it away into inner sanctuary, while at the same time, destroying her animated life in the world. It is truly both a devil and a god – a "daimon-lover."

JUNG AND FREUD ON THE PSYCHE'S DAIMONIC RESISTANCE TO HEALING

In taking an open (even appreciative) attitude towards the dark side of the numinosum in this case, and showing how, as self-care system, the patient's inner vampire personified a dissociative defense against unbearable psychic pain and anxiety, Jung finally was able to coax this woman out of her vampire's clutches and back into the world of reality. What for Freud were only "carefully cultivated daydreams," insignificant compared to the rewards of reality, represented for Jung a fascinating world of unconscious fantasy that opened onto the great vistas of religious iconography and mythology. With this appreciation of the mythopoetic basis of his Moon-lady's fantasies, Jung could offer her a genuine interest in the inner world of her traumatized psyche, and we must imagine that this interest was an essential part of a psychotherapy that allowed the patient to eventually leave her vampire-haunted diabolical sanctuary.

It is important to note that Jung is describing, in this case, his work with a much more severely disturbed patient than the traumatized hysterics behind whose "strangulated affects" (Freud, 1894: 49) Freud had found sexual trauma and "carefully cultivated (Oedipal) daydreams." (Freud, in McGuire, 1974: 429). For Jung, this more severe level of trauma led to severe fragmentation of the ego, primitive defenses, and the "possession" of the personality by a diabolical imago from the collective psyche. Such designations were for Freud too close to the occult for comfort. To him they represented a regression from the science of psychoanalysis back to what had already been known by Janet, Charcot and the early Mesmerists, whereas for Jung, they represented a re-discovery of enormous importance – in his own language, the "reincarnation of ancient wisdom in the shape of Psychoanalysis" (Jung, in McGuire 1974: 439).

Freud did not like Jung's version of "reincarnated ancient wisdom" and by 1912, the tension so obvious in the previously cited correspondence had led to an irrevocable split between the two men. This was a tragic rent in the fabric of developing theory and practice from which I believe we are still recovering in psychoanalysis. Jung went on from this point to elaborate a dissociative model of the "plural" psyche much more consonant with recent findings in work with the victims of serious trauma, especially patients with narcissistic, borderline, or schizoid personality disorders, or those showing the extreme dissociative defenses of Multiple Personality Disorder. This model *includes a religious or numinous background to the imaginal psyche* which seems to me crucial in understanding severe forms of character pathology and the primitive defenses (self-care operations) which characterize these conditions.

Meanwhile, Freud and the rest of psychoanalysis continued to reduce religious imagery in unconscious material to wish-fulfilling fantasies and to focus optimistically on those milder forms of trauma and psychopathology explainable through repressive (as contrasted to dissociative) defenses. Only with the so-called "pre-Oedipal" conditions and the work of Klein, Fairbairn, Winnicott, and Guntrip on archaic forms of unconscious fantasy did the tradition of Freudian psychoanalysis begin to consider the inner world of trauma and its diabolical representatives (see Chapter 6). By this time, the rift with Jung and his tradition was so wide that no dialogue was possible.

FREUD AND THE DAIMONIC DEFENSES OF THE UNCONSCIOUS

After the separation from Jung, Freud *did* encounter a "daimonic" element in the psyche and it is interesting to note how closely his discoveries fit with our notion of the self-care system and archetypal defenses coordinated by the Self. This daimonic element presented itself to Freud in two places: (1) as a counterpoint to his original optimism about analytic interpretation of the *resistance*, and (2) in his later theories about the "severe superego." In the final part of this chapter we will take up each of these in turn.

Freud and "daimonic" resistance

Freud found to his consternation that certain "primitive resistances" in his patients did not seem to give way when their putative libidinal strivings were made conscious through interpretation. In these "daimonic" inner forces Freud found the equivalent of Jung's archetypal vampires and possessing spirits, although he never would have acknowledged this. Freud's theoretical speculations in this area "beyond the pleasure principle" provide an important bridge to the psychoanalytic theories outlined in Chapter 6 (see Freud, 1920b).

Freud introduced the idea of resistance in his early work on hysteria to describe a phenomenon he had observed during the treatment of a 24-year-old patient, Fraulein Elisabeth von R., namely, her inability to remember and her failure to cooperate. He realized that this resistance was the same psychical force that had created the symptom in the first place, and he saw these resistances as ego resistances. They stemmed from the same source as repression, i.e., the ego's refusal to allow certain libidinal strivings into awareness because of their forbidden (unconscious-fantasy) meaning. The analyst only had to be patient and "work through" these resistances to an optimistic result. This presumably worked fine for neurotic patients. Later, however, Freud's optimism about resistance analysis began to wane. Cures did not follow working through. Resistance no longer appeared so simple as the ego's "anti-cathexis" of erotic wishes (repression). By 1926 Freud had become interested in resistances from beyond the ego, i.e., from the id or superego (Freud, 1926: 160). These resistances were more archaic, more daimonic, and much more difficult to treat. In the language of the present work, *they represented archaic defenses coordinated by an unconscious "agency" which appeared "daimonic" in its intent.*

The first of these primitive resistances (of the id) Freud called the *repetition compulsion*. Freud was struck by the fact that both inside and outside analysis, many people seemed caught in a compulsive repetition of self-destructive behavior – a kind of undertow which made them seem fated for a negative destiny. Freud's explanation for the repetition compulsion was the tendency of the psyche to mistake a benign situation in the present for an originally traumatic one. A young woman's traumatic early abandonment by her father, for example, will lead her to interpret every analogous situation with a man whom she begins to love (such as the transference) as equally dangerous, so she will reject the man and suffer the trauma of "abandonment" once again (see ibid.: 153).

This is very similar to the notion of Leopold Stein (1967) that the Self acts like the body's immune system and can be tricked in an analogous fashion. In other words, the self-care system inadvertently repeats the dissociative action of its original defense to primal trauma in later, otherwise benign, situations. It is not educable.

So diabolical did this compulsion seem to Freud that he linked the repetition compulsion with the death instinct:

> I drew the conclusion that, besides the instinct to preserve living substance and to join it into ever larger units, there must exist another, contrary instinct seeking to dissolve those units and to bring them back to their primaeval, inorganic state. That is to say, as well as Eros there was an instinct of death.
>
> (Freud, 1920a: 118–19)

So the "daimonic" intent of the repetition compulsion was none other than to do away with life altogether – to reduce it to its original inorganic state. Such was Freud's pessimistic conclusion.

The second resistance – one Freud attributed to the superego, he described in this way:

> There are certain people who behave in a quite peculiar fashion during the work of analysis. When one speaks hopefully to them or expresses satisfaction with the progress of the treatment, they show signs of discontent and their condition invariably becomes worse... they get worse during the treatment instead of getting better. They exhibit what is known as a negative therapeutic reaction.
>
> (Freud, 1923: 49)

And then, speaking like a contemporary object-relations analyst describing primitive internal object images, Freud said: "There is no doubt that *there is something in these people that sets itself against their recovery*, and its approach is dreaded as though it were a danger" (ibid.; emphasis added).

In other words, an unconscious intra-psychic "complex" functions in these people as an active inner agency trying to prevent change and growth. Freud called

80

the diabolical inner agency of the mind the "archaic superego" and believed that it operated in people who suffered from a deep sense of unconscious guilt (today we would say shame) – a feeling of "badness" that impelled them to blindly repeat self-destructive behaviors as though to bring punishment on themselves for some nameless crime. This seemingly perverse tendency, Freud believed,

> came from a piece of aggressiveness that had been internalized and taken over by the superego . . . when the superego was first instituted, in equipping that agency use was made of the piece of the child's aggressiveness towards his parents for which he was unable to effect a discharge outwards. . . . [this aggression is then] internalized and taken over by the superego.
>
> (Freud, 1933: 109)

If Freud had followed this line of thinking to its logical conclusion, it would have led him to internal object-relations theory and (possibly) back to the traumatic roots of "persecutory" inner objects such as Fairbairn's "internal saboteur" or Klein's "bad breast." But Freud's was an instinct-based meta-psychology (like Jung's) and his insight that a "daimonic" quality of primitive resistances came from the child's unexpressed aggression at the moment of a trauma provides the basis for much later theory about the psyche's "diabolical" inner objects. The role of aggression in these archaic defenses was also something that escaped Jung. We will see in Chapter 6 how much of Freud's understanding has been incorporated in other theories about the self-care system and how it contributes to a necessary revision in Jungian thinking about the inner world of trauma.

Freud's severe superego

In Freud's original theory, the dyadic structure we have been describing – one part alternately sadistic or benevolent, the other part "innocent," – boils down to the relationship between the superego (inclusive of the ego-ideal) and the ego. Freud's original theory of the superego as the introjection of the parental attitudes – both comforting and prohibitive – could not account for the extreme hostility – even sadism – of the superego against the ego in many of his cases. The severity of parental criticism – the sometimes abusive, even humiliating reproach of some parents – was indeed always mirrored in the superego's attitude toward the ego, but often the sadism of the superego far transcended even the worst kind of parental negativity.

In his *Mourning and Melancholia* (1917), Freud added another element to account for the superego's sadism. He hypothesized that the severe self-reproach found in melancholics derived from their ambivalence toward a lost love-object, this ambivalence becoming enshrined in the inner world as an ego, identified with the lost love-object, and another part representing the original hatred and reproach of the abandoning object rebounding upon the self, thereby adding to the superego's sadism. According to this theory, then, the worst aspect of self-attack was a derivative of aggression originally directed outward but unconsciously "boomeranging" against the ego. The ego's masochism in relation to the superego was derived from a previous sadism toward the abandoning object. However, even this explanation did not satisfy Freud. It still did not account for the extreme aggression manifested by the superego in many cases, and for the compulsion of some patients to repeat self-destructive behavior as if in obedience to some "daimonic" destructive power inside themselves.

As we have seen in his thoughts on the resistance, Freud was so affected by the self-destructive "repetition compulsion" of some patients, and by their "negative therapeutic reaction," that he proposed in *Beyond the Pleasure Principle* (1920b) a "death instinct" (Thanatos) as an equal partner in the unconscious with the libido or life instinct (Eros). The death instinct manifested itself as destructive aggression, a force in the psyche which endeavored to destroy or dissolve all the integrated "unities" that Eros strove to create. This was Freud's dualistic theory of the instincts, one he traced back to the ancient Greek philosopher Empedocles, who proposed that the two basic principles governing the universe and the mind, eternally at war with one another, were love and strife (see Freud, 1937: 244f.).

Then, in a final effort to explain the superego's sadism against the ego, Freud (1924) linked the death instinct with his superego theory by proposing a *primary masochism* in the ego which amplified the sadism of the superego (see Freud, 1924: 163–70). This "original" or primary masochism (*Ur-masochismus*) owed its origin to that portion of the death instinct that was not converted by Eros into outward aggression or sadism, remaining inside the organism, fused with erotic energies (sexual pleasure from pain). As a result, says Freud, "the sadism of the superego and the masochism of the ego supplement each other" (ibid.: 170), leading to a masochistic ego that both provokes and takes satisfaction in the punishment of a sadistic superego (repetition compulsion).

In this formulation, Freud bypasses the benevolent aspects of the superego, except to acknowledge that the superego carries a "model" of perfection for the ego in the form of an "ego-ideal." Subsequent psychoanalysts have emphasized the positive, loving aspects of the superego, especially as found in its ego-ideal. Nunberg (1932) was one of the first to point out that the superego's capacity to restrict instinctual life is based upon the child's love and idealization of the parental objects, introjected as ego-ideal. Modell (1958) pointed out that the auditory "voices" of the superego included loving and supportive voices as well as accusatory ones, and Schaefer (1960) described the "loving and beloved superego" in Freud's structural theory, arguing for the neglected comforting and supportive nature of the superego.

In this brief summary, we can see three ways in which the superego concept parallels Jung's concept of the primordial ambivalent Self and how it is initially carried in projection by the parent.

1 The superego takes shape around the original parental imagos, both positive and negative, and to these imagos are later linked the influence of teachers and

other authority figures who carry ego-ideals or the fear of punishment for the individual (see Freud, 1924: 168). Beyond these personal imagos, the positive aspect of the superego extends into unconscious fantasies of a loving and protective God-figure who is more powerful by far than the real father, and in its negative aspect, the superego becomes coincident with the "dark powers of Destiny" (ibid.: 168). Thus, the superego avails itself of those primordial, magical, or "transpersonal" powers in the unconscious – both benevolent and malevolent, libidinal and aggressive, Eros and Thanatos – just like Jung's archaic ambivalent Self-structure.

2 The superego performs a regulatory (guiding) function with regard to the ego (in health), assisting the ego by holding up ideal images towards which it strives, and by putting a damper on those impulses that are destined not to be gratified – thereby protecting the child from undue privation or frustration. This regulatory or "defensive" function depends upon an optimal balance between the forces of Eros, which conspires to unify the elements of the psyche, and Thanatos, which threatens to fragment, dissociate, or dissolve the integrations which Eros effects. Such an optimal balance, in turn, depends upon many factors, but especially upon the child's integration of both love and hate in relation to its primary objects, i.e., the personalization of those archaic instinctual elements of the primitive psyche. Finally, a loss of the superego's sustaining self-regulatory relationship to the ego can be experienced by the ego as abandonment and alienation (similar to what we would describe in Jungian language as a loss of ego–Self axis). Freud's regulatory or defensive aspects of the superego parallel Stein's and Fordham's "defenses of the Self" (see Chapter 5).

3 The projection of the positive aspects of the superego (as ego-ideal) onto the analyst has a stabilizing influence on the psyche of the patient, is the basis of positive transference, and makes possible the gradual modification of more archaic, negative superego aspects, as these are also projected onto the analyst and then worked through in light of the prevailing positive transference. This parallels Jung's understanding of how the archaic idealized Self is projected in psychotherapy leading to the caricatured idealization of the doctor and eventually to the internalization of this imago as an internal "center" within the patient's inner world (see Jung, 1934a: paras 206–20).

4

JUNG'S CONTRIBUTIONS TO A THEORY OF THE SELF-CARE SYSTEM

In many cases in psychiatry the patient who comes to us has a story that is not told, and which as a rule no one knows of. To my mind, therapy only really begins after the investigation of that wholly personal story. It is the patient's secret, the rock against which he is shattered.

(Jung, 1963: 117)

In this chapter we will have a more extended look at Jung's later understanding of the "daimonic presences" which people the self-care system of individuals who have suffered life-shattering trauma. Then, in the next chapter, we explore the ideas of other contributors within the *œuvre* of analytical psychology. We begin with Jung's personal encounter with the daimonic and with his unconscious ritual "efforts" in the face of early trauma and its "dark God," to preserve what we have called the inviolable personal spirit. As we might expect, these experiences made Jung very sensitive later to the "secret rocks and stories" against which his patients lives were "shattered."

JUNG'S TRAUMA AND ATMAVICTU

In his autobiography, *Memories, Dreams, Reflections*, written when he was 83 years old, Jung (1963) describes his childhood in a very straight-laced, religious Swiss family where mother and father were estranged and feelings were never discussed. A deeply imaginative, sensitive, and serious young boy, he began to be plagued with terrifying nightmares, the content of which made him feel ashamed and "unendurably lonely." His efforts to talk about these inner experiences with his dogmatic minister father or his distracted, depressed mother left him feeling even worse about himself, so he stopped trying to communicate his feelings and retired into himself. By his latency years, Jung began to realize that he was really two persons in one body. One of these persons, he said:

went to school and was less intelligent, attentive, hard-working, decent, and clean than many other boys. The other was grown up – old, in fact – skeptical, mistrustful, remote from the world of men, but close to nature, the earth, the sun, the moon, the weather, all living creatures, and above all close to the night, to dreams and to whatever "God" worked directly in him. As soon as I was alone I could pass over into this state. At such times I knew I was worthy of myself. . . . I therefore sought the peace and solitude of this "Other," second personality.

(ibid.: 45)

One time, during his early school years, Jung had entered a writing competition with his classmates on a subject he felt passionate about. When the teacher, who usually discussed the papers in order of merit, mentioned him last, he was crushed. Then the teacher brought out Jung's paper and said, "We have one paper here which ought to have been given first place, but unfortunately it is a fraud. Where did you copy if from Carl? Confess the truth!" Jung shot to his feet horrified and furious, vainly protesting his innocence. But the teacher turned away contemptuously and Jung's classmates threw odd glances at him, thinking to themselves, "Aha, so that's the way it is." "I felt now," Jung reported, "that I was branded, and that all the paths which might have led me out of unusualness had been cut off" (ibid.: 65).

The pain of this event in his life was excruciating. He became obsessed with it, but he couldn't bring himself to share his pain with anyone. This went on for days. "And then," he reported,

something happened that I had already observed in myself several times before: there was a sudden inner silence, as though a soundproof door had been closed on a noisy room. It was as if a mood of cool curiosity (and detachment) came over me, and I asked myself "What is really going on here? All right, you are excited. Of course the teacher is an idiot who doesn't understand your nature – that is, doesn't understand it any more than you do. One gets excited when one doesn't understand things."

(ibid.: 65–6)

At times like these, Jung said later,

it was as though a breath of the great world of stars and endless space had touched me, or as if a spirit had invisibly entered the room – the spirit of one who had long been dead and yet was perpetually present in timelessness until far into the future. Denouements of this sort were wreathed with the halo of a numen.

(ibid.: 66)

Around this time, Jung's disunion with himself and general uncertainty in the world led to a ritual enactment of a fantasy which at the time he did not understand.

I had in those days a yellow, varnished pencil case of the kind commonly used by primary-school pupils, with a little lock and the customary ruler. At the end of this ruler I now carved a little manikin, about two inches long, with a frock coat, top hat, and shiny black boots. I colored him black with

85

ink, sawed him off the ruler, and put him in the pencil case, where I made him a little bed. I even made a coat for him out of a bit of wool. In the case I also placed a smooth, oblong blackish stone from the Rhine, which I had painted with water colors to look as though it were divided into an upper and lower half, and had long carried around in my trouser pocket. This was his stone. All this was a great secret. Secretly I took the case to the forbidden attic at the top of the house and hid it with great satisfaction on one of the beams under the roof. I felt safe, and the tormenting sense of being at odds with myself was gone. In all difficult situations, whenever I had done something wrong or my feelings had been hurt, or when my father's irritability or my mother's invalidism oppressed me, I thought of my carefully bedded-down and wrapped up maniken and his smooth, prettily colored stone. . . This possession of a secret had a powerful formative influence on my character; I consider it the essential factor of my boyhood.

(ibid.: 21–2)

In these moving childhood experiences we see the seeds of all Jung's later authorship. First came traumatic dissociation of the psyche – simply unbearable pain that could not be held in the vulnerable ego of a young child, resulting in defensive splitting that encapsulated a part of the self which we might call Jung's personal spirit and assured its safety in the "other" world of the unconscious. Then came the miraculous self-healing as the collective unconscious psyche "took care" of Jung through the elaboration of a symbolic ritual. This ritual served the function of unifying the fragmentation-prone psyche of the small boy by preserving an image of his spirit, safely bedded down in the pencil box and hidden away with the round stone that was divided, like the young boy's psyche into two halves, light and dark. This stone, Jung recognized much later, was a Self-symbol, a *coniunctio oppositorum*. And the ritual enactments that creatively saved Jung's spirit and sequestered it in a safe place did not end with the carving of his manikin. Much later, in 1920 when he was 45 years old, while in England, he carved two very similar figures. Later he had one of them reproduced in stone and placed it in his garden in Kusnacht. "Only while I was doing this work," said Jung, "did the unconscious supply me with a name. It called the figure Atmavictu – the 'breath of life.'" Breath of life, of course, means "spirit."

We see in this example how the creative unconscious with its remarkable symbolic ritual-process came to the rescue of Jung's traumatized childhood psyche. This seemingly intelligent inner world Jung described as "numinous," referring to its uncanny feeling qualities and the apparent wisdom in its transcendent symbolic unfolding – something Jung later called the "transcendent function." In these early experiences of rescue and self-healing, Jung had an experience of the psyche's reality and saw the meaning in his suffering – a meaning which redeemed his suffering and allowed him to see it *sub specie aeternus* – from the standpoint of eternity. This makes suffering bearable in a way that cannot be achieved within the ego's narrow boundaries.

But there was another aspect to Jung's numinous world and its rescue of his spirit, which we have passed over in our description thus far – and this was found in Jung's terrifying nightmares, especially the one nightmare which was to "preoccupy me all my life" – the nightmare of the undergound phallic God who fed on human flesh and seemed like a subterranean counterpart to the Lord Jesus who sat on his throne in the sky. In this dream Jung was in a meadow and came upon a hole in the ground like a grave. "Hesitantly and fearfully" he descended into this hole via some stone stairs.

> At the bottom was a doorway with a round arch, closed off by a green curtain. . . . Curious to see what might be hidden behind, I pushed it aside. I saw before me in the dim light a rectangular chamber [of stone] and in the center a red carpet ran to a low platform. On this platform stood a wonderfully rich golden throne. . . . Something was standing on it which I thought at first was a tree trunk twelve to fifteen feet high and about one and a half to two feet thick. It was a huge thing, reaching almost to the ceiling. But it was of a curious composition: it was made of skin and naked flesh and on top there was something like a rounded head with no face and no hair. On the very top of the head was a single eye, gazing motionlessly upward. . . . The thing did not move, yet I had the feeling that it might at any moment crawl off the throne like a worm and creep toward me. I was paralyzed with terror. At that moment I heard from outside and above me my mother's voice. She called out, "Yes just look at him. That is the man-eater!" That intensified my terror still more, and I awoke sweating and scared to death. For many nights afterward I was afraid to go to sleep, because I feared I might have another dream like that.
>
> (Jung, 1963: 11–12)

Jung had this dream when he was only 3 years old. He says it was his "initiation into the realm of darkness." It was Jung's first experience of the dark side of the numinous – what he later called "the other face of God" – the dark side of the God-image. The phallus, representing his emergent awareness of sexuality and its powerful "otherness," carried what Jung called the "chthonic spirit." Reflecting on this much later, Jung said:

> It is a widespread error to imagine that I do not see the value of sexuality. On the contrary it plays a large part in my psychology as an essential – though not the sole – expression of psychic wholeness. But my main concern has been to investigate, over and above its personal significance and biological function, its spiritual aspect and its numinous meaning. . . . Sexuality is of the greatest importance as the expression of the chthonic spirit. That spirit is the "other face of God," the dark side of the God-image. The question of the chthonic spirit has occupied me ever since I began to delve into the world of alchemy.
>
> (ibid.: 168)

ʻard the end of Jung's life, he was especially passionate about the essential
ʻalence in the Godhead and the Self, in other words in the essential reality
ʻil. His major treatise on this subject is "Answer to Job" (1952), where he
describes the Old Testament Yahweh's sadistic tyrannical side and its slow
transformation through Job's suffering into the loving God of the New Testament
who is incarnated as Christ. So Yahweh starts out as both Persecutor and Protector
– then evolves into his positive side. Despite this "development," Jung always
complained that Christianity had given over all the dark side of life to the Devil
and left him out of the Trinity, which was therefore a kind of incomplete mandala
or image of the Self. He preferred the dark, grounded imagery of Alchemy, where
the Self (as pearl or philosopher's stone) was found *in stecore* – in the shit. And
instead of Christ as mediator of the Godhead, Jung always preferred Mercurius
Duplex, who was both a saviour and a destroyer, both good and evil, both a
diabolical Trickster and life-saving messenger of the gods.

JUNG'S MATURE THOUGHT ON TRAUMA

We turn now to Jung's later thought as it applies to the self-care system and early
trauma. The reader will understand that what follows is a compilation of different
elements of Jung's theory relevant to the current topic.

The role of affect in the creation of the complex

Early in his professional career, Jung made a definitive statement about his
understanding of the psyche: "The essential basis of our personality is affectivity. Thought and action are, as it were, only symptoms of affectivity" (Jung,
Collected Works 3, para. 78). This makes Jung's psychology an affect-based
psychology, despite the fact that much of the later writing of Jungian theorists
tends toward the "spiritual" and mental functions – especially the search for
"meaning" – thus moving away from the affective foundations of Jung's thought.
For Jung, affect is the *central organizing principle of psychic life* because it links
together otherwise discrepant components of the mind (sensations, ideas, memories, judgments) by lending each of them a common "feeling-tone." If a life
experience (such as an early trauma) is accompanied by a strong affect, all the
associated perceptual and mental elements of that experience will accumulate
around this affect, thereby forming a *feeling-toned complex* (see Jung, 1907: para.
82). Feeling-toned complexes are the basic functional units of the psyche and,
because human affects are universal, these complexes tend, in their most regressed
form, to take on certain "archaic," "typical" – hence "archetypal" – forms. In
the language of one well-known contemporary Jungian theorist, complexes have
a personal "shell" and an archetypal "core" (Whitmont, 1969: 65). The
archetypal core lends the complexes their typical, universal character such as, for
example, the "inferiority/superiority complex," the "parental complexes,"
various sexual complexes (Oedipus, Electra), and so on.

I have intentionally begun this section with Jung's focus on affect, because severe trauma always leaves in its wake "a lifelong disturbance of affectivity" (Krystal, 1988: 142). If we want to understand trauma and its inner "objects" we must understand its impact on affect development and affect-tolerance. While Jung's later writings do not elaborate a comprehensive theory of affects – concerning themselves more with the archetypal *images* which give affects *meaning* – nevertheless, a theory of affects and their corresponding inner object-images is discernible, especially in the early writings.

Basically, Jung started with archaic or "archetypal affects" – what Henry Krystal (1988) calls "affect precursors," typical of infancy and regressed states in the adult. These are "volcanic," undifferentiated "proto-affects" which tend to be bipolar, reflecting their derivation in psychosomatic states of contentment (love) vs. discomfort and pain (hate). Such affects reach the image level of the mind in archaic and typical (archetypal) forms which are "transpersonal," i.e., spiritualized, aggrandized, caricatured, or otherwise mythologically amplified. They flow into the primordial narrative motifs supplied by unconscious fantasy – also mythological. In other words, they find their "images" in story. Gradually, these undifferentiated affects mature and differentiate in relation to caretaking persons who help "metabolize" them by identifying, naming, and interpreting the infant's experience, by containing the infant's chaotic agitation (in projection), neutralizing toxic states, and helping to provide both plastic and verbal "forms" to embody the infant's unconscious fantasy – all this within a warm and supportive relationship. Out of this dialectical process, specific emotions differentiate, and gradually, with the help of language, become *feelings* that communicate inner states of the self to others, including those affects which pertain to mankind's primal religious experience (ecstasy, awe, mystic identity, gratitude). For Jung, religious experience was a defining aspect of the human.

One of the reasons that Jung's affect-orientation has been underappreciated is his confusing use of the word "feeling." In his later writing, "feeling" came to stand for valuing, and was used to designate one of the major orienting function-types of consciousness, along with sensation, intuition, and thinking. However, when he refers to the "feeling-toned complex," Jung uses "feeling" to stand for emotion or affect. It is unfortunate that the later popularity of Jung's typology with its "feeling types," "thinking types," etc. has partially eclipsed the affect-foundation of his psychology.

Jung's notion of possession by the complex

The role of the complex in what we have called the self-care system and its protective/persecutory inner objects emerges with greater clarity when we consider that, for Jung, complexes have a universal tendency to *image them-selves* in dreams and other fantasy material as animate beings (persons) in dynamic interaction with the ego. The psyche's natural symbol-forming function (if adequately constellated by "good-enough" parental care) automatically *personifies affects* in the form of recognizable images. Every complex is an inseparable unity of a dynamic energic factor deriving from an instinctual and somatic base (affect), and a form-giving, organizing, structuring factor making the complex available to consciousness as a mental representation (image). Every complex is therefore an "affect-image" (see Perry, 1976: 28) or, as Jung once said, the "image of a personified affect" (Jung, 1926: para. 628). Complexes constitute the "persons" of our dreams, the "voices" in our heads, the visionary figures that appear at times of stress, the "secondary personalities" of neurosis, the daimons, ghosts and spirits that haunt or hallow the so-called primitive mind.

Complexes have a more or less disturbing effect upon the ego, depending upon the extent of their "autonomy," which in turn depends upon the strength of their *affect* (see Jung, 1913: para. 1352) and whether this affect is *bearable* or not. If the complex originates in a severe or early trauma, its affect will be strong *anxiety*, and such anxiety has a dissociative effect upon the ego because it disturbs the homeostatic balance of those bodily sensations upon which the ego depends for its coherence (see Jung, 1907: paras 82–3). In the most severe cases, the ego can be completely displaced or "assimilated" by the secondary complex and the result is a state of "possession" by the complex in which only a remnant of the former ego remains behind as an "affect-ego" (see Jung, 1934b: para. 204). Jung makes the following distinctions along a continuum of complex-severity:

> Certain complexes arise on account of painful or distressing experiences in a person's life, experience of an emotional nature which leave lasting psychic wounds behind them. A bad experience of this sort often crushes valuable qualities in an individual. All these produce unconscious complexes of a personal nature. A great many autonomous complexes arise in this way. But there are others that come from quite a different source . . . the collective unconscious. At bottom they are irrational contents of which the individual had never been conscious before. . . . So far as I can judge, these experiences occur . . . when something so devastating happens to the individual that his whole previous attitude to life breaks down.
>
> (Jung, 1928b: para. 594)

Jung then contrasts how we experience these two levels of the complex and how they were experienced by primitive man:

> [If a complex from the personal unconscious is dissociated] the individual experiences a sense of loss. . . . (A primitive would rightly speak of a loss of soul, because certain portions of the psyche have indeed disappeared.) Conversely, when [such a] complex is made conscious again, for instance through psychotherapeutic treatment, he experiences an increase of power. Many neuroses are cured in this way. But when, on the other hand, a complex of the collective unconscious becomes associated with the ego . . . it is felt as strange, uncanny . . . fascinating . . . [but also dangerous]. The association of a collective content with the ego always produces a state

of alienation . . . . The irruption of these alien contents is a characteristic symptom marking the onset of many mental illnesses. The patients are seized by weird and monstrous thoughts, the whole world seems changed, people have horrible, distorted faces, and so on. [Primitives experience this level of complex as *possession by a spirit.*]

We therefore have to postulate the existence of unconscious complexes that normally belong to the ego (the loss of them appears pathological) and of those that normally should not become associated with it (their dissociation from the ego brings recovery). Accordingly, primitive pathology recognizes two causes of illness: loss of soul, and possession by a spirit.

(ibid.: paras 587–91)

According to the hypothesis we are exploring in these pages, the "possessing spirit" of Jung's "collective" complexes is precisely that "daimonic" figure encountered so often in the preceding clinical material who serves as the persecutory/protective "agent" of the self-care system. "He" or "she" comes from the archaic level of the psyche and is therefore all the more uncanny and terrifying to the ego, which easily gives way to its power.

As the affect-images of the collective layer of the psyche, archetypes structure the most archaic and primordial (primitive) emotional experience in images and motifs which are typical of mythology and religion the world over. If we can imagine the volcanic storms of affect that rampage through the traumatically abandoned or overstimulated infant's psyche, we get some inkling as to why the forms given such affect are themselves archaic, i.e., images of daimons or angels – of titanic, god-like "great beings" which threaten to annihilate the immature ego. Potentiated by severe trauma, these inner figures continue to traumatize the inner world.

To make matters worse, complexes originating in personal experience tend to "mythologize" themselves through a process Jung calls the "self-amplification" of the complex. He notes that once an autonomous complex is formed in the unconscious it does not change in the same way that it does if associated with the conscious ego, i.e., owing to dissociation, the complex is not corrected by reality. Instead, it takes on the uninfluenceable and compulsive character of an automatism, an increasingly "uncanny" or "numinous" aspect (see Jung, 1947: para. 383).

In the end, such complexes – presumably in proportion to their distance from consciousness – assume, by self-amplification, an archaic and mythological character and thus a certain numinosity, as is perfectly clear in schizophrenic dissociations. Numinosity, however, is wholly outside the realm of conscious volition, for it transports the subject into the state of rapture, which is a state of will-less surrender.

These peculiarities of the unconscious state contrast very strongly with the way complexes behave in the conscious mind. Here they can be corrected: they lose their automatic character and can be substantially

91

transformed. They slough off their mythological envelope, and by entering into the adaptive process going forward in consciousness, they personalize and rationalize themselves to the point where a dialectical discussion becomes possible.

(ibid.: paras 383–4)

In order to understand how complexes and their archetypes come to possess the individual and structure the self-care system, two additional elements in Jung's thought must be brought into focus. The first is his analysis of how, in psychopathology, the superior *mind* (analogous to Freud's superego) becomes an internal attacker of the inferior *feeling-self* and the second is his emphasis on the duplex nature of all archetypes, especially the central archetype he called the Self.

JUNG AND THE ATTACKING "MIND"

For Jung, all archetypes are bipolar dynamic structures combining opposites within themselves. One pole of the archetype represents *instinct* and related *affects* rooted in the body; the other pole is represented by a form-giving *spiritual* component made up of images produced by the mind. The *psyche* exists between these two opposites and represents a "third" factor combining instinct/affect and spirit into *unconscious fantasies* that create *meaning*. (see ibid: para. 407). As Jung puts it, "the image represents the meaning of the instinct" (ibid.: para. 398). When functioning healthily the polarities inherent within the archetype are mediated by the symbolic process which enriches and energizes a flexible ego.

One of the effects of severe trauma, however, is *to split the archetype within its own structure*. We might say that one pole (mentation) attacks the other (affect), thereby destroying the psychological structure and leaving an already fragile ego further undernourished. *Trauma both stirs up volcanic affect and at the same time severs it from its image-matrix*. The traumatized infant's raw experience is unmediated by parental figures and remains imageless, hence meaningless. The capacity for fantasy is destroyed. Experience degenerates into somatic sensation or empty mental images and ideas. Joyce McDougall, an object-relations analyst describes patients with severe psychosomatic disorder for whom "meaning is of a presymbolic order that circumvents the use of words":

the thought processes of the psychosomatic sufferer frequently appear to have drained language of its emotional significance, [whereas] the body appears to be behaving in a "delusional" fashion, often overfunctioning excessively to a degree that appears physiologically senseless. One is tempted to say that the body has gone mad.

(McDougall, 1989: 18)

In a similar vein and from a Jungian standpoint, Mara Sidoli has described patients who somatize at crucial moments in analysis where insight or change is close at hand. Sidoli speculates that these patients *cannot let infantile affects acquire symbolic mental representation* because "certain experiences in infancy were not attributed any psychic meaning by the mother" (Sidoli, 1993: 175):

> My observation is that such patients produce archetypal images all right, but these are disaffected (as in the case of alexithymia). These patients are emotionally detached observers of their own images. They defend themselves against feeling the horror, panic, and despair evoked by the archetypal image in relation to their own personal experience, and tend to view it as an artistic creation.
>
> (ibid.: 175)

Both McDougall and Sidoli describe patients in whom dissociative defenses have ravaged the capacity for integrated experience. This seems to involve an attack by one "pole" of the archetype on the other pole, i.e., an attack of the "spirit" on affect/instinct or of the mind on the body-self. In the language of the present investigation an "archaic defense" seems to rupture the integrated functioning of the archetype, severing the links between affect and image, thereby rendering experience meaningless. When possible integration or insight begins, the potential re-experiencing of unbearable affect threatens the ego, triggering the splitting defense.

In many of Jung's early cases, and in his later theory about the "negative animus" archetype, he describes how the patient's intellect, with its differentiated logos functions, becomes the source of just this sort of attack on the vulnerable feeling-self which is always "inferior" to the mind's ideal. With characteristic clinical acumen, Jung provides the following description of this "possession" by an attacking superego or "supermind" in a young male patient:

> The patient strikes us at first as completely normal; he may hold office, be in a lucrative position, we suspect nothing. We converse normally with him, and at some point we let fall the word "Freemason." Suddenly the jovial face before us changes, a piercing look full of abysmal mistrust and inhuman fanaticism meets us from his eye. He has become a hunted, dangerous animal, surrounded by invisible enemies: the other ego has risen to the surface.
>
> What has happened? Obviously at some time or other the idea of being a persecuted victim gained the upper hand, became autonomous, and formed a second subject which at times completely replaces the healthy ego.
>
> (Jung, 1928c: paras 499-500)

Jung firmly believed that this kind of encapsulated paranoid system had a psychogenic and not a biological or physical causation, i.e., that it originated in an earlier traumatic psychological moment or moments. Moreover, these moments were traumatic because the patient's usual hypersensitive emotional life had led to certain sustaining unconscious fantasies which broke down in the face of attack by his precocious intellect. The critical traumatic moment for Jung's young patient occurred when the "spiritual form which his emotions needed in order to live

finally broke down. It did not break by itself, it was broken by the patient"
(ibid.: para. 501).

> It came about in the following way. When still a sensitive youth, but already
> equipped with a powerful intellect, he developed a passionate love for his
> sister-in-law, until finally – and not unnaturally – it displeased her husband,
> his elder brother. His were boyish feelings, woven mostly out of moonshine,
> seeking the mother, like all psychic impulses that are immature. But these
> feelings really do need a mother, they need prolonged incubation in order
> to grow strong and to withstand the unavoidable clash with reality. In
> themselves there is nothing reprehensible about them, but to the simple,
> straightforward mind they arouse suspicion. The harsh interpretation which
> his brother put upon them had a devastating effect, *because the patient's
> own mind admitted that it was right*. His dream was destroyed, but this in
> itself would not have been harmful *had it not also killed his feelings. For
> his intellect then took over the role of the brother and, with inquisitorial
> sternness, destroyed every trace of feeling*, holding before him the ideal of
> cold-blooded heartlessness. A less passionate nature can put up with this for
> a time, but a highly-strung, sensitive nature in need of affection will be
> broken. Gradually it seemed to him that he had attained his ideal, when
> suddenly he discovered that waiters and suchlike people took a curious
> interest in him, smiling at one another understandingly, and one day he made
> the startling discovery that they took him for a homosexual. The paranoid
> idea had now become autonomous. It is easy to see the deeper connection
> between the pitilessness of his intellect, which cold-bloodedly destroyed
> every feeling, and his unshakable paranoid conviction.
>
> (ibid.: paras 501–2; emphasis added)

Jung's case is an outstanding example of what Corrigan and Gordon (1995) call
the attacking "mind-object" (see Chapter 6) with its associated fantasy system.
Jung describes the earlier traumatic moment upon which the unconscious fantasy-
system is constructed by the patient's mind. The young man's illusory "love"
(moonshine) and unconscious identification with the elder brother had been
traumatically disparaged. His "dream" had collapsed and, in the vacuum left by
his fragmented illusion, the patient salvaged his loving identification with the
brother by now joining the brother in hating himself (identification with the
aggressor). This constituted no less a fantasy than the moonshine love, but where
there had been love, now there was hate and a new "story" to go with it. In order
to hate himself, Jung's patient had to split himself in two. His affective experience
of humiliation and disillusionment was no doubt unbearable. None the less, his
"mind" stepped in and "made meaning" out of this unbearable experience, albeit
a nefarious meaning. The result of his fantasy was the preservation of the cruel
brother as a lovable object, while the patient took on the hated image. Identified
with perfection and the brother's ideal image, the "mind" disparaged his fragile

feeling-self as "bad," loathsome for his misplaced love, a "Mama's boy" who was unable to love a real woman in the world. Within this defensive structure, love and hate cannot be experienced toward the same object, i.e., ambivalence is impossible. The brother is "good" and he himself must remain "bad," at least in his secret feeling-self. It is intolerable for him to experience hate toward the idealized brother and equally unbearable if he starts to let in compassionate feelings toward his own (loathesome) weakness.

Finally, this split in his self-representation received outer "confirmation" in the reaction of the waiters who started to imagine him as homosexual. Now his secret loathesomeness had been confirmed by "reality." The persecutory fantasy had now been "proven." This is an example of how complexes grow by accretion, pulling in more and more "reality," like a black hole in space, grinding up bits of experience in a "system" of destructive meaning.

Trauma and "meaning" in Jung's case

Jung's case is an excellent example of how trauma is not just rupture of the stimulus barrier but is intimately related to "meaning" or to psychical reality. *The neurosis develops not in response to the trauma* per se, *but in reaction to the fantasies through which it gets an attributed meaning.* Similarly, the defenses themselves have a meaning in relation to the inevitable task of preserving the human spirit. By weaving a humiliating negative fantasy about his own loathe-someness, the patient's mind was "trying," so to speak, to keep him in relation to a reality worth living in and loving, even if his ego was rendered unlovable in the process. To the psyche, a negative meaning is apparently preferable to no meaning at all; a negative fantasy better than no fantasy whatsoever. His relentless perfectionism (despite the self-attack implied in it) became an exoskeleton which held his collapsing self together in the absence of those "transitional" processes that might have secured a true self. Also, if one's self-representation is "bad" one can always work to be better.

Unfortunately, however, the capacity to tolerate unbearable affect is only further eroded by these archaic defenses. Designed to protect the personal spirit from annihilation by reality, the self-care system provides a fantasy that "makes sense" out of suffering but splits the unity of mind and body, spirit and instinct, thought and feeling. The "mind" becomes a tyrannical perfectionist, persecuting its weaker feeling-self, all the while hiding it as its shameful secret partner until finally, with all contact lost between the ego and this victim-self, a dreaded triggering word is mentioned ("Freemason"). The ego is now totally displaced by the loathesome weakling inside, who now becomes the only self and the whole world turns tyrannical, persecutory, perfectionistic. The ego has been "possessed" by the split-off victim-self. Here we see the ultimate (unaided) result of the self-care system in operation – gradual amplification of the complex leading finally to severe psychopathology.

JUNG'S DUPLEX SELF: LIGHT AND DARK

In most of Jung's early writings, the Self is usually described as the ordering principle which unifies the various archetypal contents and balances the opposites in the psyche during the analytic process, leading toward the "goal" of individuation or "self-realization." Jung reached this hypothesis empirically. In his own dreams and those of analysands, he found himself confronted by a source of apparent wisdom in the unconscious that seemed to present a very different image of the patient's true life than that held by the patient's ego. This "center" in the unconscious seemed to compensate for the ego's one-sided attitudes as if it had the "intention" of correcting the patient's imbalanced attitude and envisioned a "goal" that seemed to embrace the patient's whole personality – not just his ego. Moreover, this "center" of wisdom in the psyche seemed to "present itself" in dreams through numinous imagery that connoted a sacred "otherness," imperishability, resolution of conflict, wholeness, ineffable beauty.

For these reasons, Jung decided that, whereas the ego was the center of consciousness, the Self represented the subject of the psyche's totality which includes both conscious and unconscious.

> Intellectually the Self is no more than a psychological concept, a construct that serves to express an unknowable essence which we cannot grasp as such, since by definition it transcends our powers of comprehension. It might equally well be called the "God within us." The beginnings of our whole psychic life seem to be inextricably rooted in this point, and all our highest and ultimate purposes seem to be striving towards it."
>
> (Jung, 1934a: para. 399)

Following from these definitions, many of Jung's followers have tended to emphasize the Self's prescient "unfolding" through the individuation process – its nudging the sometimes resistant ego toward its prespecified "plan" of individual wholeness. These authors acknowledge that this "nudging" can be disagreeable, even terrifying, but the implication is that the Self knows best what is good for the ego (see Whitmont, 1969). Sometimes the Self is presented as an oracular voice which speaks in the interior world, forcing the "host" into moral conflict with the collective values if he or she is to realize a unique personal truth (see Neumann, 1969). Others, following up Jung's idea that the Self is a "prefiguration of the ego," emphasize the dialectical relationship between the ego and the Self and the slowly developing "axis" between them, analogous on an individual level to the relationship between the incarnate Christ and his transpersonal Father (see Edinger, 1972). In all these approaches, the Self is imagined as the supreme authority, the longed-for transcendent unity of life, a unity of opposites, the eternal One having entered time.

How, then, are we to square these descriptions with the axe-murderers, shotgunners, and zombie-doctors of our previous clinical cases? These figures hardly seem to be "transpersonal guides" along the path of individuation – yet, we are suggesting in these pages that these hideous destructive images are also images of the archaic Self in its defensive function.

The answer to this question is straightforward enough. Benificent descriptions of the individuating self are found in clinical situations where the ego is relatively well established, indeed, the ego is often too well developed, i.e., hypertrophied, one-sided. In analysis with such individuals, the compensatory dialectical process between conscious and unconscious unfolds in precisely the way Jung and his followers have described. It is otherwise where the ego has suffered severe trauma and is therefore only provisionally established, fragile, riddled with anxiety, and in a constant struggle to survive. Such patients live in constant dread that the original traumatic state will return, and they expect it. Vigilant scanning of the environment replaces play for them and they live in constant fear that everything will collapse, which indeed it often does. In this case, for reasons that are not altogether clear, horrific and destructive imagery of the Self predominates. We might distinguish this Self as a *survival Self* in order to distinguish it from the *individuating Self* found in psychological health. The *survival Self seems to be the form taken by the Self when its otherwise individuating energies have been diverted to an earlier developmental task, i.e., assuring the individual's survival.* We have seen in our prior cases how this survival Self attacks the dissociable ego, splitting affect from image, dismembering experience, and have speculated that these very attacks are the Self's (often misguided) "efforts" to preserve the personal spirit of the individual from the unbearable affect of the original trauma which now seems to threaten at every turn. This, at least, would be one way to explain the apparent disintegrative urge within the psyche, as seen so often in what Jung (1928b: paras 597-91) calls "possession by a spirit" complexes.

YAHWEH AND THE DARK SIDE OF THE SELF

Jung makes it clear that, developmentally speaking, the original primal Self is an integrate of extremely powerful energies (love and hate, creation and destruction) and that we see images of this primitive Self in the earliest images we have in Western culture of a monotheistic God, i.e., the Hebrew Yahweh. In Yahweh, says Jung, we not only "see" the primal bipolar Self, *we see it in a process of transformation* (humanization) in relation to its "other" side, the people of Israel. Yahweh starts out as a tyrant. With one wrathful hand he rages against the people, persecutes them, kills their first-born, sends floods and disease to punish them, even sadistically tortures them without provocation, all the while demanding constant bloody sacrifices to propitiate his wrath. And yet this tyrannical death-dealing God is also loving in his own primitive way. After his wrath, he makes a covenant with the people never to destroy them again and provides continual guidance and protection in their Exodus from captivity. According to Jung (1952) this is all (apparently) because the Self "wants" to incarnate as man! It is just that Yahweh cannot "get to" his own loving nature until he sees the effects of his own destructiveness. This is where poor Job (and all humanity) comes in – to

97

suffer the antinomies in God and in this way to "help" God incarnate. If we were to put this in a Kleinian metaphor, we would say that the omnipotent God-identified ego cannot come into life until its love and hate can be experienced toward the same human person. Edward Edinger makes this same point without the developmental object-relations metaphor when he says in his commentary on Jung's book:

> Yahweh is both kind and wrathful, just and unjust, and he contains these opposites without contradiction because no consciousness has ever inter-vened to challenge the contradiction. Job, in his encounter with Yahweh, becomes that consciousness, perceives the contradiction and thereby gener-ates the challenge to Yahweh.

> (Edinger, 1992: 12)

Edinger's point is that in confronting Yahweh's cruelty, Job neither retaliates (talion response) nor does he collapse in defeat and humiliation. He stays astride his humanity, *suffering God as God is unable to suffer himself*. He expresses his anger, but also his humility in the face of Yahweh's power, and he never loses sight of Yahweh's potential goodness. This may give us some clues as to how to work with the archetypal defenses of the Self in psychotherapy. In his *Answer to Job*, Jung says:

> This is perhaps the greatest thing about Job, that, faced with this difficulty [the awareness that Yahweh can be unjust], he does not doubt the unity of God. He clearly sees that God is at odds with himself – so totally at odds that he, Job, is quite certain of finding in God a helper and an "advocate" against God. As certain as he is of the evil in Yahweh, he is equally certain of the good. . . . He [Yahweh] is both a persecutor and a helper in one, and the one aspect is as real as the other. Yahweh is not split, but is an antinomy – a totality of inner opposites – and this is the indispensable condition for his tremendous dynamism.

> (Jung, 1952: para. 567).

According to Jung, the primoridial ambivalent Self or God-image in the collective psyche has undergone an historical transformation parallel with its *developmental* transformation within each individual person (ontogeny recapitu-lates phylogeny). This movement, as we have seen, is toward humanization and incarnation in the body. Jung goes so far as to say that Job's suffering of the opposites in God leads to his incarnation in Christ, i.e., as the "God-man." This mythological development, we might say, records a developmental achievement in which the transpersonal powers are "tamed" (God was supposedly "tamed in the lap of the Virgin") and become available to the ego in modulated form. At this point, the problem of good and evil is no longer "in God," for "God so loved the world that he gave his only begotten son," i.e., the New Testament God has become exclusively loving and benevolent and his son also. The problem of evil has now been transferred to Christ's dark twin brother, the Antichrist or Devil.

Jung never liked this development in Christianity. He felt it too easily relieved man of his suffering and struggle. He preferred his God to be a duplex God.

All opposites are of God, therefore man must bend to this burden; and in so doing he finds that God in his "oppositeness" has taken possession of him, incarnated himself in him. He becomes a vessel filled with divine conflict (Job, par. 659). One must be able to suffer God. That is the supreme task for the carrier of ideas.

(Jung, 1973: 65)

5

ADDITIONAL JUNGIAN
CONTRIBUTIONS

Therapy is not about relieving suffering, it's about repairing one's relationship to reality.

(anonymous)

In this chapter we turn to other Jungian theorists, each of whom has tried to account for our benevolent/malevolent daimon in the language of analytical psychology. The theorists discussed represent only a sample of the many contributors who have addressed the problem of early trauma and its defenses, and I focus only on those who have, in one way or another, expanded our central notion of the dyadic self-care system and its supervising ambivalent Self figure.

ERICH NEUMANN AND THE DISTRESS EGO
OF TRAUMA

One of Jung's most creative followers, Erich Neumann describes the normal mother/infant situation as a "dual unity" and the child's first year as a "post-uterine embryonic stage" during which the child is psychically contained in the mother in total participation mystique and does not yet "exist" as a separate person (see Neumann, 1976). During this phase, the superordinate center and wholeness of the personality that Jung called the Self resides in two places: in the child's body and in the mother. Gradually, with increasing reality-contact, that part of the Self carried by the mother "migrates" into the child, partially ending the participation mystique with the mother and establishing the ego–Self axis as an interior polarity within the child's psyche, thereby assuring normal ego growth. Neumann points out that a successful primal relationship and securely established ego–Self axis are the basis for all experiences of ecstasy, religious or otherwise, in which the numinosum is allowed to dissolve ego-boundaries and the ego lets its own dominance be suspended while being temporarily taken back into the Self.

If trauma interrupts the primal relationship, the numinosum constellates negatively as the Terrible Mother and a negativized, distress-ego, bearing the imprint of distress or doom, results. A central feature of the disturbed primal relationship is a primary feeling of guilt. The unloved child feels abnormal, sick, "leprous" and "condemned" (ibid.: 86). And paired with this "bad, filthy" child is a daimonic masculine spirit (patriarchal *uroboros*) representing a violent superego, now confused with the Self, which continually attacks the "bad" child who can never live up to its demands.

Throughout Neumann's description is an awareness that all children exist on a level of "mythological apperception" and that this gives a wholly mythic dimension to the traumatic disruption of the primal relationship which cannot be adequately apprehended in denotative language. The Great Mother figure of the primal relationship, Neumann writes,

> is a goddess of fate who, by her favor or disfavor, decides over life and death, positive or negative development; and moreover, her attitude is the supreme judgment, so that her defection is identical with a nameless guilt on the part of the child.

(ibid.: 86–7)

The mother's "defection" leads to a defective development in the ego–Self axis and correspondingly to a "negative Self-figure," i.e., the Terrible Mother image (ibid.: 49).

Neumann does not attribute a defense function to the negative Self-figure but rather conceives of defenses as residing in the ego. In other words, there are no "primitive defenses" in his theory – only primitive negative images which derive from the disturbed primary relationship with the real mother now giving way to the fantasy-imagos of the Good Mother or the Terrible Mother.

THE LONDON SCHOOL AND ARCHETYPAL DEFENSES

Leopold Stein

Stein was the first to introduce the idea of archetypal defenses (Stein, 1967); he used the analogy of the body's immune system to support his contention that "the self . . . as a 'commonwealth of archetypes'. . . carries out defence actions on a much more basic level [than the ego]" (ibid.: 103). Stein proposed the fascinating idea that the extreme negativity and self-destructiveness present in people who are primitively defended, might be understood as an attack by the primal Self on parts of the ego that it mistook for foreign invaders. He points out that proper immunological response depends on the ability of the body's immune system to accurately recognize not-self elements and then attack and kill them. Similarly, for the psyche, Stein proposed that in defenses of the Self, parts of the personality were mistaken as not-self elements and attacked, leading to self-destruction in a kind of auto-immune disease (AIDS) of the psyche. Why the psychosomatic Self ends up attacking parts of itself Stein does not elaborate, except to say that proper functioning of the Self's "immune system" depends on the "fit" between the baby's archetypal expectations and the environment. When trauma occurs, the "fit" is annihilated, rendering the infant's self "immunologically incompetent."

Michael Fordham

Michael Fordham explored some of the clinical implications of Stein's immune system analogy in his classic paper "Defences of the Self" (Fordham, 1974). Earlier in his authorship, Fordham was led to hypothesize defenses prior to ego-development through his work with early infantile autism, where catastrophic impingements of unbearably noxious stimuli (for example, the mother's death-wishes toward the infant) were "defended" against by austistic encapsulation and total withdrawal *even in the first days of life, i.e., prior to the infant's ego-consolidation*. This clinical fact seemed to imply that archetypal defenses of the Self must operate to protect the traumatized infant by cutting it off from life altogether.

Fordham noticed, for instance, that if a baby is submitted to noxious stimuli of a pathogenic nature

> a persistent over-reaction of the defence-system may start to take place; [attacks on not-self objects] may become compounded with parts of the self by projective identification, so that a kind of auto-immune reaction sets in: this in particular would account for the persistence of the defence after the noxious stimulus had been withdrawn. [When this happens] ... little or no inner world can develop; the self-integrate becomes rigid and persists ... all later developments based on maturational pressures result not in deintegration but disintegration and the predominance of defence systems leads to the accumulation of violence and hostility, which is split off from any libidinal and loving communication with the object that may take place.
>
> (Fordham 1976: 91)

The combined ideas of Stein and Fordham have always struck me as being extremely promising as applied to our diabolical figure and his role as a possible archetypal defender of the personal spirit in trauma. For example, if we imagine that a defense of the Self is organized very early, then its function might be to attack all elements of experience and perception that are linked with the child's "reaching out" into a world of objects that traumatized it. This would lead to a persecution of the child's need for objects and an attack at the threshold between self and other. It would also mean an attack within the psyche on all integrative connections between the components of experience in order to break the child's desire. This would constitute what Bion describes as an "attack against linking" (Bion, 1959) – something he attributed to the death instinct. Such an explanation would explain why the inner world of the trauma victim is so unremittingly negative and why these people keep repeating their self-abuse to the point of recurrent re-traumatization (repetition compulsion). If we add to this the possibility that the archaic defense of the Self is not educable, i.e., as Jung suggested of all complexes, that it does not learn from experience, then we come very close to Stein's notion of psychological auto-immune disease. In other words, the Self "mistakes" all later hopeful developments in self–world relations as new editions of the old traumatic "reaching out" by the child and attacks accordingly. Here we have a defense which serves as a major resistance to change, to individuation, and to psychotherapy.

Others in the London School

Defenses of the Self and their accompanying "negative therapeutic reactions" were further explored by others in the London School, such as Proner (1986), who emphasized, as did Klein, these patients' inner spoiling envious attacks upon the good inner object, and Hubback (1991), who explored the archetypal basis of the repetition compulsion. Samuels (1989) has written extensively in criticism of the monistic/perfectionistic image of the Self. Jane Bunster (1993) speculates that traumatized and therefore difficult to reach patients remain de-personalized within an autistic core. Rosemary Gordon (1987) explored psychic masochism as the shadow-side of the universal need to worship or venerate something transcendent and to surrender to it; and finally, Joseph Redfearn (1992) described a specific primitive defensive "complex" originating in trauma and acting between two inner subpersonalities, one a vulnerable child, the other "the omnipotent, apocalyptic God subpersonality" who threatens to annihilate everything with "the bomb."

AMERICAN JUNGIANS

In American Jungian circles, our daimonic inner dyad has been discussed by a number of analysts. These theorists' contributions are followed by a short summary of some of the more popularized versions of the defense, found in best-selling books in America.

James Hillman and the Senex/Puer split

Of special interest for its "treatment implications" for early trauma (although these must be painstakingly drawn out of his mythological idiom) is "archetypal psychology" and its creative originator James Hillman. Hillman does us a service by pointing out that most archaic images which come up from the unconscious psyche are not single images, like the Great Mother, but are structured in tandems, pairs, dyads, couplings, polarities, or syzygies (Hillman, 1983: 166), for example mother/child, victim/perpetrator, Puer/Senex. He notes a tendency among Jungians to ignore this fact and simply to explore the static image of archetypal figure such as the Great Mother, Puer Eterus, etc. Such an approach, he points out, ignores the pathos, plot, and dynamic relationship between pairings that essential to myth and imagination.

There is a second tendency which Hillman decries. Polarities, he says, naturally incline toward oppositionalism, for example, "good" child, "bad" mother. "The inherent opposition within the archetype splits into poles when it enters ego-consciousness" (Hillman, 1979: 12) so that the duality of love and hate is always present, leading to stereotypy, polemics, side-taking and one-sidedness.

Of all the tandems Hillman explores, his analysis of the Senex/Puer dyad is especially close to our daimonic inner figures (see ibid.: 20). Close to the tyrannical side of our inner duality is the Senex. If analyzed by himself (instead of properly within his dyad with Puer) the Senex represents the Old King and his tyrannical order, the patriarchal structure, all that is cold, dry, distant, abstract, petrified. He is master of artifice and deceit, secrecy and solitude, and he is conservative, limited, pessimistic. This negativity, says Hillman, reflects a split in the primary archetype Senex et Puer. "The negative senex is the senex split from its own puer aspect. He has lost his 'child.'" (ibid.: 20). This "child" in turn, is an "avatar of the Self's spiritual aspect" – "a vision of our own first nature . . . our affinity to beauty, our angelic essence as messenger of the divine, as divine message" (ibid.: 26).

> Because the puer gives us connection to the spirit it is always concerned with the eternal aspect of ourselves and the world. When this concern becomes only-puer, exclusive and negative, the world as world is itself in danger of dissolution into the otherworldly. This danger is especially present in the psyche and history of this fraction of our era. Therefore it is of immense importance that the puer be recognized and valued, for it carries our future – positive or negative.
>
> (ibid.: 28)

The Senex et Puer archetype is no doubt one of the form-giving structures behind the archetypal defenses we are exploring, even though Hillman does not address the issues of trauma or defense and despite the fact that he makes a split within this archetype "normal," whereas we see it as a function of psycho-pathology. He says, for example, that "the inherent opposition within the archetype splits into poles when it enters ego-consciousness" (ibid.: 12). According to our analysis, this is not true of people whose psyche's have matured under "good-enough" parental care. In them, the archetype functions as it should to link up affect and image. The splitting Hillman justifiably dislikes is a function of traumatogenic environments where splitting rage predominates, and with it the defenses we have described.

Nathan Schwartz-Salant and the sado-masochistic dyad

Nathan Schwartz-Salant describes how the negative side of the numinous constellates in borderline patients and, following Jung, uses the image of the Old Testament Yahweh and his encounter with Job as one of the archetypal dyads that structure the borderline's inner self-attack. This dyad, before its transformation, is sado-masochistic. The resulting annihilating affects lead to a death-like helplessness of the "immanent self" in the borderline, analogous to the *nigredo* in Alchemy (see Schwartz-Salant, 1989).

Schwartz-Salant's focus is on the transference/counter-transference field and he helpfully describes how, when this sado-masochistic dyad constellates, the therapist and patient may enact the roles of Job or Yahweh in rapidly oscillating fashion (ibid.: 24) – or the therapist may split off from the negative energies and conduct a false-self analysis. Alternatively, the therapist may "add a third thing, an imaginal awareness of an afflicting Job–Yahweh dyad and a deeply felt caring for the soul" (ibid.: 26). This imaginal awareness in the therapist leads to potential "coniunctio processes" between therapist and patient and an eventual resulting positive constellation of the numinous.

Schwartz-Salant's analysis is important in that he recognizes the negatively constellated numinosum (and its tyrannical introject) as a critical factor to be reckoned with in the inner world of trauma. However, his assumption that the borderline has extraordinary "inherent potential ... to have a transcendent connection to archetypal processes and numinous energies, to a transcendent Self" and his reliance upon imaginal "coniunctio" experiences in the bi-personal field between himself and his patients are problematic, I believe. My own experience is that the borderline patient is not "terrified of engaging the positive numinosum" (ibid.: 33); rather, I have found that these patients are addicted to the positive (spiritualized) side of the numinosum as a defense and will exploit it wherever possible. What they are terrified of is dependency on the therapist as a real object or of the rage that follows the frustration of this dependency. I know of no way around the negative therapeutic reaction with these patients as archetypal negative energies are constellated by the frustrations of the analytic situation. In my experience, it is true that gradually this stormy process does lead to a more positive coloration to the inner world as Schwartz-Salant describes and possibly also to a more positive *relationship* to the numinous. But this never happens, in my experience, without enormous grief work in the transference and elsewhere (see Chapter 7). This important work of mourning certainly needs a warm and human connection with the therapist to be sustained, but, the necessary "separatio" is not made easier by imaginal "coniunctio" experiences.

Sherry Salman and the guardian Horned God

Sherry Salman (1986) has found our diabolical figure in the Celtic image of the Horned God, an archetypal image of sacred masculine power and protection (also a Trickster). Of him, she says:

> the Horned God represents the guardian, healer, and shapeshifter who mediates the world of the objective psyche. He is the elusive, transformative substance of the psyche itself – the adversary (Devil or Anti-Christ) *and* the savior who, with one hand, protects the Mysteries from destructive

105

influences and, with the other, protects the human psyche from contact with what it cannot bear. Encountering him involves a confrontation with the objective psyche and our own limitations, one of the essential tasks of psychotherapy.

(Salman, 1986: 7; emphasis in original)

Salman says that this image is activated whenever the psychoid layer of the psyche is touched. The Horned God has one constant function and that is to protect (ibid.: 11). In a male psyche, therefore, this figure frequently compensates for inadequate fathering and is encountered initially as a powerful dangerous male, often daimonic – sometimes as the hairy chthonic wildman, possessed of kindness and intelligence. As shamanic shape-shifter, the Horned God is able to take on animal forms and in its shadow aspect is sometimes the werewolf. When this energy has been repressed or split off in an individual's life, the Horned God appears as king of the Otherworld, – as Hades, abducting Persephone through a fissure in the earth opened for him by Gaia herself. As such, he represents the initiating life force, the essential phallic creative energy in the psyche – breaking through and abducting the ego into darkness. In Christianity he rules over the underworld, Hell. On the other hand, as Lucifer, he is the light-bringer and mediates the unconscious in a positive way.

In its negative form, says Salman, this image is with us in acted-out violence, drug addiction, compulsive perverse sexuality, and substance abuse. If integrated, this figure gives a man an effective masculine ego *in possession of its own destructiveness* (ibid.: 16); it gives a woman an effective animus connected both to the outer world, the world of the body, and to the "other" world of the psyche.

Sandner and Beebe and the daimonic Trickster

In an important clinical article, Donald Sandner and John Beebe (1982) elaborate on Jung's two levels of the complex, distinguishing between the ego-aligned complexes (those where the projected contents have been a part of the ego and been repressed) vs. the ego-projected complexes, i.e., those that are usually experienced not as parts of the ego's identity but rather as projected qualities in other people. These complexes are "located at deeper levels of the unconscious than the shadow complexes" (ibid.: 304). The ego-projected complexes, say the authors, are also usually bipolar, "split" between such qualities as "dominant harshness and vulnerable woundedness. Each pole may be represented in a dream" (ibid.: 305). Here we have our dyadic structure.

Following Jung, the authors reiterate how possession of the ego by the "ego-projected" complexes leads to archetypal affects and primitive forms of projection and projective identification. The basis for such archetypal forms of projection seems to lie in the archetypal cores of the complexes. For example, the archetypal core of a man's father complex (the father was an alcoholic, sociopathic, ruthless, unethical man) was the "daimonic trickster." The patient became so identified with this figure that he eventually killed himself (cf., ibid.: 311–12).

Further elaborating on the Trickster archetype, the authors suggest that "Mania often represents possession of the ego by an archetypal aspect of the shadow, aptly called the trickster" (ibid.: 321). This results in major manipulative splitting maneuvers, and these "must be recognized as daimonic effects of the trickster archetype at work. . . . the trickster is a crazy-maker, and patients in the grip of a manic episode regularly try to drive others, including the analyst, crazy" (ibid.: 322).

Consistent with our own analysis, the authors point out that

> demonic manifestations of the [ego-projected complexes] . . . emanate from the dark side of the Self and are defenses of the Self. The function of these powerful defenses seems to be to maintain, against the analyst's uncovering efforts, repressions that became necessary during development to permit at least partial Self-survival in the face of crushing parental demands and intrusions. As demonic defenses, these negating aspects of the Self lead the anima or animus to make projections that can be ruinously effective.
>
> (ibid.: 326–7)

Subsequent to his collaboration with Donald Sandner, John Beebe (1993) suggested an expansion of Fordham's idea of "defenses of the Self" to include a less autistic, vulnerable (small s) self capable of aligning either with or against the Self. It is possible that this interesting "dialogical" idea might be brought into line with the dream material of the present investigation where the attacking inner object (Self) is always paired with a vulnerable counterpart who it both hates and "loves" (and vice versa).

Joseph Henderson and the inferior/superior Self

Joseph Henderson, one of the few living analysts who studied extensively with Jung himself, has given much attention to Jung's concept of the shadow in its personal and impersonal (archetypal) forms. Henderson (1990: 66) feels that Jung derived his idea of the shadow from the Self, i.e., from his experience of the dark destructive side of life and God, and not from the ego. This accords well with what we find in Jung's autobiography, where, repeatedly, the sheer evil destructiveness of life (and of God) clearly perplexed Jung. Later, as a psychiatrist, he encountered in dreams dark figures who seemed to embody unregenerate evil, and he was at pains to explain them. Henderson says:

> Jung asked why the shadow appears in such a destructive form. The answer is that having denied God, the God appears in a place where one would expect it least: the shadow [as the Devil]. If one does not fear God, that is, if one plays for safety, one is haunted by the uncanny aspect of what would seem a perfectly harmless personal shadow. The more one rationalizes the personal shadow, the greater the impersonal shadow becomes, finally

becoming the container of the Self and providing an experience of the whole conscious and unconscious. My own view is that this impersonal shadow always has to be encountered in its destructive aspect before one can come to terms with the inferior function.

(ibid.: 65–6)

Henderson's clinical experience convinced him, as it did Jung, that there may be an absolute power of evil in the psyche that cannot be rationalized, and that this archetypal shadow is "inseparable from a universal religious problem" (ibid.: 97). He cites Old Testament scholarship which shows that the original idea of Satan was not personified as a figure but was a verb meaning "to obstruct." Only later did this figure become "the adversary," and still later it was included in the Godhead (Self) as the "other hand" (wrath) of God. Says Henderson:

Jung's original formulation may be paraphrased as follows: the [true] individual is one in whom the primary ego-complex has been replaced or profoundly modified by a manifestation of the Self. This implies that a widening of consciousness has occurred through assimilation of contents of the collective unconscious by means of the transcendent function. In this process of development, the individual has encountered two primary archetypal figures – one might almost say personalities – and has become acquainted with them in many forms. One is *the superior aspect of the Self*, which Goethe represented as Faust and Nietzsche as Zarathustra. The other is the *inferior aspect of the Self*, represented by Goethe as Mephistopheles and by Nietzsche as the Ugliest Man. Whoever has experienced the individuation process knows that one of these figures conceals the other . . . giving rise to the old saying, "If God is present, the Devil is not far behind."

(ibid.: 64–6; emphasis in original)

Other American contributors

In drawing attention to a "daimonic" figure in psychological life, this chapter builds upon well-known discoveries by many other investigators whose contributions cannot be summarized adequately for sheer lack of space. Among the more important is Jeffrey Satinover's (1985) early description of the archetypal defense and Jung's retreat into it during his painful separation from Freud; Peter Mudd's (1989) articulation of the lethal aspect of the Self in faulty parent/child relations; Carol Savitz's (1991) evocative description of the terrifying minotaur imprisoned at the center of the schizoid patient's labyrinthine inner world; and Ann and Barry Ulanov's (1987) portrayal of the blood-draining Witch archetype and the dangers of identification with the psyche's life-threatening images. Many more could be mentioned. The following popularized versions are included here because they explore the relevance of our diabolical figure to common everyday problems ranging from the addictions to compulsive creativity.

POPULARIZED VERSIONS

We begin this section with three of the most influential woman writers of the Jungian world: Marion Woodman, Linda Schierse Leonard, and Clarissa Pinkola Estes, and end with an important new work by John Haule on the "divine madness" of romantic love. Each of these writers makes extensive use of literature, myth, and fairy tales in elaborating the phenomenology of our archetypal self-care system or "dyad."

Marion Woodman and the daimon-lover

Marion Woodman's designation for our ambivalent caretaker-self is the "daimon-lover," which she describes as a derivative of a malignant father–daughter complex. The daimon-lover functions as an inner seducer and stands between [the woman] and any real man in the outer world. Says Woodman:

> at the core of that father-lover complex is the father-god whom she worships and at the same time hates because on some level, she knows he is luring her away from her own life. Whether she worships him or hates him makes no difference, because in either case she is bound to him with no energy going into finding out who she herself is. So long as she can fantasize her love, she identifies with the positive side of the father-god; once the fantasy is crushed, however, she has no ego to sustain her and she swings to the opposite pole where she experiences annihilation in the arms of the god who has turned against her.
>
> (Woodman, 1982: 136)

Woodman makes the important contribution that the daimon-lover complex for a woman usually compensates and defends against inadequate internalization of the mother owing to a failed psychosomatic bonding between herself and her mother in early life. This leads to inadequate somatic "indwelling" of the feminine self and to a compulsive "spiritualization" and sexualization of her deeper chthonic nature – a problem which is very refractory for creative women in particular and for women in general later trying to resolve this complex with male analysts or mentors (see Woodman, 1985).

Linda Leonard and the "Perverted old man"

Also exploring the father complex of the "puella woman," Linda Leonard describes the activities of an inner "perverted old man" who represents a critical, judging, inner masculine figure that Jung described as the "negative animus."

> Just as every Persephone has a Hades who abducts her and pulls her underground, so in the psyche of the puella dwells a sick manifestation of the rigid authoritarian side of the masculine. He is potentially a wise old

man who has become sick and nasty because he has been neglected. In my view this neglect is due to a wounded father development in which the father has not been there for his daughter in a committed and responsible way.

(Leonard, 1985: 87)

In a later work, Leonard describes a similar inner complex in terms of the Dracula/vampire theme and its associated oral eroticism (another version of the daimon-lover) indicating this figure's pre-Oedipal origins (Leonard, 1986). And in two subsequent works, Leonard explores various Trickster figures at play in her own personal struggle with addiction (Leonard, 1989 and 1993). In the first of these she makes an autobiographical comment:

Before I reached the turning point in my life, I had a series of relapses. In every single relapse there was a cunning and powerful archetypal figure working against me instead of with the creative forces of my psyche: the Trickster. Every addict knows this figure well. The Trickster is the highly seductive energy at play in the beginning of addiction. As the disease progresses he pops up whenever denial, hiding, and self-deception take place. In addiction the seductive Trickster frequently allies himself with the other underworld characters – the Moneylender ... the Gambler ... the Romantic ... the Underground Man, the rebellious Outlaw, the chaotic Madwoman, the critical Judge, and ultimately the Killer.... Acknowledging this demonic force in ourselves and the ego's powerlessness to fight it alone may lead us to reach out for help, thereby breaking through the imprisoning ring of power into the ring of love.

(Leonard, 1989: 95)

Finally, Leonard's most recent bestselling book (1993) picks up the theme of the ambivalent Trickster in the psyche presenting itself as a "mad" destructive, potentially creative feminine image in the unconscious material of both men and women.

Clarissa Pinkola Estes and the "innate predator"

In another recent bestselling book, Pinkola Estes (1992) has added her voice to those women writers who wish to describe and help us deal with diabolical, negative "forces" in the psyche. For Pinkola Estes, our ambivalent Protector/Persecutor is not someone to "befriend" as containing creative energy, because – at least for women – he represents an innate *contra naturam* aspect, opposing the positive, opposing development, opposing harmony, and "opposing the wild" (ibid.: 40), by which the author presumably means the "wildish urge within us that desires our souls lead our lives [not our egos]" (ibid.: 270). As a *contra naturam* factor, Pinkola Estes points out how the patient's ego must have the courage to name and confront this figure and learn how to say "no" to it.

According to Pinkola Estes, our "innate predator" is not related to trauma or

110

"negligent fostering," but is a malignant force that simply "is what it is" (ibid.: 46).

> It is a derisive and murderous antagonist that is born into us, and even with the best parental nurture the intruder's sole assignment is to attempt to turn all crossroads into closed roads.
>
> This predatory potentate shows up time after time in women's dreams. It erupts in the midst of their most soulful and meaningful plans. It severs the woman from her intuitive nature. When its cutting work is done, it leaves the woman deadened in feeling, feeling frail to advance her life; her ideas and dreams lay at her feet drained of animation.
>
> (ibid.: 40)

An "ancient and contemporary foe of both genders," this malignant formation acts "in opposition to the instincts of the natural Self." (ibid.: 46). And one such "instinct of the natural Self" – in fact the most central such instinct – is what Pinkola Estes calls the "wildish urge within us" of the ego for the soul, and ultimately for the spirit (which, she points out, in fairy tales is always born out of the soul) (ibid.: 271).

Ultimately, then, the "innate predator" in the psyche opposes the deepest urge of all, the urge for new life – for what Pinkola Estes describes as the "spirit child" (and what we have called the inviolate personal spirit of the individual).

> This spirit child is *la niña milagrosa*, a miracle child, who has the ability to hear the call, hear the far-off voice that says it is time to come back, back to oneself. The child is a part of our medial nature that compels us, for it can hear the call when it comes. It is the child rising out of sleep, out of bed, out of the house, and out into the wind-filled night and down to the wild sea that causes us to assert, "As God is my witness, I shall proceed in this way," or "I *will* endure."
>
> (ibid.: 273)

Here, Pinkola Estes provides a beautiful description of the inviolable personal spirit which we have described as the "client" of the Protector/Persecutor Self. For all the beauty and depth of her descriptions, however, the author fails to see the malignant inner figure as "duplex," and she denies its relationship to trauma or "negligent fostering," preferring to see this figure as simply a being in the psyche that "is what it is." While this attitude certainly honors the basic negativity and destructiveness of the figure, by de-linking it from the vicissitudes of personal development, Pinkola Estes ignores the findings of clinical investigators and undermines therapeutic possibilities.

One of the troubling aspects of Pinkola Estes's view is that it can contribute to a mystifiction and reification of archetypal reality as though this reality is not intimately connected with the ego's object-relations and environmental provision. Not everything in the psyche "is what it is." Images change, and change radically, in relation to environmental factors, therapeutic and otherwise.

111

John Haule and the "tiger pit" beneath the Self's synthesis

John Haule's subject is romantic love, including that compulsive, addictive form of love that often leads to death and destruction. Haule takes the view that "love of God" lies at the root of human love and is the "foundational and central activity of the human psyche" (Haule, 1992: 8). Romantic love seeks fusion with the beloved (loss of ego) and ultimately this longing points to a deeper longing, *"fana"*, an Arabic verb referring to "the passing away of the individual self in Universal Being" (ibid.: 11). This in turn leads us into dangerous territory, says Haule, because loss of ego-functions is characteristic of psychopathology. How, then, do we distinguish between the undertow of destructive love that pulls at us in the beguiling form of the daimon-lover (our self-care defense), and the real thing which has to do with the "higher function" of the anima and its mediation of the Self (ibid.: 20)?

Haule's answer is familiar to Jungians because it explains the darkness of the unconscious in terms of the "shadow" personality. Hence,

> The demon lover results from failure to differentiate our anima or animus from our shadow. The numinous contrasexual other within us whose job it is to relate us to the Self (anima or animus) is contaminated with everything we wish we did not have to deal with (shadow).
>
> (ibid.: 107)

Elsewhere, Haule suggests that the "demonic power" of the anima or animus "resides in its bewitching mask," and that once this is "depotentiated" she no longer has control over us like an autonomous complex (ibid.: 20). In a similar vein he suggests that,

> what distinguishes the demon lover from the beloved through whom we love God is the degree of wholeness experienced. In genuine *fana*, we are connected with our beloved through our Self and our anima or animus acts as a lens to bring her or his being into focus . . . whereas . . . in relationship with a demon lover, the connection turns on our respective wounds.
>
> (ibid.: 83)

It is clear that Haule wants to keep true love, rooted in the "love of God" and the Self, as distinct as possible from daimonic love (contaminated by the shadow). And yet he has to admit that even in daimonic love, there is a power of fascination – even a mysterious promise of transcendence through self-surrender – that mimics "true" romantic love. Both forms of love share in the "numinous" dimension of the psyche. Yet Haule eschews the obvious solution to this dilemma and one very consistent with Jung's writings, namely, *that the Self contains the shadow.* Instead, he proposes a model of the collective unconscious psyche that describes the "lowest" level of the psyche as a riot of instincts or archetypes ("innate releasing mechanisms") in disintegrated profusion (the "tiger-pit"), whereas the next layer up is reserved for the synthetic activity of the Self (ibid.:

51). If there is a "flaw" or "wound" in the Self's synthesis, we get a glimpse into the abyss, the disjointed world of chaos from which the daimon-lover beckons. If we should fall into his clutches, regressing morally and otherwise into a hideous shadow of our former selves, then "we know that at least one of the IRM's has broken loose from the Self's synthesis and has taken possession of consciousness" (ibid.: 86).

Using the literary example (from Dostoyevsky's *The Insulted and Injured*) of a sexually obsessed woman who is a model of propriety on the outside but leads a secret life of sordid sensuality, laughing "like one possessed . . . in the very heat of voluptuousness," Haule says:

> She is possessed – by one of the inborn releasing mechanisms; she has brought the considerable forces of her well-developed ego into the service of that sexual instinct run amok. We hear in her laugh the painful conflict between the Self and the tiger pit. She has sided with the tigers. For that reason, she is a particularly grotesque example of the demon lover.
>
> (ibid.: 87)

Haule's analysis is typical of those analysts (many of them deeply religious people) who wish to reserve Jung's concept of the Self (and God) for those processes in the psyche that are synthetic, integrative, and healing. However, I think this theoretical move gets us into some trouble clinically (because it mistrusts darkness) and theoretically, because, ironically, it is not true to Jung's psychology – at least as I read it. What Haule accomplishes with his model is effectively to install a Freudian metapsychology in the unconscious. On the lowest level are the instincts (id) and above them is the salutory synthetic organ of the psyche (Freud's ego, Haule's Self) which in health organizes and harmonizes (higher, secondary process) the lower chaos but does not participate in its primary process. As I understand Jung, he meant something radically other than this, namely, that the Self (God-image) is ambivalent, containing both good and evil and, correspondingly, that both good and evil, spirituality and sexuality, *structure the primary process, i.e., are a part of the deep psyche*. This would mean that every dark impulse in the unconscious (innate releasing mechanism) has its spiritual *image*, (transcendent function) and hence, is a part of the Self.

This same point is made by Jung in describing his break with Freud. When Jung was finishing *Psychology of the Unconscious* in 1911, he was working with mythological material that seemed to have both a destructive and a constructive aspect. The "Hymn of Creation" (about the positive unfolding of creative energy) produced by Miss Miller was quickly followed by "Song of the Moth." Jung says:

> In the moth the libido is shown to burn its wings in the light it has created before; it is going to kill itself in the same urge that brought it to birth. With this duality in the cosmic principle, the book ends. It leads up to the pairs of opposites, that is, to the beginning of the Types.
>
> (Jung, 1989: 28)

Freud could see nothing in the book but resistance to the father, and the point in it to which he took the greatest exception was my contention that the libido is split and produces the thing that checks itself. This to him as a monist was utter blasphemy. From this attitude of Freud's I felt more than ever convinced that his idea of God was placed in sexuality, and that libido is to him only an urge in one direction. As a matter of fact, however, I think it can be shown that there is a will to die as well as a will to live.

(ibid.: 24–5)

Sexuality and spirituality are pairs of opposites that need each other.

(ibid.: 29)

It is a widespread error to imagine that I do not see the value of sexuality. On the contrary, it plays a large part in my psychology as an essential – though not the sole – expression of psychic wholeness. . . . Sexuality is of the greatest importance as the expression of the chthonic spirit. That spirit is the "other face of God," the dark side of the God-image.

(Jung, 1963: 168)

6

PSYCHOANALYTIC THEORY ABOUT THE SELF-CARE SYSTEM

With the gravely ill person one is rarely dealing, at first, with the authentic illness of the patient. What one has to negotiate some sort of alliance with is the patient's practice of self-cure, which is rigidly established by the time he reaches us. To treat this practice of self-cure merely as a resistance is to fail to acknowledge its true value for the person of the patient. It is my belief from my clinical practice that few illnesses in a person are difficult to handle and cure. What, however, is most difficult to resolve and cure is the patient's practice of self-cure. To cure a cure is the paradox that faces us in these patients.

(Masud Khan, 1974: 97)

In the preceding chapters we have seen how an archaic, often dyadic, internal self-care system operates in the clinical situation to preserve, protect, and persecute the vulnerable personal spirit of the individual in an effort to keep it "inside" and out of reality. We then traced the discovery of the "daimonic" inner imago(s) in the collaboration between Jung and Freud, showing how an integration of their respective approaches leads to a fuller understanding of the archetypal nature of defensive processes in those cases where early experience has been "unbearable." In Chapter 4, Jung's later thought was explored, as were the writings of a number of his followers in Chapter 5. In the current chapter we review the work of other clinicians outside the Jungian field who have discovered a similar situation of Protector/Persecutor and his/her "client" in the inner world of patients with significant early trauma.

Our goal in this chapter is threefold: first, to fill out the many facets of this inner self-care system as it has been discovered by clinicians across theoretical disciplines; second, to demonstrate by a comparison of clinical/ theoretical evidence that the archetypal inner figures we have discussed are "universals," found everywhere that depth psychotherapists work with the so-called "primitive" mental states; and third, to offer a critical commentary on the work of other investigators in order to bring their ideas into dialogue with the Jungian approach presented thus far. If psychotherapists from widely different theoretical outlooks independently confirm the presence of our diabolical inner

115

figures and their self-preservative activity, this will be persuasive support for their archetypal roots.

EDMUND BERGLER AND THE SELF-DAMAGING "DAIMONION"

Of all Freud's students and later disciples, perhaps no-one developed the theory of psychic masochism so thoroughly – one might even say obsessively – as Edmund Bergler (1899–1962). In a total of twenty-four books and some 300 scientific papers, Bergler developed his idea that self-damage by a sadistic superego was the core of all neurosis – making it far more serious than other investigators had recognized. Bergler's superego lacks benevolence altogether, it is, in fact, a monster – a "daimonic" internal agency bent on a campaign of sheer torture and lifelong abuse of the helpless masochistic ego (see Bergler, 1959).

How this tormenting inner situation comes about derives from a developmental theory which has elements of the later Kleinian idea of the infant's original (pre-Oedipal) condition, which Bergler says is one of magical omnipotence or infantile megalomania, demanding instantaneous gratification. When this infantile wish runs into reality's "no," the infant experiences a frustration which leads to unbounded rage – aggression that cannot find adequate expression owing to the infant's undeveloped motoric equipment. This aggression is first projected outside the self and attributed to the Bad Mother, but then it "boomerangs" against the ego, becoming incorporated in a sadistic superego which mercilessly attacks the self from within. By establishing an inner agency of abuse, the child unconsciously defends its megalomania and self-sufficiency in the face of an environment which seems hostile to its every wish, preferring its own depression to the "humiliation" of being subject to someone else's will. The final stage in this sequence is the libidinization of the pain caused by the superego, i.e., its defensive conversion into pleasure (psychic masochism). Patients with this background will present themselves as innocent victims seeking support, but they are really unconsciously engineering self-damaging situations which they inwardly enjoy. Until they realize this and break the self-destructive pattern, supportive psychotherapy will not help them.

In Bergler's theory, there is one additional intra-psychic agency, besides the superego, which helps the child protect its illusion of omnipotence, i.e., the ego-ideal. In the ego-ideal the child holds onto its archaic image of perfection and self-glorification, frustrated in reality but now enshrined in this inner department, made up mostly of infantile narcissism. This egoideal now becomes a major instrument of torture in the hands of the sadistic superego because the child is always falling short of it.

This leads to Bergler's final formulation. The accumulation of cruelty and aggression directed against the ego he calls "Daimonion," a term adopted from Socrates who described it in Plato's *Apologia* as "a godlike and daimoniacal something . . . some kind of voice that deters me from things I wish to do, but never gives positive advice" (Bergler, 1959: 46). Daimonion, says Bergler, is a malignant spirit, an internal angatonist with uncanny power. It tricked Socrates into drinking the hemlock (by remaining silent) when he might have escaped imprisonment.

Expressed psychoanalytically, Daimonion is an internal "something" which is the individual's own worst enemy. It is a cruel jailer and tormenter composed of the child's rebounding aggression. It is always at work in the human being's inner world despite all conscious strivings for happiness or pleasure. It is an unsuspected inhabitant of the human psyche, adverse to enjoyment of life, contentment, and success, always aiming for misery, unhappiness, and self-destruction.

These two unconscious forces – ego-ideal and Daimonion – combine to form the unconscious conscience (superego). Daimonion uses the ego-ideal for its campaign of torture, constantly presenting to the ego the ego-ideal's exaggerated infantile claims of all-power and grandiose achievements, constantly asking the unchanging question: "Have you achieved all the aims you promised yourself as a child?" If the answer to this question is in the negative, the result is guilt (ibid.: 46–7).

Bergler's idea that the "Daimonic" voices of the superego *use* the ego-ideal's images to create a more demanding *perfectionism* which only further persecutes the ego, finds corroboration in much current clinical literature. Marion Woodman (1982) has attributed most eating disorders to an "addiction to perfection," and Sidney Blatt (1995) has shown persuasively how many contemporary suicides committed by seemingly healthy, accomplished people derive from a form of "neurotic perfectionism" in which the self-critical, often overly self-reliant individual is "stalked by his own impossible standards of perfection" (ibid.: 1003). The harsh punitive superego is indeed a terrible "force" in the psyche of men and women across the spectrum of psychological adjustment and mal-adjustment.

ODIER AND THE MALEVOLENT/BENEVOLENT "GREAT BEINGS"

Charles Odier, a long-forgotten, though brilliant psychoanalytic theorist, was a contemporary of Jung's. His book *Anxiety and Magic Thinking* (Odier, 1956) explores the relationship between certain primitive forms of thinking investigated by Jean Piaget (the "magical," prelogical, a-dualistic phase) and Freud's theory of traumatic anxiety. All psychic anxiety, says Odier, has its origin in the infant's unbearable experience of early trauma. Trauma, in turn, creates a regressed portion of the ego which fails to participate in the mental development of other parts of the self. Anticipating D.W. Winnicott (see p. 124), Odier defines trauma in terms of those wounds to psychic equilibrium that paralyze or dissociate consciousness when the helpless infant is deprived of the mother's care and protection – leading to abject states of profound *insecurity*. These traumatic states of insecurity are not "remembered" by the infant, but in later childhood they are revived by analogous threatening conditions, and they amplify the current distress, flooding the ego with the disorganizing anxiety of the early trauma.

Once fear or distress begins, the regressed part of the ego always returns in both thought and affectivity to the magical level of infancy with its associated conviction of imminent catastrophe and its terrors of malevolent "forces" or "beings." Anxiety replaces fear. A vicious circle is established because the malevolent thoughts are usually so awesomely terrifying to the regressed ego that they themselves are traumatogenic factors in the patient's experience. Long after the outer trauma has ceased, malevolent magical thinking continues and, with it, a constant expectation of total catastrophe and death. The negative thoughts and convictions of catastrophe and death become inner objects of terror and the individual is repeatedly traumatized, not by outer reality but by his or her own nefarious malevolent expectations (see ibid.: 58).

For Odier, the magical level is one characterized by superstition, omnipotence of thought, and primitive affects. It exerts two opposing actions on the psyche: at times an action of destruction and at times an action of protection. On the one side is nefarious or destructive magical thinking (black magic), the legacy of a traumatized childhood; on the other, positive, beneficial magical thinking (white or pink magic) that surrounds the first years of happy children. Corresponding to these two opposing forms of magical thinking are what Odier calls the "great beings" which come to haunt or hallow the traumatized child's inner world. Just as magical thinking exerts two opposing actions – destruction and protection, these gigantic, fantasized "beings" are of two types: malevolent and destructive on the one hand, benevolent and protective on the other. In other words, they represent an objectification of the primal affects of childhood (see ibid.: 37–113). In Jungian language, they represent archetypal images.

Odier gives the example of a patient, Ariane, who dreamed of both a benevolent, protective "great being" and then shortly thereafter of a malevolent one. The patient had been abandoned many times in childhood and later brutally criticized by her father. In the first dream:

> I am alone in a strange land. Before me a dark expanse of water spreads out endlessly. I feel afraid – a nothingness – before such immensity. But a god appears – a huge giant, half nude. I try to follow him, to attract his attention so that I can be under his protection. Then, showing me my family in deep mourning, he tells me: "Stay with them, they also have nobody." I awoke with a feeling of having a great mission to accomplish.

> (ibid.: 104)

In the second dream:

> I am on the terrace of our house lying on a couch in a magnificent moonlight. Behind my head is a dark corridor instead of the living-room door. At the entrance of the corridor is a huge black frog, monstrous and horrible. I am

seized with an inexpressible terror. Suddenly things change. Not the horrible frog, but my father emerges from the shadows of the corridor with a gun in his hand – like a common murderer. I feel paralyzed with fear! Awakening, I remained in the unpleasant atmosphere of my childhood and it was a long time before I could get out of it.

(ibid.: 105)

This patient's father was an irascible and violent man who for some reason loved frogs and toads. As a little girl, seeking greater closeness with her remote father, Ariane had befriended these animals, feeding and protecting them in her garden – even playing the flute to them in the evening. "Thus," says Odier,

she would make friends and proteges of these strange and disgusting animals, and turn the malevolent beings into benevolent ones – something she could never do with her terrible father. . . . It is obvious why the frog and the father are one in the nightmare.

(ibid.: 106)

A Jungian interpretation of these dreams might question Odier's assumption that frogs were "disgusting" creatures to his patient and would add an important archetypal element to our understanding of her dreams' content. Through a Jungian lens the "great beings" in Ariane's dreams would represent personifications of unconscious fantasy/structures – just like the "vampire" we witnessed in Jung's "Moon-lady" fantasy (Chapter 3) and would not necessarily be interpreted as "stand-ins" for known personal content (the father). Unconscious fantasy is the unconscious "meaning" the psyche makes out of its often unbearable experience with real objects. The structures/images through which this "meaning" reaches consciousness are archetypal and mythological. Moreover, these mythological image/structures in the unconscious are not just idle cross-cultural "curiosities" but, because the psyche has primordial roots, they are informative about what the psyche "intends" by presenting archaic affects in such "typical" (archetypal) form. Limitations of space prevent us from expanding on this point here.

SANDOR FERENCZI AND THE CARETAKER SELF'S TRANSPERSONAL WISDOM

We have seen how Freud tended to emphasize the negative, persecutory side of what we are calling the self-care system (superego) and how Odier adds to the picture by focusing on the benevolent/protective role of the "great beings" as well as their malevolent aspects. Sandor Ferenczi brings a different perspective to bear on the inner world of trauma. In his famous paper "Confusion of Tongues" (1933), Ferenczi illustrates one of the most remarkable features of what we have called the self-care system, namely, its ability to accelerate one part of the personality's development precociously, making use of seemingly miraculous

119

wisdom, while leaving yet another part of the personality behind in a regressed state. Faced by the unbearable affects of severe trauma, says Ferenczi,

> part of the person regresses into the state of happiness that existed prior to the trauma – a trauma which it endeavours to annul. [Yet] more remarkable is the working of a second mechanism. . . . I mean the sudden, surprising rise of new faculties after a trauma, like a miracle that occurs upon the wave of a magic wand, or like that of the fakirs who are said to raise from a tiny seed, before our very eyes, a plant, leaves and flowers.
>
> When subjected to a sexual attack . . . the child can develop instantaneously all the emotions of mature adults and all the potential qualities dormant in him that normally belong to marriage, maternity and fatherhood. One is justified – in contradistinction to the familiar regression – to speak of a *traumatic progression*, of a *precocious maturity*.
>
> (Ferenczi, 1933: 164–5; emphases in original)

As evidence of this "traumatic progression," Ferenczi cites the frequently reported typical dream of the "wise baby" in which an infant or young child gives prescient advice to its caregivers (ibid.: 165). He explains much of this "wisdom" as a function of the child's "identification with the (adult) aggressor" (ibid.: 162), but not all of it. Ferenczi was also intrigued by the possibility that, in trance states, extraordinary capacities of the mind are also tapped into by the traumatized psyche.

The apparently transpersonal (paranormal?) capacities of the traumatically progressed self and its simultaneous protection and persecution of its regressed "partner" (our dyadic self-care system) are beautifully illustrated by Ferenczi's clinical process notes on his work with a sexually abused woman named Elizabeth Severn. The case is reported in *The Clinical Diary* (Ferenczi, 1988) under the name "R.N." and the following description is condensed and paraphrased from the text.

The first traumatic shock befell R.N. at the age of 1½, when the patient's father drugged her with an injected narcotic and sexually abused her. The memory of this experience – long forgotten before her analysis – but present underneath as primitive agony and a death-wish, was recovered only later in analysis while she and Ferenczi were exploring a trauma that had occurred when she was five. At this age the brutal attacks from the father were renewed, her genitals were artificially dilated, with insistent suggestions that she be compliant to men and again the stimulating intoxicants were administered. Ferenczi reports that with the recovery of this memory there was an awareness of enormous, unbearable suffering, abject helplessness, and despair of outside help, with a suicidal death-wish accompanied by total relinquishment of control – a vacating of herself and total identification with the aggressor. But on the brink of "giving up the ghost" (ibid.: 39), something new came into play in this patient's inner world. What Ferenczi called "the organizing life instincts" (ibid.: 8), otherwise known as "Orpha", awakened and, in place of death, chopped up the personality, dispersing it into fragments – thereby driving it insane in order to prevent death. (Here we see the persecutory aspect.) The person now, according to Ferenczi, consists internally of two parts – one that is destroyed – the regressed feeling component – and one that *sees* the destruction – the progressed intellectual component. The "destroyed" child-part is

> a being suffering purely psychically in his unconscious, the actual child, of whom the awakened ego knows absolutely nothing. This fragment is accessible only in deep sleep, or in a deep trance ... It behaves like a child who has fainted or given up the ghost, completely unaware of itself, "dead" who can perhaps only groan, who must be shaken awake mentally and sometimes also physically.
>
> (ibid.: 9)

But then there is "Orpha" – the part that "sees" the destruction. "She" is a supra-individual being, apparently without time and space (ibid.: 13), who, at the moment of unbearable pain, "passes through a hole in the head into the universe and shines far off in the distance like a star"(ibid.: 206), seeing everything from outside, all-knowing. This "Astral fragment," Ferenczi says, leaves the selfish spheres of earthly existence and becomes clairvoyant – "beyond understanding the aggressor, to an 'objective understanding' of the entire universe, so to speak, in order to be able to grasp the genesis of such a monstrous thing" (ibid.: 207).

Orpha, says Ferenczi, has only one concern and that is the preservation of life. She plays the role of the guardian angel. She produces wish-fulfilling fantasies for the suffering or murdered child, she scours the whole universe seeking help (R.N. was convinced that Orpha, in her omniscience, had tracked Ferenczi down as the only person in the world who could help her). But for R.N., when her most shattering trauma struck at the age of 11, even Orpha was forced to admit her helplessness. At this age, R.N.'s father, who had repeatedly hypnotized and sexually abused the girl, now abandoned and cursed her, leaving the deserted child with an indelible sense of her own filthiness and contemptibility. With this, says Ferenczi, Orpha could not help any longer and sought to arrange for R.N's suicide. When this was made impossible because of confinement in a hospital, the only alternative was the complete atomization of psychic life.

The patient remembered the sensation of exploding into the universe, with images of brilliantly shining constellations, hallucinatory, seemingly unconnected images and words, such as, "I am a universal egg" (ibid.: 29). This lava-like eruption came to an end in total "incineration" – complete temporary insanity, catatonic stupor. But, says Ferenczi, this person did not stay insane. Like Isis, looking for the lost and dismembered body of her beloved Osiris, Orpha returned and managed, "as if by a miracle, to get this being back on its feet, shattered as it was to its very atoms"(ibid.: 10), and even succeeded in re-establishing unity with the pre-traumatic personality, although this was accomplished by memory lapses and retroactive amnesia of varying duration (ibid.: 39).

Ferenczi comments on this "dissolving in the universe" and the "re-coagulation" that was engineered by Orpha:

> The point at which external control is completely abandoned and inner adaptation sets in (where even death as adaptation becomes conceivable) is perceived inwardly as deliverance, liberation. This moment probably signifies the relinquishing of self-preservation for man and his self-inclusion in a greater, perhaps universal state of equilibrium.
>
> (ibid.: 7)

> The tendency, widespread in schizophrenics, to create their own cosmogonies, which often strikes us as fantastic, is a part of the attempt to incorporate their own "impossible" suffering into that greater unity.
>
> (ibid.: 33)

> In any event these reflections open the way to an understanding of the surprisingly intelligent reactions of the unconscious in moments of great distress . . . including the notoriously familiar "wise baby" dreams [and the] regressive powers of spiritualist mediums.
>
> (ibid.: 81)

> Whether one should go further and search for supermaterial, metaphysical intuitions in the form and content of mental disorders (like physicists, in whose view substances are finally reduced to energy) is something each must decide for himself.
>
> (ibid.: 29)

And he further speculates:

> To what extent do those who have "gone mad" from pain, that is, those who have departed from the usual egocentric point of view, become able through their special situation to experience a part of that immaterial reality which remains inaccessible to us materialists? And here the direction of research must become involved with the so-called occult. Cases of thought transference during the analysis of suffering people are extraordinarily frequent, . . . and it is possible that even the intelligence of which we are so proud is not our property but must be replaced or regenerated through the rhythmic outpouring of the ego into the universe, which alone is all knowing and therefore intelligent.
>
> (ibid.: 33)

Ferenczi's suggestion here, that Orpha is part of a regenerative universal "intelligence," or makes use of a deeper wisdom in the psyche at moments of traumatic distress, reminds one of Jung's conviction that the Self, representing the wholeness of the psyche, including its "psychoid" depths, represents a "destiny" factor for the individual and has the ego-transcendent capacity to guide and regulate the individuation process. It represents a factor truly "superior" to the ego.

OBJECT-RELATIONS THEORISTS

Melanie Klein and Wilfred Bion

Both Melanie Klein and Wilfred Bion are significant to our discussion because of their emphasis upon the death instinct and its *personification* as a terrifying "object" in unconscious fantasy-systems of very young children and/or psychotic processes. Both use Freud's construct of the superego to describe this tyrannical inner attacker but both extend the idea of the superego far beyond what Freud intended. Klein was one of the first to do analytic work with children, and she was shocked to find how much violence occurred in the spontaneous play of her young patients (see Klein, 1946). She attributed this to a pre-Oedipal superego which was much harsher and more cruel than the superego described by Freud. This superego, she felt, originated in potentially psychotic levels of anxiety. In order to escape being destroyed by its own death instinct, the child ejects its hatred outward onto the (bad) breast or penis (projective identification) where it can then "locate" its otherwise unbearable anxiety as persecutory fears of attack (paranoid/persecutory position). The child's loving feelings are similarly projected (good breast or penis) and the stage is set for the child's ultimate discovery that good and bad breast/penis belong to the same person (depressive position and achievement of whole object-relations). In the process of the child's working through its love and hate with the real/fantasied mother (or later the analyst) and her different parts, the superego is modified and becomes less harsh, evolving into a capacity for guilt (conscience) and resulting in reparative efforts to make good the imaginary damage the child has done to its objects.

But at the beginning of this stormy process, the projected hateful feelings and their associated fantasy elements are projected onto the mother/analyst who then becomes a partially hallucinated horrendous "being" or, split into parts, a terrifying "thing." If the mother/analyst cannot receive and modify these projections, reintroducing the loving feelings, then this hateful introject gets internalized, so the child (and later the psychotic adult) feels him or herself persecuted in the internal world by a menacing sadistic breast/penis, thing/person.

Wilfred Bion takes Klein's analysis a step further into adult psychotic processes by hypothesizing that Klein's sadistic superego perversely attacks not only the child's ego, but all "linking" processes in the mind which allow the child to have an experience of a coherent self (see Bion, 1959). Because the breast and penis are linking objects, as well as primary objects of the infant's experience, attacks upon them generalize into attacks on what they symbolize, i.e., relationship to objects in the world and integration among objects internally. This results in an attack upon the very capacity for integrated, whole experience. Thoughts are severed from feelings, images from affects, memory from consciousness – even the capacity to think is attacked. What results is an "ego-destructive superego" taking the place of normal ego-development and usurping normal ego-functions (see Bion, 1957).

Bion is convinced that a malignant figure stalks the inner worlds of psychotic patients and creates huge resistance to their improvement in psychotherapy. This malevolent inner force is a "bizarre formation" or a "bizarre object" which systematically strips all experience of its meaning. Bion writes:

> If the mother cannot tolerate ... projections the infant is reduced to continued projective identification carried out with increasing force and frequency. The increased force seems to denude the projection of a penumbra of meaning. Re-introjection is effected with similar force and frequency. Deducing the patient's feelings from his behaviour in the consulting room and using the deductions to form a model, the infant of my model does not behave in a way that I ordinarily expect of an adult who is thinking. It behaves as if it felt that an internal object has been built up but has the characteristics of a greedy vagina-like 'breast' that strips of its goodness all that the infant receives or gives leaving only degenerate objects. This internal object starves its host of all understanding that is made available. In analysis such a patient seems unable to gain from his environment and therefore from his analyst.
>
> (Bion, 1962b: 115)

Bion's assumption of a malevolent hypertrophied superego that hates and attacks all linking processes in the psyche corresponds closely with our hypothesis of how the primitive survival-Self institutes an "auto-immune" attack upon those vulnerable opportunities for self-expression and relatedness which it mistakes for threats of re-traumatization. To this hypothesis, Bion adds a rich but sobering analysis of how what Jung called the "transcendent" function (for Bion the "alpha" function) is itself broken down by inner hatred so that in the worst cases, *the psyche's very symbolic capacity to process its own affects is attacked*. This is a radical hypothesis, and one which raises questions about our assumption within analytical psychology of the psyche's symbol-forming function *sui generis*. Bion's analysis would suggest that even this capacity is relative and depends upon unpredictable variables such as the mother's projection-metabolizing ability and also the level of innate aggression in the infant requiring metabolization.

D. W. Winnicott

Winnicott's whole authorship is about trauma in one form or another, so what we review here is only one part of a much larger whole, some of which has already been cited. For Winnicott, trauma is always about a failure of the environment/ mother to provide care that is "good enoough" to sustain an active, creative relationship between inner and outer reality. If the mother's care is erratic, overstimulating, or grossly neglectful, a split starts to open up between the infant's psychosomatic "true" self and a (primarily mental) "false" self that is pre-cociously organized to screen the true self from further trauma and to act as a *substitute* for the environment which has become unbearable. For Winnicott, this division of the whole psychosomatic self results from the intervention of primitive defenses designed to prevent the experience of "unthinkable agonies" associated with early trauma. In the language of the present investigation, such "primitive defenses" are equivalent to the dyadic self-care system – one part of the personality as a "progressed" false self, located in the mind, with a regressed true self as its "client."

Winnicott's true self carries what we have called the personal spirit. It appears before the organization of "inner objects," at the very beginning of life and initially is "little more than the summation of sensori-motor aliveness" (Winnicott, 1960a: 149). Its "omnipotence" is another way of acknowledging its numinous, archetypal basis, which must be slowly "humanized" within the mother–infant dyad. If this does not happen in an optimal way, then according to Winnicott, the true self ceases to incarnate in the body and the (mostly mental) false self, based on compliance with outer demands, takes over the life of the individual, hiding the still omnipotent, but now traumatized true self as its shameful secret.

Winnicott sees a spectrum of false-self dominance. At one extreme the true self is completely hidden, even from the false self. Further toward health, the true self is "acknowledged as a potential and is allowed a secret life" (ibid.: 143). Still further toward health, the false self searches for the optimal conditions that will allow the true self to come into being. At this level the false self becomes a caretaker self, caretaking the true self.

Winnicott cites the case of a woman who had a false self but who never had the feeling throughout her whole life, that she really existed:

> I found I was dealing with what the patient called her "Caretaker Self". This "Caretaker Self": (1) found psychoanalysis; (2) came and sampled analysis, as a kind of elaborate test of the analyst's reliability; (3) brought her to analysis; (4) gradually after three years or more handed over its function to the analyst. . . . (5) hovered round, resuming caretaking at times when the analyst failed (analyst's illness . . . holidays, etc.).
>
> (ibid.: 142)

Winnicott emphasizes the positive (caretaking) side of what we have called the self-care system. Its persecutory dimension is not discussed, except to say that if the caretaker self cannot find a way for the true self to exist, then it becomes its lot to organize the patient's suicide – because the true self must never be betrayed, an analysis identical to Ferenczi's description of Orpha and the regressed ego. "Suicide in this context," says Winnicott, "is the destruction of the total self in avoidance of annihilation of the true self" (ibid.: 143).

Corrigan and Gordon and the "mind-object"

The persecutory side of Winnicott's false self, located in the mind, is emphasized by Corrigan and Gordon (1995) in their concept of "the mind-object." The authors propose that for a certain subgroup of patients, what Ferenczi called the "progressed" self becomes precocious, grows up too soon and becomes identified with the mind – including the mind's perfectionistic ideals. This perfectionistic "mind" becomes personified as an internal "mind-object" and ruthlessly attacks the psychosomatic self which can never keep up with its relentless demands. The result is depression, Obsessive-Compulsive Disorder, or various forms of schizoid withdrawal. In our language, the self-care system takes over and prevents all further dependency which would allow for growth.

Michael Eigen

Among the various psychoanalytic writers reviewed here, Eigen comes closest to an archetypal understanding of the so-called primitive defenses of our self-care system. Eigen focuses on Bion's ideas of how early trauma, with its "psychotic agonies" stimulates a "malevolent mind" which ultimately wreaks havoc within the psyche and leads to potential damage of the very capacity to process our own experience. A malevolent "life-hating superego" virtually commandeers otherwise normal thinking to justify its destructive intent and sets about deconstructing the psyche's symbolic capacity. Condensing Bion's ideas, Eigen summarizes:

> As a metaphor for massive destructiveness, Bion imagined [psychic evolution] working in reverse. Instead of feeding trauma into primary process, where traumatic impact may be worked into images, which give rise to symbols, which give rise to thought, a stunning reversal occurs; any achievement gets deconstructed back into originary trauma elements, which remain unprocessable. Raw, everlasting catastrophe takes the place where a psyche might have been. The psyche (what there is of it) becomes a "catastrophe machine," grinding any bits of possible experiencing into horrific nothingness.
>
> (Eigen, 1995: 114)

Eigen, however, is not content to let the matter rest with Bion's "catastrophe machine." In a passage that Jung himself could have written, Eigen says:

> It is easy to imagine an infant unable to process turbulence it undergoes. But I think it helpful to confess a processing incapacity all life long. Our religions and psychotherapies offer frames of reference for processing unbearable agonies, and perhaps, also, unbearable joys. At times, art or literature brings the agony-ecstasy of life together in a pinnacle of momentary triumph. Good poems are time pellets, offering places to live emotional transformations over lifetimes. There are moments of processing, pulsations that make life meaningful, as well as mysterious. But I think these aesthetic and religious products gain part of their power from all the moments of breakdown that went into them.
>
> (ibid.: 117)

Here Eigen is suggesting something about the psyche that was central to Jung's differences with Freud, namely, that the very unconscious fantasies in terms of which the infant mind tries to defend itself from early trauma are structures of meaning already present, at least *in potentia*. They are not "made up" in order to make the infant/child feel better – quite the contrary, their often diabolical presence, as we have witnessed, frequently makes the trauma victim feel worse. In other words, the mind has an archetypal basis. Its frames of reference which structure the psyche are "released" on the occasion of the infant's early experience with the mother (including trauma), but are shared by humanity as a whole and are also "released" along the path of each individual's suffering the human condition. Therefore, when our traumatized infant later encounters these same "categories" in the narrative symbol-systems (stories) of religion, poetry, and art, they carry transformative potential and "meaning" *precisely because they were present at the beginning*. In fact, it is in these later analogous archetypal images or re-enactments that the early trauma is "re-membered." Psychopathology, in this view, is relative and universally human. Even its trauma-generated "repetition compulsion" is a part of human experience across the board, and need not imply a "death instinct," although this *fantasy* of Freud's is part of the meaning he and others have made of clinical experience with trauma.

Ronald Fairbairn

Among the theories which best account for the coincidence of a vulnerable "innocent" inner object and a violent Protector/Persecutor of that object is Fairbairn's discussion of how the internal saboteur comes to have such a sadistic relationship with the "libidinal ego." Fairbairn worked with children who had been victims of sexual assault during World War II and found, to his astonishment that these innocent children felt ashamed of being assaulted and resisted the memory of their trauma because it made them feel "bad." Fairbairn concluded that the dependent child's motive in becoming bad was "to make his objects good" (Fairbairn, 1981: 65), and that this was accomplished by internalizing the "badness" associated with these objects and then repressing the self- and object-images carrying this "badness." Fairbairn contributes to our understanding here by his emphasis that *the child's aggression is the agent of this repression*. He says:

> It is the experience of libidinal frustration that calls forth the infant's aggression in relation to his libidinal object and thus gives rise to a state of ambivalence ... Since it proves intolerable to him to have a good object which is also bad, he seeks to alleviate the situation by splitting the figure of his mother into two objects. Then, in so far as she satisfies him libidinally, she is a "good" object, and, in so far as she fails to satisfy him libidinally, she is a "bad" object.
>
> (ibid.: 110)

127

Once [this] ambivalence has been established, however, the expression of feeling towards his mother involves him in a position which must seem to him singularly precarious.

(ibid.: 112)

If, on the one hand he expresses aggression, he is threatened with loss of his good object, [she rejects him all the more] and if, on the other hand, he expresses libidinal need, he is threatend with the singularly devastating experience of humiliation over the depreciation of his love, shame over the display of needs which are disregarded or belittled, [or] . . . at a still deeper level, an experience of disintegration and of imminent psychical death.

(ibid.: 113)

[In this precarious situation] . . . the child seeks to circumvent the dangers of expressing both libidinal and aggressive affect toward his object by *using a maximum of his aggression to subdue a maximum of his libidinal need.* In this way he reduces the volume of affect, both libidinal and aggressive, demanding outward expression. . . . The excess of libido is taken over by the libidinal ego; and the excess of aggression is taken over by the internal saboteur. The child's technique of using aggression to subdue libidinal need thus resolves itself into an attack by the internal saboteur upon the libidinal ego.

(ibid.: 115)

In Chapter 1 we found good examples of this internal attack in the cases of Mrs. Y. and the shotgunner and in the female artist and her dream of the axeman. Both such persecutory inner objects would represent, according to Fairbairn, personifications of the patient's inverted aggression – aggression that should have been available for adaptation, but wasn't, leaving these patients with an ingratiating "false self" to negotiate relations in the world and aggression turned inward.

One of Fairbairn's important ideas is that in the psychoanalytic situation the goal must be to help the patient take the risk of releasing his or her internalized "bad" objects so that their libidinal cathexis can be resolved. The resistance to this is the patient's constant "temptation to exploit a 'good' relationship with the analyst as a defence against taking this risk" (ibid.: 69). "I feel convinced," says Fairbairn,

[that] it is to the realm of these bad objects, rather than to the realm of the super-ego that the ultimate origin of all psychopathological developments is to be traced; for it may be said of all psychoneurotic and psychotic patients that, if a True Mass is being celebrated in the chancel, a Black Mass is being celebrated in the crypt. It becomes evident, accordingly, that the psychotherapist is the true successor to the exorcist, and that he is concerned, not only with "the forgiveness of sins," but also with "the casting out of devils".

(ibid.: 70)

Harry Guntrip

Fairbairn's analysis is amplified by Harry Guntrip, who finds the same "internal saboteur" and its innocent "client" in the dreams of traumatized patients (see Guntrip, 1969). Fairbairn and Guntrip are alone among these theorists in their use of dreams to confirm the internal world of trauma. The neglected or traumatized child, Guntrip says,

> must feel that it is too frightening to be weak in an unfriendly and menacing world. . . . and if you cannot change your world, you can try to change yourself. Thus he comes to fear and hate his own weakness and neediness; and now he faces the task of growing up with an intolerance of his immaturity.
>
> (ibid.: 187)

This "intolerance of immaturity" is represented by an "antilibidinal ego" which Guntrip sees as an internal representative of the child's identification with the dependency-rejecting "bad parental object." This antilibidinal ego "hates" the dependency that got the child into such trouble with the intolerant parents and thus is an "introjection" of them now established as a "5th column" in the internal environment. Guntrip points out that the antilibidinal ego is one of the main sources of resistance in psychotherapy.

> The hostility . . . of the antilibidinal ego to direct dependence on anyone for help, and its hating to admit needs, is the most stubborn source of resistance to psychotherapy and of resistance to the psychotherapist. It hates the needy child inside and hates the therapist to whom he desires to turn for help.
>
> (ibid.: 196)

To illustrate the opposition of the antilibidinal ego to emergent dependency needs, Guntrip cites the dream of a female patient that contains attacking figures reminiscent of the sadistic dream figures in cases such as Mrs. Y. and the shotgunner.

> I was a little girl, standing at the door of a large room trembling with fear. I saw you inside and thought "If only I could get to him I'd be safe." I ran across the room but another girl strode up and pushed me back to the door.
>
> (ibid.: 196)

Guntrip continues:

> Some two years later, when the patient was trusting me much more fully, she dreamed this same dream again. This time she got to within an inch of being able to touch me when the other girl emerged, as it were, from nowhere at the last moment, smacked her viciously across the face and drove her away again.
>
> (ibid.: 196)

Both Fairbairn and Guntrip focus exclusively on the malevolent persecutory activity of the internal saboteur or antilibidinal ego and view the regressed or libidinal ego as its innocent victim. From a Jungian standpoint, we might question this one-sidedness and the tendency – especially in Guntrip – to see only hatred and violence in the antilibidinal ego, and only goodness and innocence in the "lost heart of the self" which is the victim of its persecution. As we have seen illustrated in several cases, there seems to be a telos or intention within the archaic defensive system's violence, even though it is one that may go awry, leading to totally senseless violence against the psyche.

James Grotstein

In language reminiscent of Klein and Bion, American object-relations theorist James Grotstein also describes various malevolent inner figures that resist the progress of analysis in narcissistic, depressed, or addicted patients. "Narcissistic patients" says Grotstein,

> have a fear of transformation. [With the progress of analysis] . . . there is a growing disparity . . . between the progressive self and the yet remaining immature self. When the schism between these two portions of the personality achieves a critical differentiation, sometimes a negative therapeutic reaction with critical acting out takes place. It is as if the unprogressed portion of the personality undermines the progress of the progressive self in order to call attention to itself.
>
> (Grotstein, 1987: 325)

In one case, Grotstein reports a patient who had internalized the manic, grandiose aspect of his mother as a Nazi-like inner figure that tried its best to defend him from further catastrophe. It propelled the patient to great success vocationally, but it made ruthless, sadistic demands on him also. When the patient began to improve in analysis, this manic self began to fight back, by attacking the therapist's interpretations, undermining the therapy, minimizing the importance of the analyst, and generally conducting "the real analysis" in between sessions (ibid.: 329). This would be a classic example of what Freud meant by the negative therapeutic reaction.

This "manic" part of the patient, says Grotstein, sometimes becomes a virtual "living phantom," seeming to hold a more dependent, helpless self "hostage within its powerful snare" fighting for its own autonomous destiny.

> I have seen patients suffering from chronic depressive illness who seemed addicted to their depression and who would ultimately reveal that they were experiencing their depression as a split-off internal persona that was fighting for its own life and that feared the patient having any link with hope, progress, and happiness. I have termed this depressive persona the "Madonna of Sorrows." It is experienced as an autistic self-mother who

130

pities and soothes the narcissistic patient in the presence of ill treatment by others and in the presence of an unhappy life generally.

(ibid.: 330)

In one case of an anorexic girl, Grotstein reports with apparent chagrin that the patient's anorexia

> was personified virtually as an autistic "mothering self" who seemed to protect the enfeebled patient in a state of sanctuary, understood her, and was able to soothe her by the very redoubtability of her disciplining agenda. The therapist was seen as a helpful person on one level, but as an enemy to her "anorectic mother" and self on the other level. In one case, the patient's neurotic personality engaged me in analysis most ably until there was a sufficient differentiation between her normally progressive self and the still lagging anorectic-primitive self. At this time her vomiting became worse and she precipitated a program of such severe weight loss and chemical imbalance that her life was in danger. Her resistance to analysis subsided only when I acknowledged the positive importance of her anorectic self as a protection for her against her disappointing childhood objects

(ibid.: 325)

One of Grotstein's important discoveries is how the "Madonna of Sorrows" becomes a soothing, seductive inner figure that casts an addictive "spell" over the patient's individuating ego and carries on a kind of internal "co-dependency" relationship with it. This analysis is reminiscent of Janet's early discovery that some of his patient's possessing daimons conducted a kind of auto-hypnosis of the patient from within, and that until he had the daimon's cooperation, he could not successfully hypnotize the patient.

Otto Kernberg and his associates

Kernberg and his associates describe the internal world of the borderline patient as made up of caricatured, fragmentary, and exaggerated part-object representations, either loving or hateful, interacting with distorted, stereotyped part-self representations. Primitive defenses keep these part-self and object images from integrating into whole self and object representations. For loving and hateful feelings to coexist within a whole self or object image would arouse more anxiety than these patients can tolerate.

These part-self and part-object images arrange themselves in dyads, which become "roles" the patient plays outwardly in his or her interactions with others. This gives the analyst access to the inner imagos, because they are externalized in the transference. Typically, these dyads involve a vulnerable child or infant part-self representation and a caretaking "parental" part-object representation. Typical dyads are:

Loving parent – spontaneous uninhibited child
Punitive sadistic parent – bad, filthy child

131

Uncaring, self-involved parent – unwanted child
Sadistic attacker – abused victim, etc.

(see Kernberg *et al.*, 1989: 103)

Therapy consists of identifying the split inner actors as they are projected or identified with, naming them and their linked affects, and then helping the patient tolerate the anxiety of holding contradictory good and bad self or object images. The goal in this process is enhanced tolerance for ambivalence. Gradually, the patient is able to perceive himself or herself, as well as the therapist, as a more complex human being and thus a new dimension of depth in the perception of self and others signals the transformation of part into total object-relations (ibid.: 122).

Of interest in Kernberg's object-relations approach is the use of terms like "caricatured, distorted, unmodulated," etc., for what we have been describing as archetypal fantasy elements in the internal world. Jung was very clear that when one confronted these kinds of opposite images, one was in the area of archetypal "numinous" energies. But he did not articulate very clearly how these opposing inner images manifested in the psychotherapeutic situation and how, through the process of repeated projective identification and interpretation, they were worked through, i.e., humanized. For this, Kernberg's practical treatment suggestions are very useful.

Davies and Frawley and childhood sexual abuse

In the object-relations tradition of Kernberg and associates, Jody Messler Davies and Mary Gail Frawley have recently published their views on the treatment of adult survivors of childhood sexual abuse (see Davies and Frawley, 1994). They view the transitional space of the therapist/patient dyad as a "field" within which otherwise unavailable (dissociated) self-and object-representations split off in the early trauma are externalized (projective identification) together with their unconscious fantasy components, thereby reconstructing the "forgotten" traumatic situation in the transference/counter-transference situation. Among the paradigms enacted back and forth in this co-created space are various internal self- and object-relational dyads reminiscent of Kernberg's child and parent images. For example:

the uninvolved nonabusing parent – neglected child
the sadistic abuser – helpless, impotently enraged victim
the idealized, omnipotent rescuer – entitled child demanding rescue
the seducer and the seduced

(see ibid.: 167)

Within these four relational matrices, each one of which represents what we have called the dyadic self-care system, there are eight "positions" for the patient and therapist to identify with or to enact in complementary fashion. If the patient takes up the role of sadistic abuser, the therapist will experience the impotent rage of the victim in his counter-transference, for example. Ultimately, these paradigms must be made explicit through interpretation so that the affects associated with them can be identified, expressed, and worked through. This requires the active involvement of the therapist as well as his/her observational neutrality.

One of the most useful illustrations of the patient's identification with the sadistic, abusive side of the sado-masochistic dyad in psychotherapy is the authors' point that the victims of early trauma often try to destroy hope in their analysts.

> In most cases, adult survivors are terrified that good things cannot last, that promises will always ultimately be broken. Rather than waiting for the inevitable disappointment to occur, patients. . . . often intervene in the buildup of anxiety that accompanies hope by assuming control of the situation and shattering what they are convinced is only an illusion anyway. . . . Identifying with the victim, the therapist experiences the despair and deflation once held by the victimized child.
>
> (ibid.: 174)

The approach of Kernberg *et al.* to borderline states in general and of Davies and Frawley to childhood trauma in particular, illustrate how what we have identified as a dyadic, archaic self-care system gets organized in the transferential field and how it can be worked with relationally. From a Jungian perspective, we would want to emphasize that the imaginal "field" within which the dyadic self-care structures are manifested is not limited to transference and counter-transference. The dream itself is such a field, as is the sand tray and all other media of the so-called "creative arts" therapies which engage the patient in "active imagination." No less than the relational technique of Davies and Frawley, these therapies require the active involvement and playful engagement of therapist and patient alike in a process which seeks to uncover encapsulated affect which does not yet have word-forms for expression.

James Masterson

James Masterson (1981) has developed a developmental object-relations theory which shows how sado-masochistic dyads are created in the inner world as normal separation/individuation processes are traumatically ruptured. In normal development, says Masterson, the fused mother/infant self-object unit goes through an intermediate stage where part-images (a good and a bad self-representation) differentiate and then later coalesce into a whole self-representation, both good and bad. The same process applies to the object-representation.

The problem comes when the mother fails to allow the child to separate and rewards only the "good" compliant child, withdrawing from the child's individuated, self-activating thoughts and wishes. Self-expression is greeted with abandonment by the mother; compliance, dependence, and passivity are rewarded. This alternating rewarding/withdrawing imago is internalized and with each aspect of the maternal object-image goes a self-representation. The "withdrawing object-relations unit (WORU)" attacks and criticizes a "bad," ugly child and the rewarding object relations unit "loves" and rewards a "good" compliant child. So we find the Protector/Persecutor and his "client" seen as either a "good" or "bad" child (see ibid.).

In such a situation, the child becomes internally critical of his or her own genuine needs for self-expression (WORU) and retreats into pathological self-soothing by the rewarding unit (this would be equivalent to Winnicott's false self). In therapy, the borderline patient projects the rewarding unit onto the therapist and seeks his or her approval for "good" behavior in order to avoid the abandonment-depression that is associated with any act of true self-expression. When the therapist confronts this, then the withdrawing unit is projected, the patient feels devastated, "bad," etc. and the therapist is now indistinguishable from the persecutory inner object. Therapy proceeds back and forth as these split internal images are projected and interpreted in the transference, although Masterson presumably does not explicate his counter-transference reactions as do Davies and Frawley.

The reader will note that Masterson's analysis is in some respects just the opposite to that of Guntrip, Fairbairn or Winnicott in how the personal spirit pole of the dyad is defined. Guntrip *et al.* see the despised vulnerable true self, loving and needy, rejected by the internal saboteur; Masterson believes that it is the individuating active self, rejected by the WORU. These two positions can be reconciled if it is recognized that some dependency needs, if gratified, serve separation/individuation needs, whereas others do not. No doubt the personal spirit is also both vulnerable and actively self-expressive. Internal self-attack can undermine both.

Jeffrey Seinfeld

American object-relations theorist Jeffrey Seinfeld has combined the theories of Winnicott, Fairbairn, Klein, Masterson, Jacobson, Searles, and others to describe the activities of what he calls "the Bad Object" in its destructive rampages through the inner world of borderline and narcissistic patients (Seinfeld, 1990). Seinfeld is more sympathetic to the role of unconscious fantasy in the formation of inner objects than either Masterson or Kernberg, and also more sympathetic to the genuine needs of the vulnerable developing self for a holding environment (and a symbiotic period in the transference) before the separation needs that Kernberg and Masterson emphasize. He also makes especially creative use of Fairbairn's notion of the "Exciting Object" and points out how frequently parents who fail to offer their children satisfying holding, mirroring, and soothing, provide substitutes in food, toys, sexual stimulation, money, etc. thereby generating insatiable needs in the child. This Exciting Object becomes allied with the Bad Object leading to insatiable addiction, sado-masochistic obsessions, and deepening inner convictions of badness.

Most of Seinfeld's excellent case studies demonstrate how the awakening of vulnerability in the patient and a craving for an outer "good object" activates an "anti-dependent defense" (again our self-care system). In part, this represents the possessiveness of the internal Bad Object which fears losing the self component (the disgusting vulnerable child-self) to the potential good-object therapist. It therefore attacks the vulnerable feelings (often projected onto the therapist or others). This internal attack on vulnerability was demonstrated in several of the cases cited in the preceding chapters.

It is noteworthy that none of these object-relations theorists, with the exception of Fairbairn and Guntrip, look to dreams to corroborate their inner *dramatis personae*. Rather, they infer them from the study of recurring patterns in patients' interactions within the transference. This is one area where the present investigation offers some corroborative imagery to support what can otherwise begin to sound and look like a purely mechanical description of the inner world of trauma.

Colin A. Ross

Colin A. Ross, who does not consider himself an object-relations theorist, has worked extensively with Multiple Personality Disorder (MPD) patients and has witnessed the intricate, complex, multi-layered structure of the inner personality system with its complicated switching sequences and amnesia barriers. He himself and others he has trained have been struck by the unconscious intelligence of the psyche and its intricate mapping, and gatekeeping functions. Ross also notes that MPD patients regularly report more paranormal experiences than other diagnostic groups. Having read Jung's doctoral dissertation, Ross is aware that dissociative disorders go together with spiritualism, mental telepathy, telekinesis, clairvoyance, poltergeist contacts, and so on.

Ross has discovered typical alter-personalities in MPD cases, one of which he calls the Protector/Observer personality. This figure, he says, can be calm, mature, rational, and abstract, often with only the information component of the traumatic memory, not the feeling, the physiological arousal, or the sensory intensity associated with it (Ross, 1989: 114). The physiological arousal of the trauma, says Ross, is frequently given over to child-alters who abreact these memories in treatment. Protector/Observers sometimes control the switching sequences of the system and are in charge of which alter is out at a particular time. Occasionally, says Ross, the Protector may resort to persecution of the host personality in order to "keep it in," so to speak, or, it may try to prevent the patient from changing, by burning the host personality with cigarettes, cutting his or her wrists, or forcing him or her to take pills when a crucial change is immanent. Finally, the Protector (now Persecutor) personality may try to kill the host personality in a misguided attempt to protect it from future suffering (ibid.: 115). Here we see another independent confirmation of our Protector/Persecutor self-care system with its uncanny self-preservative capacities.

Susan Kavaler-Adler and the Daimon-lover

Examining the compulsive aspects of creativity, Susan Kavaler-Adler (1993) applies an object-relations approach to what she calls the "daimon-lover complex" in the unconscious of women artists. This malignant image of an internal father is retained in the psyche in archaic unintegrated form because of traumatic experiences which leave a predominance of hostile aggression in the psyche and which are unmourned. This aggression, in turn, prevents part-self and part-object images from integrating – a process she calls "mourning integration" based on Klein's "depressive position." In mourning integration, tolerance for the loving affects of grief permit the otherwise split imagos of archaic inner objects to integrate, modulate, and ultimately to be given up for new attachments.

What we have referred to as the ambivalent Trickster-like Protector/ Persecutor and his vulnerable personal spirit client, Kavaler-Adler refers to as the daimon or muse forms of the internalized part-object father, both idealized and malevolent:

> Perhaps that is why when we consider creative literature, we find myths that reflect both the idealized and malevolent father in the form of the demon lover. The demon lover can appear in one moment of self-expressive experience as a muse god and at the next moment as a devil. The muse is both inspirational and erotic. He can inspire the "creative ecstasy." Yet for the creative woman suffering from preoedipal psychic arrest, the villainous demon takes possession of her, turning the creative ecstasy into a suicidal frenzy or into the cold frigidity of isolation and death. Images of death then abound. Alternatively, an idealized muse father is once more recreated through manic and narcissistic modes of defense. The vicious cycle must continue. Only despair, sickness, death, or suicide can end the cycle, as long as the preoedipal arrest is not modified.
>
> (ibid.: 75)

Kavaler-Adler's insight that early trauma leaves an internal world menaced by archaic, alternately malevolent or benevolent images falls at the center of our concern in these pages. She makes the further point that, for women who have suffered early trauma in relation to the mother, substitution by the father for the missing maternal experience will not work. The father will tend to an "exciting object" (Fairbairn) and the woman will try to recreate the missing experience on a "spiritual" level *through her creativity* – knowing no other way to communicate. She will thus be compelled to create and yet will remain equally frustrated in ever getting what she needs by way of response to her creativity. This reactivates the early pre-Oedipal trauma with the mother and a vicious circle results.

On the basis of my own clinical experience, I agree with Kavaler-Adler's formulations as applied to the unmourned trauma of female patients and the tendencies toward addictions to exciting inner-paternal objects – often leading to especially refractory forms of transference-addiction. One would need to add, however, that the pattern Kavaler-Adler has illustrated is not limited to the female psyche, and the Trickster components of her diabolical inner objects are not only found attached to the father-imago. The problems presented by the archetypal self-care system are not confined to gender roles.

Part II

INTRODUCTION TO PART II
Fairy tales and the two-stage
incarnation of the Self

A young male patient was recently struggling out loud in his session with his seemingly fateful and compelling love for a young woman he had been dating. He kept trying to escape his feeling for her and its implied commitment by having affairs with other women. Yet each time he came out of these sexual encounters more empty and full of longing for this one steady woman, Mary. What was it that she held for him, he wondered. Why did it feel "deep" with her and "shallow" with all the others? Suddenly, his eyes filled up with tears and he said very movingly, "You know what it is – more than anything else, when I'm with Mary, I feel a sense of potential for my life! Things seem possible that otherwise don't – that's the difference. When I'm with her I feel potential for my life!" I told him I could not imagine a better description of being in love than that.

To feel potential for one's life – shared with a beloved other – is what a certain group of patients (generally called "schizoid") cannot allow themselves to experience in the real world – precisely because their nascent longings to do so were traumatically disappointed as children. The links with the world – mediated by significant others – were broken, and hope was lost. The word "potential" is one of those linking words. It has two Latin roots, *potis* or latent power, and *posse*, to be able, from which we get our word "possible." So, the *American Heritage Dictionary* defines potential as "the inherent capacity or ability for growth, development, or coming into being." Something "inherent," an "inward potency," crosses a boundary and becomes real – is actualized in the world.

D. W. Winnicott has helped us to understand that this process occurs in the individual lives of children whenever there is a good-enough "fit" or empathic match between the spontaneous gesture of the baby and the mother's mediating response. The child is made real in this optimally facilitating environment as gestures of the true self get linked up with the world and the flow of love into life begins. If the original situation was traumatic, the individual is left with an obsessional *object-hunger* in order to get the developmental process back on track again. Occasionally, this object-hunger is satisfied in the psychoanalytic trauma of early rapture of those transitional processes so essential to the personal spirits emergence can be repaired.

141

TRANSITIONAL PROCESSES BETWEEN THE HUMAN AND DIVINE

A purely personalistic psychology, however, does not capture the true mystery of that *coming into being* of the personal spirit in the face of trauma to which Winnicott's otherwise accurate imagery pertains. This is because it leaves out the transpersonal element or it interprets the transpersonal element as infantile omnipotence and neglects the primacy of the numinosum in human experience.

From the standpoint of Jungian psychology, the miraculous processes at the boundary between potentiality and actuality in human development must be seen against the backdrop of archetypal processes, which means against the backdrop of mythology. Mythology and all the great religions of the world are preoccupied with one essential question – the question of relationship between the human and divine and how it is maintained in the face of human suffering. How, and through what agencies is a connection maintained between the transcendent world, with its life-giving divine energies, and the mundane temporal world bound by time, space, history, and routine? Where do we come from? Does our existence have a meaning beyond everyday life? Does God manifest himself in history? These are all linking questions and remind us that the word "religion" contains the notion of "re"-flection and "ligeo," ligament or connection – hence reconnection. It is, of course, paradoxical to say that the stories of myth are concerned with this linking, because when they are told, they themselves are the link. The symbol is itself a bridge or link between us and the mystery of existence – but then, within its own imagery, it further portrays this link.

Many examples come to mind, but one or two will illustrate the point. In the mythic tale of Demeter and Persephone, Demeter and her daughter, known initially as "Kore," are out picking Narcissus flowers when Hades rides up in his chariot and abducts the young maiden, taking her down into his kingdom in the underworld, which we would interpret as the unconscious or numinous world, here in its chthonic form. In this imagery, then, we have a wrenching split, similar to that in a personality after trauma. Archetypal defenses take over and pull the innocent remainder of the traumatized self into the darkness of unconscious process, supervised by the diabolical, yet initiatory Hades himself. Meanwhile, Demeter, representing human life in all its potential fruitfulness, wanders the entire universe searching for her daughter, but to no avail. Finally, still inconsolable at the loss of Kore, she retires to her temple at Eleusis and there prepares a cruel and terrible year for mankind: she will not permit the earth to bear fruit or any crop to grow unless she sees her daughter again. In the resulting crisis, Zeus sends Hermes down into Hades' kingdom and obtains his promise to return his queen, now named Persephone; but before sending his wife up to earth, the Dark Lord tempts her to eat a few pomegranate seeds. The pomegranate was the fruit symbolizing marriage and the effect of eating it was to render the union – the link – between man and wife indissoluble. The result of this marriage means that the two worlds, the inner (divine) and outer (human) are forever wedded. Persephone thus belongs to both worlds and by spending six months in the lower kingdom and six months in the upper one, she becomes the "ligament" between the human and the divine. Balance is restored. The traumatic rupture between the two worlds is healed.

Another example comes from the Old Testament: when Yahweh became so outraged at the excesses of man that he was impelled to destroy the world, he made sure that one part of the creation was saved – this part was Noah, and to him were entrusted all the animal species, two by two. If we take Yahweh as Fairbairn's antilibidinal ego in this narrative, we have a fairly accurate picture of what happens to the inner world of trauma – devastation and annihilation except for an encapsulated core of life which is retained at all costs. The question is, then, "Will a link ever be forged between this lost heart of the self and all that transpersonal aggressive energy that has both cut it off from the world, but also preserved it for the future?" According to the Genesis account the "link" provided is a covenant – one of the most lovely images of all time – the rainbow bridge – the sign than never again will God and man go apart:

And God said, This is the token of the covenant which I make between me and you and every living creature that is with you for perpetual generations: I have set my bow in the cloud, and it shall be for a token of a covenant between me and the earth . . . and I will look upon it, that I may remember the everlasting covenant between God and every living creature of all flesh that is upon the earth.

(Gen. 9: 12–16; *Revised Standard Version*)

The Christian symbol for this magical link between man and God is the paradoxical "God/man" – the "incarnation" of the Word become Flesh. Everywhere in mythology the imagery repeats the same theme. Something of the eternal enters time and forever changes it. A child of light is born at the darkest time of the year; or waters flow in the desert; or a bush is burned but not consumed. All these libido-symbols have to do with a miraculous penetration of this world by another greater world, forging a link between the unrealized spiritual potential hidden at the core of each individual life and the mundane historical existence in this body, this place, this time.

As in mythology, so in the healthy personality we see the struggle toward a balanced relationship between the energies of the ego and the Self such that the energies of the Self infuse the ego but do not overwhelm it or provide it with substitutes for human gratifications. Libido can be transferred across the ego/Self threshold and invested in love-relations, interests, commitments etc. In trauma, however, it is another story, as we have seen already. All investment of libido in "this life" is resisted by the self-care system in order to avoid further devastation. Energies of the numinous world then became substitutes for the self-esteem that should come from embodied gratifications in the human world. The transpersonal is placed in the service of defense.

PSYCHOLOGY'S DEVELOPMENTAL QUESTIONS

If trauma ends all transitional processes and therefore all religious experience, then the question becomes how to get these processes stated again. The basic question might be expressed as follows: "Through what process of normal development is the world of transpersonal numinous experience linked up in a dialectical relationship with mundane reality, so that life becomes truly meaningful, vital and alive?" or "How is the magical world of childhood retained into adulthood?" To phrase our question somewhat differently, we might ask, "How do we live a symbolic life?"

There are many theoretical variations of this question but only Jung penetrates deeply into its spiritual dimension. Jung would have asked, "How do we keep a dialectical relationship going between the ego and the Self (the image of God in the psyche) so that we do not suffer either too much *alienation* from the Self or too much *identification* with it?" One of Jung's partial answers to this question was the psyche's natural "transcendent function," in which the tension between psychic opposites leads to the symbol, a "living third thing" intermediate between the mystery of life and the ego's struggles. But Jung did not elaborate the interpersonal process-dimension of the "transcendent function" nor did he emphasize adequately the critical role of trauma in undermining the transcendent function altogether.

Self-psychologists (see Kohut, 1971, 1977) would phrase this question somewhat differently as follows: "How does the infant's original archaic grandiose and omnipotent self, with its fragile self-esteem totally dependent on a mirroring 'other' – and its proneness to fragmentation – gradually become transformed into an autonomous coherent self with solid self-esteem regulation, realistic expectations, and genuine ideals?" Kohut's answer is an intermediate period known as the "self-object" stage – including the self-object transferences – in which there is "phase-appropriate" disillusionment and transmutation of the archaic grandiose structures into interior psychic structure – without losing contact with the self-object carrying these imagos in projection.

Object-relations theorists would ask this same question somewhat differently again, perhaps as follows: "How does the original undifferentiated unity of the mother/infant dyad (a oneness) transform into an experience of self/object separateness (a two-ness) such that the paradox of true symbolic capacity is realized (a three-ness)?" (see Ogden, 1986: 214). Winnicott's answer was a "good enough" mother holding "potential space" or "transitional space" long enough so that the subjective world of the infant could interpenetrate the objective world of reality. With optimal care, the child's experience of reality occurs within the orbit of omnipotence. Omnipotence can then be given up gradually.

It has perhaps not escaped the reader's attention that each of these theories has proposed an "answer" to our question of how the divine and human worlds are interwoven, which involves a linking term beginning with the prefix "trans-." Jung spoke of the *transcendent* function. If the opposites are held in tension, the

144

psyche will produce a symbol which is both a synthesis of the opposites, yet something which transcends them both. For Winnicott, *transitional* space, if lived in long enough, leads to creative emergence of the "True Self" which is the spontaneous self that loves paradox and humor and transcends itself through enjoyment of a cultural (symbolic) life. For Kohut, the paradoxical "self-object" stage with its union of grandiose self–idealized other leads gradually to a *transmuting* internalizition of psychic structure and hence to realistic ideals (including religious ideals). We have another "trans-" word, *"transference,"* which is important precisely because it is the "space" within which the two worlds we have discussed inevitably become co-mingled around the image of the analyst (whose humanity must eventually be discovered and a relationship can then hopefully be worked out between the real and imaginal elements).

TRANSITIONAL PROCESSES IN FAIRY TALES

It should come as no surprise, then, that the transitional processes we have found to be a preoccupation of mythology in general and depth psychology's "mythology" in particular, are also a major concern of fairy tales.

Again, one or two examples will suffice for illustration. In Cinderella, we have, on the one hand, a world of enchantment, magic, wonder, and mystery, represented by the enchanting world of the ball, with the Prince, chariot, music, etc., and on the other hand, a world of routine, banality, and Cinderella's mundane life among the cinders. These two worlds are radically separated so that the all-too-human Cinderella has no access to the "magical" world and royal Prince has no access to human suffering with its transformative potential. What joins the two worlds in "transitional reality," providing the Prince with the link to the beautiful maiden he has fallen in love with, is nothing less than the glass slipper! The glass slipper is at once mundane and human (a shoe) yet crystalline and "royal." With the aid of this transitional object, the royal Prince, representing transpersonal reality, and the common Princess, representing the all-too human world, are linked. So the tale ends "happily ever after" – which in this case means that a transitional link has been found to assure that these two worlds are now inextricably interwoven and united. The effects of trauma are transcended.

Similar examples will be found in the fairy tales that follow. In each of them, the human world of misery or innocence exists in some kind of counterpoint with another world represented by transpersonal powers, and these powers are usually introduced through an intermediate being such as a spell-casting witch or wizard, in any case a Trickster. These mediating spirits are usually "evil" as experienced by the "ego" in the tale, but often, as we shall see, it is not so easy to tell. Usually, the traumatized or innocent hero or heroine of the tale is "bewitched" by the "evil" side of the transpersonal entity and then the struggle in the tale centers on how to release this hero or heroine from bewitchment and turn this tragic state into what we might call "enchantment," which is what fairy tales mean when they end "happily ever after."

So to come back to our question, the answer offered by fairy tales to the split between human and divine is a dramatic story which usually moves from innocence or sterile misery through bewitchment and a struggle with dark powers, to transformation of the ego and the constellation of the positive side of the numinous, leading to "enchantment" – living happily ever after. In this process the "daimon" (either angel or demon) is the critical agent in what turns out to be a seemingly universal two-stage process.

TWO-STAGE HEALING OF THE SPLIT IN FAIRY TALES

The two-stage process portrayed in the fairy tales that follow describes the healing of a split betwen the human and divine, the ego and the Self, which is the inevitable result of traumatic rupture in transitional processes. Sometimes the original trauma is described. Usually only the sterility of life following *implied* trauma provides the initial condition which requires healing. In the first stage, the wizard appears on the scene of a sterile life or a witch lures a man into a garden, or a genie pops out of a bottle, etc. The narrative's hero or heroine then falls under the spell of this transpersonal figure and gets trapped in a tower, or seduced into a cottage in the woods, or swept away into a magical room. In these "transformational chambers" the traumatized ego is "bewitched" by the negative side of the primal ambivalent Self. This stage corresponds to what psychoanalysis calls "incestuous identification" and what Alchemy refers to as the "lesser *coniunctio*" – a stage of union between two substances which have not yet been sufficiently differentiated and which is therefore highly unstable (see Edinger, 1985: 211).

The dangers of the "lesser *coniunctio*" are primarily addictive. If prolonged too long, they represent what Michael Balint (1979) called "malignant regression" as contrasted with "benign" regression or regression in the service of creation. This first stage seems to be necessary for everything that follows – at least for the traumatized ego – but it is possible to get stuck here, and if this happens, then the numinosum turns negative and destructive. This is why Freud was so suspicious of religion. He saw it as a defensive fantasy used to escape from the rigors of real life. Often enough, this does occur, and in the traumatized psyche, addiction to the lesser coniunctio is the usual result and an ever-present danger, as we have seen. We might say that this preliminary "bewitchment" is a stage of twoness in oneness, but not threeness. It is not yet "potentiated" as symbolical or dialectical process.

For this threeness stage to be reached, there is a necessary violent sacrifice of the bliss and oblivion of the "lesser coniunctio." This happens in the myth of Eros and Psyche (Chapter 8), when Psyche disobeys her daimon-lover and, insisting on "seeing" him, spills hot oil on Eros. In Chapter 9 we will see how the third daughter in the story of Fitcher's Bird breaks the spell of her death-

146

dealing husband by protecting and sequestering her own vulnerability before entering his murder-chamber. In Chapter 7, Rapunzel violates the pact with her caretaking witch who then cuts off her hair and throws her out of the tower. In Chapter 10, Prince Lindworm keeps eating his wives until he meets one more violent than himself who will also love him despite his ugliness. These spell-breaking, violent processes result in a sacrifice of the God-like identity of the ego and the return of a personal spirit to the body. This perilous process can have either a destructive or a redemptive outcome. If successful, it leads out of the lesser to the greater coniunctio – out of participation mystique and into true living (enchantment) and true relationship. The daimon is then transformed and becomes an angel or, in the language of our previous chapters, the primal ambivalent Self is liberated from its defensive role as a survival-Self and sets up its guiding function as the internal principle of individuation. If unsuccessful, the ego remains addictively identified with the Self's diabolical energies (bewitched) and is eventually devoured by its negative aspects.

7

RAPUNZEL AND THE
SELF-CARE SYSTEM

In this chapter we will employ the story of Rapunzel imprisoned in her tower by the old witch or sorceress, to illustrate the mythological portrayal of the self-care system as experienced by the patients described in Part I, with its Protector/ Persecutor personality and its vulnerable client – the carrier of the personal spirit.

We will be approaching the image of Rapunzel in her tower as an image of the inner condition of these patients – a condition that is both split and walled off. In our story, the walls of the tower contain not only the innocent Rapunzel, a twelve-year-old pre-adolescent girl, but also a guardian witch – the ugly sorceress known as "Dame Gothel." This tower or "inner sanctum" provides a cocoon in which innocent Rapunzel seems to grow, like a hydroponic plant, on illusions supplied by her sorceress, who comes every day to "feed" her. Rapunzel's hair grows long, she sings every day like a canary unaware of its confinement in a cage, and everything seems innocently happy in her fantasy "bubble" until the Prince rides by on a horse and hears her singing. The Prince, representing the outer world in its "otherness," longs for the beautiful Rapunzel and her idyllic world *inside* the tower. He breaks into Rapunzel's cocoon, and when his penetration of the inner world is discovered, there follows a rage reaction from the sorceress that *almost* destroys everything in our story. Rapunzel has her beautiful hair cut, is exiled to the desert, separated from her lover, and the Prince throws himself down in despair and is blinded. Indeed, our tale would end in tragedy but for two important elements: first, Rapunzel is pregnant, giving birth to twins, and second, Rapunzel's voice once again draws the blinded Prince to her and this time, her grief heals his blindness and her own. Our story's portrayal of how grief heals the rift between imagination and reality gives us an important clue about the role of grief in the working through of trauma and the trauma defense.

RAPUNZEL PATIENTS

The patients for whom this story is a symbolic description of the therapy process are usually patients who were robbed of their childhood by trauma and forced to grow up too fast, becoming self-sufficient too early. To have a childhood requires a holding environment in which the child can fall back on caretaking parents (see

Modell, 1976). With such a holding environment, self-care of the kind we have witnessed in trauma is not necessary. The child does not have to "hold itself together;" there is someone else present to do this. D. W. Winnicott has shown that when this "good-enough" facilitating environment is provided, personality growth can occur in a "transitional relationship" to imaginally elaborated "others" in play and creative expression. For many of these patients, this *imaginal elaboration of external reality* has been cut off too early. Play ends, except as defensive fantasy; vigilant self-care takes over.

With this rupture, the need for transitional relatedness does not end. It is simply taken into the internal world and continues on an inner level as illusion. The special "other" who has abandoned the child outwardly now is replaced by a magical, all-loving, hallucinatory caretaking self who carries on a dialogue with the mortified ego inwardly. The external self-object connection becomes an internal "we" and the child becomes preoccupied with internal reality – dreamy and isolated, full of secret melancholy longings and despair. Staying green on her rarified diet of illusion, the Rapunzel patient may look good on the outside, but she cannot live creatively in the world, and she begins to lose her ability to root anywhere in reality. Instead of realistic self-esteem fed by accomplishments in the world, the ego must feed on substitute fantasies of omnipotence and a sense of inner superiority develops to rationalize not doing anything. Often tough and stubborn on the outside, these patients are increasingly plagued with feelings of de-personalization, artificiality, the "plate-glass feeling," panicky states of confusion associated with disturbance in the reality-sense, and various forms of somatization. In diagnostic parlance, these patients are "schizoid," but as Fairbairn and others have noted, everyone alive is more or less "schizoid."

These patients present special challenges and opportunities for the therapist. In my experience, the therapist is generally very moved by their courage and their fierce personal integrity, even though one comes to realize that this fierceness (Rapunzel's sorceress) in the protection of a core of selfhood is really the main source of their difficulty. These patients also capture the special interest of therapists because of their developed relationship to the inner world. For them, the inner world is not an epiphenomenon – a mere repository of repressed material – it is a treasure trove of fragile contents which have about them a numinosity which endows them with supreme value. These are individuals who take their dreams seriously, who usually keep journals of their reflections and experience, who read voraciously – and who, above all, value the hidden, the secret, and the beautiful dimensions of life which are all too easily lost to "better-adapted" people – like the Prince who ventures by Rapunzel's tower and is overcome by her singing.

I believe it can be safely said that Jung himself was such a person. In the prologue to his autobiography, Jung says:

> In the end the only events in my life worth telling are those when the imperishable world irrupted into this transitory one. That is why I speak

chiefly of inner experiences, among which I include my dreams and visions. . . . All other memories of travels, people and my surroundings have paled beside these interior happenings . . . . Outward circumstances are no substitute for inner experience. Therefore my life has been singularly poor in outward happenings. I cannot tell much about them, for it would strike me as hollow and insubstantial. I can understand myself only in the light of inner happenings.

(Jung, 1963: 5)

Perhaps it is not without meaning that Jung spent much of his later life writing about Alchemy in a tower at Bollingen, on the shores of Zurich Lake. And it is life in a tower that awaits Rapunzel as our story begins. We will go through the story in stages, with clinical and theoretical commentary on each stage.

RAPUNZEL[1]: PART 1

There were once a man and a woman who had long in vain wished for a child. At length the woman hoped that God was about to grant her desire. These people had a little window at the back of their house from which a splendid garden could be seen, which was full of the most beautiful flowers and herbs. It was, however, surrounded by a high wall, and no one dared to go into it because it belonged to an enchantress, who had great power and was dreaded by all the world. One day the woman was standing by this window and looking down into the garden when she saw a bed which was planted with the most beautiful rampion (rapunzel), and it looked so fresh and green that she longed for it, and had the greatest desire to eat some. This desire increased every day, and as she knew that she could not get any of it, she quite pined away, and began to look pale and miserable. Then her husband was alarmed, and asked: "What ails you, dear wife?" "Ah," she replied, "if I can't eat some of the rampion, which is in the garden behind our house, I shall die." The man, who loved her, thought: "Sooner than let your wife die, bring her some of the rampion yourself, let it cost what it will." At twilight, he clambered down over the wall into the garden of the enchantress, hastily clutched a handful of rampion, and took it to his wife. She at once made herself a salad of it, and ate it greedily. It tasted good to her – so very good, that the next day she longed for it three times as much as before. If he was to have any rest, her husband must once more descend into the garden. In the gloom of evening, therefore, he let himself down again.

The first thing to be noted in this first part of the tale is the division between the two worlds separated by the wall which the husband climbs over. In our tale, the world of the garden is a "splendid" world, full of great beauty, green with life and flowering plants and herbs – but also dangerous, because it belongs to an enchantress. On the other side of the wall is the mundane everyday "high-up" world of the man and his wife who, we are told, has been barren and without a child, pining away – but this situation is about to change.

150

We might characterize these two worlds as simply "the unconscious" and "the ego," but this would not be quite correct. It would be better if we thought of these two worlds in more extreme form for purposes of illustration. In this sense, the realm of enchantment would be closer to what Jung means when he talks of the "psychoid" or "magical" realm of the psyche. This is the deepest level of the unconscious, the *fons et origio* of all psychic energy – very intimately related to the instinctual and bodily realm. Jung called this level the "collective unconscious" or the "mythic" layer in which archetypal imagery and primordial affects structure events in an implicate order which reaches consciousness in the form of *numinous* images.

On the other hand, we have the time- and space-bound world of reality – this is the ego's world, as it were. This world is "real," but unredeemed and corporeal, bounded by death, by routine, by familiarity, by the ordinary. It is fraught with separation and loss, endings and beginnings, split parts but not wholes. In Buddhism it is the veil of Maya – a world in itself devoid of meaning, but a world absolutely necessary for the *creation* of meaning.

These two worlds are separated by a high wall in our story, and *this is what happens when trauma strikes the fluid transitional world of childhood.* Archetypal defenses then come in to cut the ego off from the resources of the unconscious and also from vital, lived life-in-the-world, as we saw in some of our earlier cases. The Protector-part of our inner dyad tries to compensate for this by supplying highly aggrandized interior fantasies elaborated by the collective psyche but, in the process, the capacity to relate to reality weakens (owing to a loss of adapted aggression) and with this weakening the interior world becomes increasingly persecutory. Life dries up and loses its savor. Things begin to feel dead, "unreal," and increasing anxiety stalks the inner world.

For this dissociated condition, our story is going to offer a solution. The beginning of such a solution is a state of "longing" and the longing here is for a child. The story "locates" this longing in the barren wife who becomes pregnant and then begins to crave the green rapunzel that grows in the garden beyond the wall. The symbolic equivalence of her longing for a child and her craving for the rapunzel in the garden is proven by the fact that the child's name is identical with the mother's craving. And this longing – this craving, aching desire – is what links the two worlds separated by the wall.

The witch is in the reverse plight from the mother – she is also childless. She lives in her enchanted world, walled off from reality, growing rapunzel seemingly quite content until the husband breaks in from "out there." (Note that here the incursion of the husband – a male figure from the "real" world – into the walled enclosure of enchantment prefigures the Prince's entry later into Rapunzel's tower.) So the husband is the catalyst for the witch's awareness that she, too, is missing something. Now she wants a child – something she can't have, i.e., the child she cannot bear because she is a sorceress. Only a human mother can bear a child. So both the mother and the witch end up wanting what the other has on "her" side of the wall. Envy seems a crucial link here. The witch envies the mother's "real" Rapunzel. The mother covets the Witch's enchanted rapunzel. Envy and a mutual longing are what gets our story started.

Correspondingly, the child, as the coveted link between the two worlds separated by the wall, is the carrier of the story's hope. This is often the case in fairy tales and mythology. In the child, what is still potential has a chance to actualize in-the-world. Symbolically, therefore, the child represents the potential for realization of the personal spirit in life. At the miraculous moment of a child's birth, the imaginal becomes real, incarnate, and it is for this reason, I believe, that mythology has selected the birth of the divine child as its answer to the question "Does God manifest himself in history?" The Christian answer to this question is "yes but . . ." Yes, but the divine child (God/man) will have to be born again after a period of illusion, and this second birth will be equivalent to a *sacrifice*. We will discuss sacrifice at greater length in the next chapter, where it serves as the pivotal moment in story of Eros and Psyche. Rapunzel also goes through a "sacrifice" – of both her hair and the veil of illusion of her existence in the tower. From within that walled enclosure she must be "born again."

There are some other interesting details in the first part of our story. The father, an emissary of the mother's longing, first descends into the garden "at twilight" and in twilight he is successful in returning with the rapunzel. It is when he goes in the dark that he has trouble. Now what is is the symbolic meaning of "twilight?" American readers will remember *The Twilight Zone*, a popular television show in the 1960s. Its spooky stories described uncanny events that occurred in liminal time – between the two zones of day and night when extraordinary events could happen. Twilight is a transitional area where two worlds are co-mingled – the night world, representing the unconscious, and the day world, representing the ego and consciousness. It is here, where they meet, that magical things can happen. An opening is created between two worlds and energy can flow back and forth. Longings can be satisfied, healing can occur – but the two worlds must be held in tension with each other. One must not be too greedy, which is what happens in our story. The wife cannot get enough of the green rapunzel. Having been starved for so long behind the wall, she now goes on an eating binge – a classic borderline problem.

We have already discussed how, for Winnicott, "transitional processes" of all kinds represented this "twilight" zone. For Winnicott, the paradigmatic metaphor for this is the magic moment when the baby, hungry and in need, "hallucinates the mother's breast," and the mother, representing reality, empathically puts her real breast exactly in the place of the baby's hallucination. At this moment, says Winnicott, a magical link is forged between the two worlds, and the baby has the experience of actually creating a world, his or her omnipotence is not questioned. One does not ask the baby the unbearable question, "Did you find this or did you create it?" This question can only be answered later, after enough "illusionment" experiences. The child can then begin to allow for disillusionment experiences (see Winnicott, 1951).

Despite his introversion, Jung was also aware of the importance of transitional

152

process. At times he even "placed" the unconscious psyche in the intermediate zone between self and other. For example, in reply to a question from a colleague who was asking why the dreams of a certain patient seemed to be referring always to the analyst, Jung replied:

> With regard to your patient, it is quite correct that her dreams are occasioned by you. . . . In the deepest sense we all dream not out of ourselves but out of what lies between us and the other.
>
> (Jung, 1973: 172)

So Jung was very much ahead of his time in emphasizing the importance of this interpersonal "field" as a space within which symbolic life emerged. His whole book on transference (Jung, 1946) is about the transformative processes engaged in this "field."

Treatment implications

Before we return to our story, we should take note of the fact that the psychoanalytic situation focuses the "two worlds" we have been talking about in a very intensified way, and does so especially where erotic energies and fantasies of union are constellated in the transference/counter-transference. The psychoanalytic situation often opens the unconscious very rapidly. The patient begins to dream – feels a renewed excitement in life. Fantasies are elaborated around the treatment situation and around the anonymity of the analyst's life and presence. The patient begins to hope and love again. But then there is another "world" constellated by the psychoanalytic situation – the world of the psycho-analytic frame; the world of reality (the patient's and the analyst's); the world of limitation and facticity and history. This harsh world of reality involves the fact that analyst and patient have come together to work on the patient's problems; the fact that the analyst charges a fee for this work and offers his services in time-limited segments; the fact that the analyst is not available on weekends; the fact that the analyst has a personal life to which he or she is responsibly bound (hopefully by desire also). So *the analyst rapidly becomes both an object of desire and frustration*. In this way he or she embodies the tension that exists in our story between the two worlds separated by the garden wall. The analyst becomes in this sense, a "transformational object" (Bollas, 1987: 13–29).

A patient involved in the early stages of a positive transference once said, "You're the only one who's *in here* and also *out there* at the same time." For this patient, and others like him, the burning question at this point becomes: "Can all this secret wonder and renewed hope and longing find a place in lived life, i.e., in the 'real' world?" Does the magical, interior world, have a place in outer life? Can the sacred dimension of experience in childhood be retained in adult life? Do the sacred and profane worlds go together?

To these poignant and deeply agonizing questions psychoanalysis gives a painful answer: "Yes, but only with hard work and much suffering" – suffering

153

in which illusions woven, perhaps for the first time, around an outer "object" must eventually be grieved as illusions if they are to develop into mature love. Mature love accords the object its necessary freedom and separateness. To do this requires inner sources of sustainment and these "sources" for the trauma victim are archetypal sources, not humanized ones. The process of moving from symbiotic illusion (in the tower) to mature self–object relatedness is a stormy one for the trauma victim, as our story attests.

In this gradual deconstruction of the self-care system in the transference there is a constant movement back and forth between unconscious bewitchment, on the one hand, and reality on the other. In technical language, this is a movement between projective identification or self/object identification and true object-relating. Needless to say, this *rapprochement* stage is difficult to negotiate. The danger lies always in losing the tension between the two worlds previously separated by the "wall" of the self-care system. If the therapist gets lazy, he finds himself in the garden of the enchantress and a collusive entanglement begins. If the therapist does too much interpreting, the wall comes down again and we finds ourselves in the sterile world of the wife before her pregnancy. Always the goal must be to maintain the tension between the two worlds we have discussed, so that the personal spirit, carried by the Rapunzel-part of the patient, can gradually emerge to animate life in the world. This is a slow and painful evolution from bewitchment to enchantment.

Now to return to our story.

RAPUNZEL: PART 2

In the gloom of evening, therefore, he let himself down again; but when he had clambered down the wall he was terribly afraid, for he saw the enchantress standing before him. "How can you dare," said she with angry look, "descend into my garden and steal my rampion like a thief? You shall suffer for it!" "Ah," answered he, "let mercy take the place of justice, I only made up my mind to do it out of necessity. My wife saw your rampion from the window, and felt such a longing for it that she would have died if she had not got some to eat." Then the enchantress allowed her anger to be softened, and said to him: "If the case be as you say, I will allow you to take away with you as much rampion as you will, only I make one condition, you must give me the child which your wife will bring into the world. It shall be well treated, and I will care for it like a mother." The man in his terror consented to everything, and when the woman was brought to bed, the enchantress appeared at once, gave the child the name of Rapunzel, and took it away with her.

Rapunzel grew into the most beautiful child under the sun. When she was twelve years old, the enchantress shut her into a tower, which lay in a forest and had neither stairs nor door, but quite at the top was a little window. When the enchantress wanted to go in, she placed herself beneath it and cried "Rapunzel, Rapunzel, let down your hair to me." Rapunzel had magnificent long hair, fine as spun gold, and when she heard the voice of the enchantress she unfastened her braided tresses, wound them round one of the hooks of the window above, and then the hair fell twenty ells down, and the enchantress climbed up by it.

There are many ways we could approach this part of the story. If we took it on the outer level as a commentary on incestuous relations between fathers and daughters, we could say that the father's desperation to escape his own enchantment results in the sacrifice of his daughter to the witch. Terrified of the unconscious, he lives this through his daughter. This is the basic dynamic of father/daughter sexual abuse. The daughter, herself "caught" by the inflating fantasies of specialness and the "special secret" shared with the idealized adult, falls into the father's bewitchment and is lost to her own life.

This pattern is true even without sexual abuse. In more general terms, our story suggests that the daughter who is identified with the father's unconscious (often his unconscious misery) is lost to her own life. In this connection, I recall a patient who dreamed that she was giving her father blood transfusions through their joined fingertips. She had become the only connection this unhappy man had to his life, to his feelings, and although she had a deep "love" for (identification with) her father, the dream provides a ghastly image of what this was costing her – blood, the symbol of life itself.

In our story, we have no cry of protest from Rapunzel's mother either, as her daughter disappears into the "tower" of enchantment. It seems the mother was too enchanted herself to claim the child for life in the real world, and just abandoned her as a matter of course to the father in his bewitchment. The literature on child abuse is full of these passive mothers – usually victims of abuse themselves – who sacrifice their daughters to literal or psychological incest. Indeed, we could profitably explore a whole variety of such interpersonal and family themes as related to our story. All of these outer patterns and family dramas evolve, however, from the inner object world of family members – the unconscious "complexes" that Jung found were shared by all members of a family. So we return to our story as an *inner drama* – a kind of narrative dream of an imaginary psyche. In this way, the various figures represent "part-objects" or "complexes," i.e., inner personifications of a hypothetical psyche.

Through this interpretive lens we would say that *the child* represents that "innocent" part of the psyche that carries the memory of the trauma and has gotten split off in order to preserve the whole personality from fragmentation or enfeeblement. As carrier of the personal spirit, this child is essential to the redemption of the story and the restoration of creative "enchanted" living. However, the Protector/Persecutor witch in our story prevents contact with reality, knowing only too well how devastating such contact has been in the past. There results, then, a kind of infant sacrifice on an inner level. Trapped in enchantment, the child-part exists in a suspended state, unable to die, but also unable to live – in a limbo of the "undead." Sometimes, in dreams, we find this part-personality trapped inside a glass bubble or contained in a space capsule, isolated in the attic, or buried in the ground. Sometimes it is asleep or in an altered state, bewitched, anesthetized, or autistic. In our previous cases we saw this child in Lenore's angry frightened "little girl," in Mary's vision of the "outer-space child," and in the case of the "spirit child" that floated down into the arms of Patricia and her grandmother to be "released."

In mythology, this situation is frequently represented by one part of the self getting trapped in the underworld, such as Eurydice or Persephone in Hell guarded by the Prince of Darkness. A problem then develops in the upper world where everything freezes up and nothing grows (this is Demeter's revenge until she can get Persephone back). Another image of this state is the souls of the innocents (infants and patriarchs) trapped in Limbo where they do not suffer the "deep" flames of Hell, but only the eternal, low-grade suffering of endless waiting – forever suspended – neither here nor there. Still another image for this condition is the Waste Land in the Grail legend which surrounds the Grail Castle after the Fisher King is mysteriously wounded. In terrible torment from his wound, the King is kept alive beyond his normal life-span, because no-one has asked the necessary question to link up the two worlds. When Perceval does this ("Whom does the Grail serve?") the King is allowed to die and the waters of the Waste Land flow again, making it flower.

In our story, Rapunzel represents that part of the personality that is held captive. In our earlier case of Mary, we saw that this was also the addicted part of the personality – in this case the part addicted to the witch, to a life of "bewitchment." I think the power of this negative enchantment is the most powerful resistance that therapists confront with Rapunzel patients and with the part of the therapist that identifies with their injuries. This seductive undertow in the work results from the fact that *the inner sanctuary to which the beleaguered ego repairs in time of crisis is also a world that opens onto transpersonal energies.* The retreat of Rapunzel to her inner sanctum is not just a retreat to previously introjected "archaic inner objects" or a regressive defense in pursuit of infantile omnipotence but, as Jung emphasized, a regression to a world of mythic and archetypal "objects" with its own healing order and efficacy. Although frequently beginning as a defense and later placed in service of defense, this fantasy world also provides these patients with genuine access to the collective psyche and to inward mysteries that are not easily available to "better-adapted" people. True, it also makes them inflated, self-sufficient, stubborn, and impenetrable, and we will discuss that problem when we come to the witch's reaction to the Prince's invasion of her tower. But the life-sustaining mysteries that support the forsaken personal spirit in the inner towers of our traumatized patients come from a depth of being and intelligence that far surpasses the ego's narrow concerns. This is the transpersonal or archetypal meaning of the self-care system.

So the sorceress or witch in our story is a personification of the spell-casting potential of the psyche itself – a "bewitchment mother" – an alternative to the real mother who failed to mediate the magical world to the child. One might say that she represents the Terrible Mother archetype in its spell-casting bewitching power, but this would only be partly correct. There is also a life-serving side to the witch. She says, "I will care for [the child] like a mother." Also, we know that life in the witch's care was not at all bad. The story tells us that Rapunzel grew into the most beautiful child under the sun, she had a charming voice, sang like a bird, had beautiful blonde hair as fine as gold; in short she was a princess – a *puella aeternus*, beautiful, innocent, captivating but sealed in a bubble.

The witch's caretaking role in our story is to keep Rapunzel from getting hurt by traumatic interactions with the outer world and people. This means keeping her from wanting anything and so she must attack hope or desire whenever it is felt. The witch is therefore unmitigatingly negative. Rapunzel patients are usually very familiar with his/her voice in the internal world. The witch is the one who says "it doesn't matter," "don't stick your neck out", "you don't really want it anyway", "put it off until tomorrow", "you'll just be disappointed" or, if perhaps the patient finds the courage to take a risk and has suffered humiliation or rejection, she's the one who says: "I told you so, you should have listened to me . . . that was stupid and you got what you deserved." Another interesting thing about the witch in the inner world of trauma is her perfectionism. Nothing in the real world can measure up to her rarified idealism or brilliant intellectual rationalizations: "The real world is a corrupt place," she says, "it's not worth investing in . . . You want to get married? – Look at the divorce rate . . . You want to work with a psychoanalyst? – Look at them, they're all charlatans anyway – corrupt . . . You want to make a better living? – you're compromising your principles and becoming a Yuppie." And so on.

The witch, as one part of the self-care system, is also a comforter, but the comfort she gives is of a particularly sad and melodramatic type and is really a well-meaning deceptive swindle. It is as though she reads stories to the Rapunzel side of the personality every night at bedtime, but the story she tells is of an especially sentimental type. It goes something like this: "You were an orphan and nobody loved you or recognized your soulful beauty, but I found you and took you home and together we've made it in a cruel and corrupt world in which most things are false and banal. Nobody understands you except me and therefore you can never be lonely with me in your life." This soothing self-comfort works temporarily to ameliorate and rationalize pain, but it gradually breaks down and, like all neurotic circles, the psyche's "efforts" to dissociate in order to protect itself from acute trauma leaves the personality enfeebled and chronically traumatized. So the person eventually ends up seeking help.

We reach a further understanding of Rapunzel's witch if we look into the universal, archetypal meaning of witches, i.e., if we amplify the image. Thus, we find that, universally, witches are spell-casters associated with the night and death. They personify altered states of consciousness. Frequently they have the power of prophecy, they devour children, and they do not weep. The insensitivity of witches is part of how they are recognized. If a witch is stuck with a pin she doesn't feel it. In fact, any insensitive spot on the body (like scars) may be a witch's or devil's mark. So witches are associated with psychic numbness – an inability to feel pain. They might be understood then to represent the psyche's very ability to anesthetize itself, to dissociate, freeze, or hypnotize the ego from within.

Now to return to our story.

RAPUNZEL: PART 3

After a year or two, it came to pass that the King's son rode through the forest and passed by the tower. Then he heard a song, which was so charming that he stood still and listened. This was Rapunzel, who in her solitude passed her time in letting her sweet voice resound. The King's son wanted to climb up to her, and looked for the door of the tower, but none was to be found. He rode home, but the singing had so deeply touched his heart, that every day he went out into the forest and listened to it. Once when he was thus standing behind a tree, he saw that an enchantress came there, and he heard how she cried: "Rapunzel, Rapunzel, let down your hair." Then Rapunzel let down the braids of her hair, and the enchantress climbed up to her. "If that is the ladder by which one mounts, I too will try my fortune," said he, and the next day when it began to grow dark, he went to the tower and cried: "Rapunzel, Rapunzel, let down your hair." Immediately the hair fell down and the King's son climbed up.

At first Rapunzel was terribly frightened when a man, such as her eyes had never yet beheld, came to her; but the King's son began to talk to her quite like a friend, and told her that his heart had been so stirred that it had let him have no rest, and he had been forced to see her. Then Rapunzel lost her fear, and when he asked her if she would take him for her husband, and she saw that he was young and handsome, she thought: "He will love me more than old Dame Gothel does," and she said yes, and laid her hand in his. She said: "I will willingly go away with you, but I do not know how to get down. Bring with you a skein of silk every time that you come, and I will weave a ladder with it, and when that is ready I will descend, and you will take me on your horse." They agreed that until that time he should come to her every evening, for the old woman came by day.

Here we have the addition of an entirely new element which carries the hope for a resolution of the original traumatic dissociation between the two worlds of the enchanted garden and reality. We saw earlier how the wife's longing for a child and longing for the rapunzel in the garden which became the child was the first "bridge" between the two worlds. This, we speculated, corresponded to the witch's desire for a child, suffering as she did without any access to the real world of people. Now Rapunzel is behind a wall – in her tower – and suffers the same plight as our witch, i.e., a life of "bewitchment" which prevents the possibility of a life "enchanted" by a healthy relationship between the real and the imaginal. We saw in the case of Mary how the isolation created by our diabolical Protector/Persecutor leads to fantasy instead of imagination.

Now the Prince comes on the scene and he, like the wife earlier, longs for what he hears. Rapunzel's sweet voice "deeply touches his heart" and every time he goes to the forest he is drawn to the enchanted tower. Here again we have the world of outer reality and its representative needing the nourishment that can come only from the inner world with its archetypal energies. What we hope for, and what the story seems to be preparing for through its various stages, is a relationship between these two worlds – not either one swallowed by the other which is what so far has happened to poor Rapunzel.

We note also that the Prince is a Trickster, but in his positive form. Unable to climb the tower, he waits for old Dame Gothel and observes the ritual "rite of entry" ("Rapunzel, Rapunzel, let down your hair"). Then he uses this rite to enter without an invitation. This is a good example of how the shape-shifting Trickster energy of the psyche penetrates boundaries that would otherwise be defensively closed off and brings a creative *coniunctio* before Rapunzel knows what has happened. The Prince is also tricking the Trickster, i.e., he steals in without the witch's knowledge. This is a frequent theme in fairy tales and myth when something new and fragile is about to come into existence and, always tyrannical, "ruling powers" defend against this. When the Christ child is born, for example, King Herod sends out an edict to kill all children under two years of age. Only a trick and a flight into Egypt saves the child. In our fairy tale too, the new meeting with fragile Rapunzel is hemmed round by the sorceress and her possessive "spells."

Rapunzel's hair serves as the way into and out of the tower for both Prince and sorceress. If we think of Rapunzel's hair as an image of her innocence and unconsciousness – like a head full of fantasies which exist in an uninitiated state – the image suggests that pure fantasy serves as the only link to reality at this stage. Eventually, this hair-ladder will have to be replaced by more realistic means. Rapunzel says, "I do not know how to get down," and asks the Prince to bring yarn skein by skein for her to build a ladder that would substitute for her hair. As with our Rapunzel patients, a rapport in fantasy needs to happen first (Kohut's "mirror" or "twinship" transferences) and reality must be brought in a little bit at a time (Kohut's "phase-appropriate disillusionment"). Reading ahead in our story, we know that this slow incremental process, analogous to therapy sessions week after week, is interrupted by a crisis in which Rapunzel's fantasy hair-ladder is clipped all at once. But before this crisis, the fantasy element predominates and provides the major link between the world inside and that outside the tower. Side by side with this "magical" level a more realistic connection is being woven as the prince brings yarn, skein by skein. A new reality-link is being built up by the Prince's nightly visits.

Treatment implications

In the psychotherapeutic situation, this stage in our tale corresponds to the beginning of positive transference, and there is no therapy for trauma that works without it. Here we have a description of the beginnings of trust and the renewal of hope that a connection between the inner world of the tormented patient and the "real" world might be established. The patient is beginning to relax his or her self-comfort and turn it over to the therapist. This is a moment of enormous possibility, but also of deadly peril for the patient and, as Winnicott has said, a period of deep dependency corresponding to the caretaker self turning over its functions to a real person. But, if all goes well at the beginning, a wonderful sustaining illusion forms around the person of the therapist, who now carries the imago of the Prince and the possibility of a "wedding" between the human and the "royal" Self. The patient begins to dream and hope again. Depression turns into possibility. It seems as if life can be lived again. The therapy hours become the major events of the patient's week. At this stage there may be a longing for total mutuality – an insatiable need for the therapist's love. This love is like an embrace which holds the splintered fragments of the broken-hearted child-self in the patient much like a parent would hold a child who had just been traumatized. Hope is contagious and, at this stage, the therapist may begin to look forward to hours with the patient. Often he will find himself openly available for extra needs and, sensing the patient's traumatized ego, will instinctively be more generous than usual with his or her time, attention, and caring concern.

The story says that the Prince was "deeply touched in his heart" by Rapunzel's singing, i.e., he is enchanted with her. This is the counter-transference, an altered state for the therapist, too. The story says that the Prince crawls into the tower on the long tresses of fantasy-hair. In other words, for him, too the world of reality is left behind.

What is sacrificed in this honeymoon period of therapy is the harshness of a traumatic reality which has penetrated the patient's world too soon, before symbolic capacity had developed. It is this world that is now restored in the "magical" connection between the protagonists. Just like Rapunzel and the Prince, therapist and patient tend to forget about the work they are there to do together. A mutual deception occurs, but it is a benign and necessary one. For example, in our story we notice that both Rapunzel and the Prince are slightly dishonest with each other, i.e., their meeting is sustained in illusion by a necessary splitting off of the other side of each. Rapunzel appears to the Prince as the lovely innocent victim and colludes with him against the witch, who remains her secret. She does not introduce him to old Dame Gothel. He will have to meet her later. Similarly, the Prince tricks Rapunzel into thinking that he is identical with the good (food-bringing) side of the witch, in order to get in. So he represents himself as nourishing and loving. He doesn't mention his reality-limitations, his other responsibilities in the kingdom back home. What takes place then is a great deal of powerful *coniunctio* energy, but as Edward Edinger has illustrated, this is the "lesser *coniunctio*," which in Alchemy is the union of substances that have not yet been sufficiently differentiated (see Edinger, 1985: 211ff.). Further procedures are necessary if a "greater coniunctio" is to be possible. Between Rapunzel and the Prince, or between patient and therapist, a healing "transference illusion" is established and this brings with it a renewed link with the world that had previously been devoid of fantasy – unstoried, unredeemed. But this link will have to survive a test of the dark side which has yet to emerge.

RAPUNZEL: PART 4

The enchantress remarked nothing of this, until once Rapunzel said to her: "Tell me, Dame Gothel, how it happens that you are so much heavier for me to draw up than the young King's son – he is with me in a moment?" "Ah! You wicked child," cried the enchantress. "What do I hear you say! I thought I had separated you from all the world, and yet you have deceived me!" In her anger she clutched Rapunzel's beautiful tresses, wrapped them twice round her left hand, seized a pair of scissors with the right, and snip, snap, they were cut off, and the lovely braids lay on the ground. And she was so pitiless that she took poor Rapunzel into a desert where she had to live in great grief and misery.

On the same day that she cast out Rapunzel, however, the enchantress fastened the braids of hair, which she had cut off, to the hook of the window, and when the King's son came and cried: "Rapunzel, Rapunzel, let down your hair," she let the hair down. The King's son ascended, but instead of finding his dearest Rapunzel, he found the enchantress, who gazed at him with wicked and venomous looks. "Aha!" she cried mockingly, "You would fetch your dearest, but the beautiful bird sits no longer singing in the nest; the cat has got it, and will scratch out your eyes as well. Rapunzel is lost to you; you will never see her again." The King's son was beside himself with pain, and in his despair he leapt down from the tower. He escaped with his life but the thorns into which he fell pierced his eyes. Then he wandered quite blind about the forest, ate nothing but roots and berries, and did naught but lament and weep over the loss of his dearest wife. Thus he roamed about in misery for some years, and at length came to the desert where Rapunzel, with the twins to which she had given birth, a boy and a girl, lived in wretchedness. He heard a voice, and it seemed so familiar to him that he went towards it, and when he approached, Rapunzel knew him and fell on his neck and wept. Two of her tears wetted his eyes and they grew clear again, and he could see with them as before. He led her to his kingdom where he was joyfully received, and they lived for a long time afterwards, happy and contented.

Here we have the denouement of our story, what Jung would call the "crisis and lysis" of the dream. We might call this part "rupture in the symbiotic membrane," leading to what Melanie Klein called the "depressive position" or Edinger the "greater coniunctio". Here, the two worlds that were kept apart, come together in a stormy crash, and terrible disappointment is the result. It is interesting how these two worlds intersect through a "slip of the tongue." It was Freud, who pointed out that through such parapraxes, dissociated material finds its way into consciousness – only to be re-repressed. In our story, the bewitched world of the tower is broken into through a betrayal which is instigated by a Trickster. This is mythologically equivalent to the snake in the original enchanted Garden of Eden inspiring Eve to eat the apple. There is always a desire for more than illusion – for otherness, for potentially enchanted life in the real world. And aggression is an important part of this process. Rapunzel makes a claim on the world and this betrays her beloved witch, who flies into a rage.

161

Treatment implications

In therapy, "moments" such as this usually occur when the schizoid patient finds the courage to make actual claims on the therapist, i.e., transferential demands which the therapist cannot meet, even if he or she wanted to. The therapist's honest limitations result in "disillusionment" and the patient is re-traumatized. The analyst is also traumatized and horrified. All his or her good intentions suddenly seem to have done nothing but create a hideous illusion – a co-dependency with the patient's inner Rapunzel. Both parties suffer a disillusioning loss at this stage. The patient thought the therapist would really be the link to life in the world – would really fulfill this promise and be a Prince. The therapist thought that the patient would really be healed by empathy and understanding alone and would give up the incessant demands for rapport, empathy, and soothing nourishment. Instead, to their mutual chagrin, the needs within the "symbiotic membrane" are incessant, insatiable and never seem to be satisfied. At this stage, the therapist's patience may begin to wear thin. To his or her growing irritation, the therapist finds that every interpretation is traumatic, every vacation, every reminder of his or her real life in the world seems to cause the Rapunzel patient incredible suffering. At this point there is usually some event that breaks things open. Usually, the therapist acts out.

For example, one time I raised a young woman's fee. I call this acting out because this was the first fee raise in five years and therefore it was a big one – ten dollars per hour. I announced this in the beginning of the hour. She looked at me blankly, insisting within the session that she had no particular reaction to this – everything was fine – just send her the bill; she didn't even want to think about it. An hour later she called me in a rage and broke her next appointment. Here was Rapunzel's witch. This was followed with cursing and suicidal threats. The next day I received a letter full of profuse apologies for her anger and self-recriminations about her bad temper (here the witch has been turned back inside again, blaming the child-self). In the working through that followed, this patient was able to describe the panic she felt at having ruined the relationship with her anger (this was a girl who had temper tantrums as a child and each time was punished more severely).

This eruption of rage in the patient was the beginning of countless confrontations which followed between her witch and my realistic limitations. I began to firm up my boundaries, ending the hours on time, confronting transferential demands instead of side-stepping them – each time calling the patient back to the paradoxical reality of what we were doing together.

During this very stormy phase in the work a delicate combination of reassurance and firmness is called for. It is very difficult for trauma patients to endure this without an assurance of a real relationship being possible after therapy. Often, these patients cannot get over the "cruelty" of the analytic set-up. How can they express their secret transference-fantasies, for example, when they will only be humiliated by silence from the analyst who, a few minutes later, will usher them out the door and usher in the next "case?" As painful as this experience can be for the patient with early trauma, the truth is – and sometimes the realization matters to the patient – that in psychotherapy there *is* a "real relationship" *and* an "illusory one" between analyst and patient all the time. Moreover, the tension between these two is necessary for both parties to endure, because in the patient's life the essential polarities of the human condition have been escaped in fantasy and now want to be escaped again in transference-resistance. For the therapist, holding this tension returns him or her to the human limitations of what can realistically be offered to the traumatically injured people in his or her practice – despite the therapist's deep hope/fantasy of rescuing the patient from all the "unjust" misery inflicted by life's circumstances.

In our story, this stormy phase of working through the self-care defenses is imaged as both Rapunzel and the blinded Prince wander through the desert, Rapunzel now with her twins, "living in wretchedness" and the Prince weeping and lamenting the loss of his "dearest wife," who was, of course, a wife he had met in a "towering illusion." How to recover this illusion on a different level is the question our story poses for us – in other words, how to convert bewitchment to enchantment.

Here is where a Jungian approach provides an essential element of understanding. The inner world of the archetypal self-care system is in one respect a "towering illusion" – an omnipotent, wish-fulfilling, grandiose fantasy, retreated into in order to avoid the unbearable pain of a traumatically contaminated reality. This was Freud's approach to the inner world and its "religious" imagery. But, in another way, Rapunzel's tower and its spell-casting sorceress describe the numinous reality of the archetypal layer of the psyche, and this is just as "real" as the outer reality viewed with such suspicion by Rapunzel's witch. As we have seen, Jung adopted the word "numinous" from Rudolph Otto's important study of the nature of religious experience across cultures. Otto had shown that the numinous is a *category of experience* like love or aggression, but a category of experience perhaps uniquely expressive of what it means to be human. It was a small step for Jung to theoretically "locate" this awe-inspiring mysterious power in the deepest layer of the psyche – its collective or religious dimension. So, according to the argument we are making here, when trauma strikes and the enchantress comes to rescue the human spirit, the archetypal "world" that opens up through the abyss of outer catastrophe is *a world already waiting to be discovered*. It is not "created" by the ego in order to provide necessary illusion (as Freud thought). It is placed in the service of "illusion" in order to defend the personal spirit, but these archetypal defenses are a kind of miracle in their own right and provide for the organism's survival.

The problem comes, as we have seen, in the Rapunzel-self's desperate longing for a real life from within a towered world which begins to turn more and more persecutory. The caretaking side of the numinous energies begins to give way to the diabolical, destructive side. These are the light and dark sides of the numinous and represent amplified versions of the "love" and "aggression" which the traumatized patient has not been able to "humanize" in a normal developmental process with transitional figures.

In our story, both Rapunzel and the Prince seem to have fallen under the persecutory, destructive side of the self-care system as each struggles in a split-apart, unredeemed world of misery. The separating "wall" is back now as an unbridgeable gulf which separates them – each lost to the other. But then the Prince hears Rapunzel's voice – a repeat of what happened as he rode by the tower early on. He wanders blindly toward this voice until Rapunzel recognizes him, falls on his neck, and weeps the tears which heal his broken vision. In this image we have a beautiful depiction of how grief heals the lost connection to the numinous world.

In the therapy situation there are also many tears at this time. Patient and therapist go through times when the connection seems to be utterly broken. And yet, if the tension can be held during this period, a true "coniunctio" is possible. One of the healing factors in this working-through period is the fact that this time, the therapeutic "trauma" comes after a period of essential self-object "illusion" in which a true "pregnancy" can occur in the relationship. Even with the unraveling of this illusion, there is a difference from the earlier traumatic time in the patient's life. First, a true union has occurred; second, a full protest is heard from the patient – the protest that could not happen as a child. In small doses, this is the poison that cures. We know that immunity develops only with an injection of the disease-organism. Only this diluted re-traumatization gets to the pain. And this is a mutual process. The therapist must also recognize his or her own "disillusionment." A crucial part of my work with the above female patient, for example, was acknowledging my own difficulties. The patient needed to see that I was suffering too, before she could feel the reparative side of her own anger and cry the tears which could heal the eyes of her wounded relationship to reality. She needed to see me struggle with authentic reactions to her anger and her love before she could accede to my expectation that she struggle with hers. In this process, the therapist's humanity distinguishes him from the cruel perfectionism of the patient's inner caretaker. The ensuing struggle, shared with the patient, represents the larger human reality that in one way is the larger human community that the patient has never fully entered. This is the essential grief work done during this period.

When our Rapunzel patients get better, even as their outer lives become more animated with their true selves, they go through a mournful period of dreaded loss of their inner worlds – or so it feels to them – a kind of agonizing sacrifice of what feels like their "childhoods." They do not want to give up "God's world" for the hollow superficialities of life in "this world," with its banalities and falsehoods. Yet life in the outer world is beginning to be more real and authentic. Like Rapunzel, they are challenged to give up their identification with the inflated world of bewitchment and, after the "fall," to recover a relationship to enchantment. This is what "happily ever after" means in our fairy tales – neither living in bliss, on the one hand, nor a hollow "reality" on the other, but living in a world where the wall between imagination and reality comes down and becomes a flexible boundary. This is more than Freud's everyday misery. It is living a life one can dream about and in which the struggle to realize that dream can be shared with others who are doing the same thing.

8

PSYCHE AND HER
DAIMON-LOVER

The story of Eros and Psyche, told as a short interlude in a longer novel *The Golden Ass*, by the ancient Roman writer Lucius Apuleius, has proven irresistible to Jungian theorists. Erich Neumann adapted the story (Neumann, 1956) and was the first to interpret it. He approached the story as a paradigm of female development. By contrast, both von Franz (1970) and Ulanov (1971) see it as a model for anima development in men. James Hillman (1972) sees it as an archetypal drama – a metaphorical portrayal of the longing of the Psyche for Eros and Eros for Psyche, and recently Lena Ross has interpreted the tale as the "struggle to separate from the collective while maintaining a relationship to the divine" (Ross, 1991: 65).

In relative contrast to the above analyses, we will be approaching this story as a portrayal of what we have described as the archetypal self-care system and its "rescue" (by Eros) of a traumatized innocent ego (Psyche). In this story, Psyche's rescuer turns out to be a daimon-lover and, like the tale of Rapunzel, the story describes the healing of trauma as a two-stage process in which the protective, loving aspects of Eros are encountered first and the daimonic aspects later. As the story progresses, both Eros and Psyche must suffer the loss of illusion as a relationship is finally worked out between the reality-bound ego and the ambivalent numinous powers represented by Eros in both his protective and persecutory form. Eros/Psyche, then, represent a dyad much like the witch/Rapunzel, and this archetypal structure defines the self-care system of the traumatized patient with its initial *resistance* to change and ultimate acceptance of change's inevitability (which is part of the human condition).

If we apply a gnostic metaphor to this development in our story, we might say that the two-stage process delineates a kind of two-stage descent of the spirit into matter – *an incarnation of the personal spirit (daimon) in the body*. In Chapter 4, we described this process in reference to Winnicott's notion of "indwelling." In the present chapter we see that indwelling seems to occur in a two-stage process. In stage one, the alienated (traumatized) ego of the narrative (Psyche or Rapunzel) is "captured" by a protective daimon (witch or god) and swept away into a fantasy castle or tower. After sufficient time in this transformational chamber feeding nightly on the ambrosia of her caretaking daimon, the innocent, uninitiated ego of the narrative is strong enough (both Psyche and Rapunzel are pregnant) to risk alienation from the positive side of the Self with which it has become identified. At this juncture, a *sacrifice* takes place and stage two is initiated. This sacrificial moment which we saw in Rapunzel at the moment both she and the Prince confront old Dame Gothel and are thrown out of the tower, issues in a process of suffering and alienation as (in our current story) both Eros and Psyche suffer the "dark side" of their blissful love. But this suffering includes the positive, interior element (*in utero*) and is therefore of a completely different order from the unregenerate misery with which our stories begin. It represents the suffering of a sacralized ego – an ego now under the guidance of the Self and its individuating energies.

EROS AND PSYCHE[1]: PART I

There once lived a King and Queen who had three daughters and one of them, Psyche, was so extraordinarily beautiful that men were speechless in her presence and began to worship her as though she were the goddess Aphrodite herself. Her less attractive sisters had long-since been married to kings. Yet potential suitors only admired Psyche from afar, leaving her miserable, broken in spirit, all the while loathing in her heart the very loveliness that made her so unapproachable. In this dilemma, Psyche's father consulted the oracle Apollo to find a husband for her, and received the proclamation that Psyche was to be prepared for marriage with a monstrous dragon, and so, with great weeping and mourning, she was led up a lonely mountain to await her marriage to the daimon.

Meanwhile, Aphrodite, who was deeply offended that a mere mortal should have displaced her as Goddess of Beauty, summoned her lusty little boy Eros, and implored him to avenge her by causing Psyche to fall in love with the vilest of men – "one so broken that through all the world his misery has no peer"(5). Sent on the avenging errand by his mother, Eros found Psyche trembling on her lonely mountain crag. Sweeping her away on the West Wind, he bore her gently down to a beautiful grove near a transparent fountain of glassy water. In the center of the grove stood a palace "built by no human hands but by the cunning of a god"(9).

Allured by the charm and beauty of the miraculous palace, Psyche beheld such vast wealth and provision as she had never seen. Overcome with joy, she was given instruction by disembodied voices that bade her refresh herself and served her delicious meals and wine like nectar, then sang to her as an invisible choir. That night, under the shroud of darkness, her unknown husband came, made love to Psyche and departed in haste before dawn. And so it was for many nights and days.

But meanwhile, Psyche's parents grew old and feeble with grief, and her elder sisters also. Climbing to the crag where Psyche had been left, they beat their breasts and wept for the lost Psyche until finally the young beauty, herself overcome with grief, prevailed upon her unknown husband to allow them to visit her. Granting her wish, Eros wafted the two sisters to his palace on the West Wind, but he made Psyche promise – on the threat she would lose him forever – that she would say nothing of her husband or what he was like.

Upon seeing the affluence of her heavenly wealth, Psyche's elder sisters burned with envy and, returning home swollen with rage, contrived a plan against her. Feigning grief, rending their hair and tearing their faces, they returned to the crag once again. Meanwhile, poor Psyche, missing her sisters more than ever, prevailed upon Eros to allow a second visit, then a third.

"Do you see," he said, "what great peril you are in? . . . Those false she-wolves are weaving some deep plot of sin against you whose purpose is this: to persuade you to seek to know my face, which, as I have told you, if once you see, you will see no more. And so if hereafter those wicked ghouls come hither . . . give neither ear nor utterance to anything concerning your husband. For soon we shall have issue, and even now your womb, a child's as yet, bears a child like to you. If you keep my secret in silence, he shall be a god; if you divulge it, a mortal"(18).

Finally Psyche's sisters devised an equally cunning deceit and address their sister; "Ah you are happy, for you live in blessed ignorance of your evil plight and have no suspicion of your peril . . . . For we have learned the truth . . . . He that lies secretly by your side at night is a huge serpent with a thousand tangled coils; blood and deadly poison drip from his throat and from the cavernous horror of his gaping maw. Remember Apollo's oracle, how it proclaimed that you should be the bride of some fierce beast. . . . The hour has now come when you must choose whether to believe your sisters. . . . or find a grave in the entrails of a cruel monster" (22–3).

Poor Psyche was overcome with terror at this melancholy news. Swept beyond the bounds of reason and trembling with anguish, she resolved to look upon her unknown lover and if necessary kill him in his sleep as her sisters recommended. "Impatience, indecision, daring and terror, diffidence and anger, all strove within her, and, worst of all, in the same body she hated the beast and loved the husband" (25).

None the less, when the appointed hour came and Eros was fast asleep, she lit a lamp – and there beheld the beautiful Eros, fairest of Gods. Pricking herself on one of his arrows, Psyche fell in love with love. She threw herself upon him in an ecstasy of love, but at that very moment, the oil lamp sputtered and a drop fell upon Eros. Leaping from the couch, his secret now betrayed, Eros tore himself from Psyche's kisses and flew away with never a word.

Like most fairy tales, our story begins with something out of balance between the numinous world of the gods and the human realm. In other words, something has gone wrong in the *mediation* of archetypal energies and the imbalance will have to be corrected. In the story of Rapunzel, we saw how a wall separated these two worlds (as in the schizoid disorders) and how gradually, through different mediating figures and the suffering of Rapunzel and her Prince, the two worlds were interpenetrated and eventually integrated. In Eros and Psyche we do not have a wall between the numinous and the real, but rather a *defensive use of the a wall between the numinous and the real, but rather a defensive use of the numinous by an inadequately established reality-ego*. This is the problem of narcissism, i.e., the identification of the ego with beauty, wealth, or fame – all collective values that inflate the ego with numinous, archetypal energies that do not properly belong to it. Psyche is "inflated" by everyone else's desire (she carries their projections), but her own desire is unawakened. Her "spirit is broken" and she is full of self-loathing – precisely what we have seen as the legacy of early trauma. Only her outer beauty sustains her self-esteem. Inwardly she is empty and without an authentic self.

In this dreadful situation, abandoned by human love and destined only for bondage to a daimon-lover, Psyche is in the same plight as Jung's Moon-lady after her incestuous violation by her brother (Chapter 3). However, "man's extremity is God's opportunity," and at this moment of unbearable suffering, a transcendent "being" comes to the beleaguered ego's rescue, sweeping it away into an inner mythic landscape, dissolving it in divine energies so that it can recover. In this case, Psyche's daimon-lover is none other than "Love" himself. However, this "Eros" is apparently in need of his own development, because we first meet him in our story as nothing but a mother's boy, possessed as it were, by his divine mother Aphrodite who kisses him "with parted lips." So if our story is about the rescue and transformation of a traumatized ego, it is also simultaneously about the rescue and transformation of the *daimonic partner of this ego*, who is drawn down into human affairs out of love for this very wounded feminine part of the self.

EROS AS DAIMON

Taking a tip from Grotstein (1984), we noted in the epigraph to Chapter 1 that "when innocence has been deprived of its entitlement, it becomes a diabolical spirit." In keeping with this analysis, we might best think of this god, Eros, as that inviolable personal spirit or daimon that escaped Psyche's selfhood when her spirit was broken. In Chapter 2 we explored how in early trauma, there is a reversal of what Winnicott called indwelling and the somatic and spiritual poles of the archetype are dissociated. We speculated that one reason for this split was the necessity of preserving the *personal spirit inviolate* and that the Self, reacting to trauma, was the organizing agent for a *dismemberment of experience* necessary for survival. In our clinical examples, we also saw how, when this happens, the Self constellates negatively, actually preventing integration or individuation, and how, while protecting the personal spirit, it also persecutes or imprisons it.

If we think of the Self as that potential wholeness of the personality which continually seeks incarnation in the ego and its object-relations, then the dismemberment or severing of its relationship with the reality ego which trauma forces upon it, means that the *Self has, so to speak, sacrificed itself* – i.e., sacrificed its very essence *which is relationship*. As the daimon or the god (Eros) in our narrative, it has cut itself off from its potential reality-incarnation (Psyche) – dismembered itself, so to speak, by dismembering its relationship to the ego and the world. The resulting pair Eros/Psyche, then represent two halves of an original personal/transpersonal (inner/outer) unity that has been dismembered by trauma.

169

Like Plato's original man who was cut in two, with each half forever seeking its mate, the Eros/Psyche or Self/ego pair are now radically separated and, if they are to be rejoined, it will require that the person housing this process find a new capacity for suffering the psyche's archetypal affects. This new capacity for suffering is always a *rediscovery* based on the *remembering* of earlier times in the patient's life when dependency was possible and love was welcomed. This remembering can occur only in a love relationship with another person and we have repeatedly seen the resistance to this love which the dismembered Self sets up. In psychoanalysis, this love relationship emerges in the transference and, with it, all the transpersonal uniting factors that such transferences set in motion.

In our story, and in mythology in general, the "transpersonal uniting factors" are intermediate beings or daimons who link up the purely spiritual realm of the gods and the earthbound human race. In Plato's symposium, Socrates cites Eros as just such a mighty daimon or spirit, halfway between God and man. One of his listeners asks him a more general question about what these mighty daimons or spirits do, and he replies:

> They are the envoys and interpreters that ply between heaven and earth, flying upward with our worship and our prayers, and descending with the heavenly answers and commandments, and since they are between the two estates they weld both sides together and merge them into one great whole. They form the medium of the prophetic arts, of the priestly rites of sacrifice, initiation, and incantation, of divination and of sorcery, for the divine will not mingle directly with the human, and it is only through the mediation of the spirit world that man can have any intercourse, whether waking or sleeping, with the gods.
>
> (von Franz, 1980a: 36)

So it is the daimonic that serves, then, as an intermediate area of experience, between the transpersonal, archetypal world, with its numinous dynamism – both positive and negative – and the human, mundane world of ego-functioning. Daimons represent the Self in its mediating dynamism. As both Protectors and Persecutors, they are necessary parts of the self-care system, precisely because there has been *insufficient mediation* of the raging archetypal energies that pour through the ego in traumatic circumstances. We know that the ego cannot unfold according to the promptings of a transpersonal control-point unless there is a facilitating environment – unless the archetypal world is allowed to personalize in such a way that its grandiose imagery is scaled down to human proportions. Without this, it is as though the Self turns its energies from *living* into a last-ditch effort at *preserving* what is left of the true personality for possible redemption in the future. It "supplies" a world (Eros' crystal palace) for the beleaguered child-ego in place of the lost world of life lived in relation to reality. In other words, the daimon-lover is what the Self looks like when it is ingrown – turned back on itself, unredeemed by human recognition.

In our story, Eros flies on his great wings to the mountain crag where Psyche is waiting in order to carry out his mother's bidding. No sooner does he see Psyche's suffering, however, than something comes over him which even he cannot control and he is drawn down into the human realm, betraying his own divine mother and thereby entering voluntarily into his own transformation process. This moment contains the paradox that love *awakens in the God of Love only when he approaches human suffering and limitation.* In our story, divine Eros is moved to betray his heavenly perfection only by a suffering mortal soul. This is an *incarnational* motif similar to the early Christian concept of "kenosis" (from the Greek meaning "to empty") whereby Christ, identified with the all-pervading oneness of the Godhead, without definiteness, "emptied himself" of his all-embracing plenitude to become man – to become definite. Jung thought he saw in this voluntary sacrifice a glimpse of the psyche's telos or ultimate goal, which was not just the ego's goal but transformation of the whole personality. The Self does not seem to want unlimited expression (discharge). It seeks human limitation in order to transform itself.

DAIMONIC PROTECTION VS. IMPRISONMENT

The world into which Eros sweeps the traumatized Psyche is well known to us now from Rapunzel's tower. It was to Jung's great credit that he realized the true nature of this inner sanctum following outer trauma. Unlike Freud, who saw it only as a regressive, sexual, wish-fulfilling world into which the ego retreated (incestuous regression to the womb), Jung realized that the regressing ego went deeper, into the collective layer of the psyche, and there found itself sustained by transpersonal energies that were absolutely essential if the ego was ever to "progress" again.

> The regressing libido apparently desexualizes itself by retreating back step by step to the pre-sexual stage of earliest infancy. Even there is does not make a halt, but in a manner of speaking continues right back to the intra-uterine, pre-natal condition and, leaving the sphere of personal psychology altogether, irrupts into the collective psyche where Jonah saw the "mysteries" ("representations collectives") in the whale's belly. The libido thus reaches a kind of inchoate condition in which, like Theseus and Peirithous on their journey to the underworld, it may easily stick fast. But it can also tear itself loose from the maternal embrace and return to the surface with new possibilities of life.
>
> (Jung, 1912a, para. 654)

Here we have depicted the encapsulated world of what psychopathology knows as the "schizoid defense," but with Jung's important addition of the life-sustaining energies available there. Inside this world of illusion, the mortified Psyche's fragile ego is kept alive like a hydroponic plant, feeding nightly on the nectar of Eros' love, i.e., on archetypal fantasy. It is one of the miracles of psychological life that the traumatized psyche is kept alive in this way (albeit at a tremendous price). Inside the crystalline palace of our story, Jung saw more than what D.W. Winnicott called the "cold storage" into which the true self retreats under traumatic circumstances (see Winnicott, 1960a: 140ff.) and more than the deep inner sanctum to which the "lost heart of the libidinal ego" retreats in the parallel image of Harry Guntrip (see Guntrip, 1971: Part II). Jung saw a transformation chamber in which the traumatized ego was broken down into its basic elements, dissolved, so to speak, in the nectar of the gods, for the "purpose" of later rebirth. In our story, the dissolving effect of Eros leads to a breakdown of Psyche's beleaguered "I" in the fused state of a divine/human "we," so that the first stage in her healing is equivalent to the surrender of her "old" personality and its transformative inclusion in something larger. This something larger, under whose "spell" she falls at this stage, is precisely the religious element (Eros' divinity), and Jung saw in this archaic motif a profound truth about the psyche that pointed far beyond the apparent illusory escapism of religion emphasized by Freud.

THE DAIMONIC AS JAILER

Before going on with our story, it seems important to underscore the truly dangerous aspects of those self-sustaining illusions which grow luxuriantly in what we might call the crystal palace of the daimon-lover, where Eros takes Psyche and where he imprisons her "in the dark" for a long time. Entering this psychological "space" is equivalent to entering an altered state of consciousness. This is why all witches and daimons are "spell-casters." If this "narcissistic" energy is appropriated by the ego, as it inevitably is to some extent, then a very refractory kind of inflation results, and the libido gets stuck in the underworld. The resulting constellation is both inflated (the god Eros) and infantile (the injured Psyche). People caught in this web are paradoxically both incredibly needy and proudly self-sufficient at the same time, impotent and omnipotent both – a "divine or royal person" and a "baby" simultaneously. This imperious infantilism is the dark side of the daimonic's influence over the ego – its tendency toward incest and "malignant regression."

Freud very correctly warned about the addictive quality of this stage, because the glass bubble within which Eros and Psyche remain is not only the place of transformation, as Jung so optimistically thought; it is also the place of our compulsive addictions and "co-dependencies." The "love" inside this space is incestuous, i.e., developmentally prior to self-object boundary differentiation and it is *addictive precisely because here we have access to the "ambrosia" of divine energies*. It was this fact that helped Jung to understand the "spiritual problem" behind alchohol addiction, which he saw as a misguided concretistic projection of the need for spiritual experience into the mind-altering "spirits" of alcohol.

What Jung did not see (how could he have?) was how addictive his own psychological theories would become to people whose "New Age" proclivities inclined them only to the "light" or "healing" side of the numinosum.

People who are victims of addiction know how futile their struggle often is in the "dissolving space" supervised by the daimon-lover, and how important "turning the problem over to God" is in their own recovery. It might even be said that the daimon-lover exploits the psyche's longing to surrender in the service of neurosis. He is the seducer, the weaver of illusions and he demands total obedience. He tempts us into one more drink or one more candy-bar, or one more sexual adventure. His ministrations are always temporarily soothing, as the gods' ambrosia is sweet, but they are never fully satisfying because the daimon-lover is an inner substitute for the original caretaking "other" needed in infancy, and the encapsulated space in the psyche under his (or her) self-care system is cut off from the real world. Therefore, he can offer only inflated substitutes for what is really wanted – which is the *imaginal link* between reality and fantasy, not fantasy as a soothing defense against reality. What the daimon-lover supplies is always based on a genuine need, but it never fulfills it, and the more one indulges in the substitute, the deeper the real need is obscured.

THE DAIMON-LOVER AND FANTASY

D. W. Winnicott calls the "crystal-palace" stage in our two-stage process, "fantasy" (one dimensional) as distinguished from true "imagination" which is *fantasy about something real* (two-dimensional). He understands fantasy as a defense against both dreaming and living (see Winnicott, 1971a: 26ff.), and presents the case of a middle-aged woman who spent most of her life in fantasy. This patient had very early abandoned all hope in object-relating because of a too-early disillusionment in relationship to her mother. She was the youngest of several siblings who were left to look after themselves. In the nursery she struggled to belong and play, but she could only fit in on a compliance basis. So

> while she was playing the other people's games she was all the time engaged in fantasying. She really lived in this fantasying on the basis of a dissociated mental activity... she became a specialist in this one thing: being able to have a dissociated life while seeming to be playing with the other children in the nursery... gradually she became one of the many who do not feel that they exist in their own right as whole human beings.
>
> (ibid.: 29)

Winnicott says that, in her fantasy, "omnipotence was retained" and wonderful things could be achieved, but in this dissociated state, whenever the patient began to put something into practice, such as painting or reading, she found the limitations that made her dissatisfied because she had let go of the omnipotence that she retained in fantasying. Thus, fantasying "possessed her like an evil spirit" (ibid.: 33) – precisely our daimon.

In fantasy, "a dog is a dog is a dog." Fantasy has "no poetic value," whereas a true dream has poetry in it, i.e., layer upon layer of meaning related to past, present, and future, and to inner and outer reality. Fantasy, therefore, has no meaning. It cannot be interpreted (ibid.: 35).

> The patient may sit in her room and while doing nothing at all except breathe she has (in her fantasy) painted a picture, or she has done an interesting piece of work in her job, or she has been for a country walk; but from the observer's point of view nothing whatever has happened. In fact, nothing is likely to happen because of the fact that in the dissociated state so much is happening. On the other hand, she may be sitting in her room thinking of tomorrow's job and making plans, or thinking about her holiday, and this may be an imaginative exploration of the world and of the place where dream and life are the same thing. In this way she swings from well to ill, and back again to well.
>
> (ibid.: 27)

FANTASY AS A DEFENSE AGAINST THE SYMBOLIC

In a similar vein, Thomas Ogden has distinguished the realm of fantasy as a non-symbolic stage, all symbolism requiring what he calls "the capacity to maintain psychological dialectics"(Ogden, 1986), which in turn requires what Winnicott has called *potential space*. By potential space, Ogden means an intermediate area of experiencing that lies between inner reality and external reality – it lies "between the subjective object and the object objectively perceived" (ibid.: 205). In Winnicott's language, it is the "hypothetical area that exists (but cannot exist) between the baby and the object (mother or part of mother) during the phase of the repudiation of the object as not-me" (Winnicott, 1971a: 107) that is, at the end of being merged in with the object. In other words, it is the "space" of the interpenetrating mix-up between subject and object that aways precedes threeness and constitutes a "twoness in oneness." The central feature of potential space is the paradox which both joins and separates baby and mother. The baby gets to the separateness of the object only through this intermediate area and its symbolic creativity.

This intermediate area of "twoness in oneness" is what the healing of trauma requires, whether in the transference or elsewhere. Ogden gives a beautiful example of the symbolic capacity developed within "potential space" after a trauma – a capacity that Eros and Psyche have not yet realized in their crystal palace, i.e., the "third" factor of their union in "twoness" (the baby) has not yet been born.

> A two and a half year old child, after having been frightened by having his head go underwater while being given a bath, became highly resistant to taking a bath. Some months later, after gentle but persistent coaxing by his

mother, he very reluctantly allowed himself to be placed in four inches of bath water. The child's entire body was tense; his hands were tightly clamped onto his mother's he was not crying, but his eyes were pleadingly glued to those of his mother. One knee was locked in extension while the other was flexed in order to hold as much of himself out of the water as he could. His mother began almost immediately to try to interest him in some bath toys. He was not the least bit interested until she told him she would like some tea.

At that point the tension that had been apparent in his arms, legs, abdomen, and particularly his face, abruptly gave way to a new physical and psychological state. His knees were now bent a little; his eyes surveyed the toy cups and saucers and spotted an empty shampoo bottle, which he chose to use as milk for the tea; the tension in his voice shifted from the tense insistent plea, "My not like bath, my not like bath," to a narrative of his play: "Tea not too hot, it's okay now. My blow on it for you Tea yumm." The mother has some "tea" and asked for more. After a few minutes the mother began to reach for the washcloth. This resulted in the child's ending of the play as abruptly as he had started it, with a return of all of the initial signs of anxiety that had preceded the play. After the mother reassured the child that she would hold him so he would not slip, she asked him if he had any more tea. He did and playing was resumed.

(Ogden, 1986: 206–7)

Ogden comments:

[Here is conveyed a sense] of the way in which a state of mind was generated by the mother and child in which there was a transformation of water from something frightening to a plastic medium (discovered and created by the child) with meanings that could be communicated. In this transformation, reality is not denied; the dangerous water is represented in the playing. Nor is fantasy robbed of its vitality – the child's breath magically changed dangerous water into a loving gift. There is also a quality of "I-ness" that is generated in play that differs from the riveted stare and desperate holding-on that had connected mother and infant prior to the beginning of play.

(ibid.: 208)

To reach a place where "reality is not denied" and "fantasy retains its vitality" is the goal of psychotherapy with all trauma survivors because with trauma, there is a collapse of what Ogden describes as the dialectical tension necessary to generate meaningful experience. In the case of our tale, this collapse is in the direction of fantasy, and reality is kept out of the encapsulated numinous world by the archetypal self-care system, which resists the loss of its control over inner feeling states. This resistance is vested in the diabolical side of our Protector/Persecutor and this destructive resistance is seen in Eros' obsessive concern with secrecy about himself and his insistence that Psyche remain unconscious of his true nature.

In psychoanalysis, an analogous danger is sometimes seen in the analyst's refusal to become more "known" and human to his or her patient, i.e., the analyst's insistence on complete anonymity or, alternatively, in the analyst's refusal to allow his patient any negative feeling. Nothing maintains "transference addiction" so much as the analyst's continued refusal to divulge anything flawed or personal to a patient who desperately needs contact with his or her partner's *reality*. The "spell" of transference can only be dissolved through encounters with the analyst's reality limitations and often the patient's curiosity about the analyst and insistence on penetrating his or her anonymity become especially strong towards the end of the work. Analysts who are always sympathetic, never confront their patients, and retain their idealized image as long as possible, keep their patients (and themselves) in a crystal palace and out of life and its inevitable suffering. In our story, the "call" of reality comes from Psyche's sisters in the tale and what this "call" ultimately wants is a *sacrifice*. This is what both the patient and the analyst caught in a seemingly endless unconflicted positive transference would like to avoid.

INDIVIDUATION AND THE TUG OF REALITY

We come now to that charming part of the tale where Psyche's sisters visit the mountain crag where she was left and begin to grieve for her. The sisters here represent the "call" of reality to the blissfully imprisoned Psyche. Eros makes Psyche promise she will not answer them, but left alone again, Psyche becomes unbearably lonely and begins to feel a captive in the walls of her luxurious prison, deprived of all real human conversation. Finally, she prevails upon Eros to allow her sisters to visit, and the three are tearfully reunited. This is the beginning of a series of visits by the sisters (three in all), the ultimate result of which is the break-up of the one-dimensional fantasy-world in which Psyche has been living with her unknown husband.

Curiosity is a major part of this process – curiosity about what is *really* going on underneath (shadow-side) all the one-dimensional blissful "love." Curiosity is part of consciousness and the root of consciousness is "to know with another," i.e., a "twoness" is necessary. The crystal palace of the daimon-lover is a one-dimensional space in which Psyche feels a "oneness" with her lover (projective identification) but she is not separate from him. She cannot *see* him and thus cannot *know* him. So, just like the serpent in the Garden of Eden tempted Eve to eat the fruit of the tree of knowledge, Psyche's sisters represent the individuation urge toward wholeness by emphasizing the shadow-side (dragon) of her blissful love.

Finally, Psyche's curiosity gets the best of her and in a moment similar to that *slip of the tongue* where Rapunzel's secret love for the Prince is betrayed to Dame Gothel, Psyche lights a lamp and illuminates the darkness surrounding her daimon-lover. In this paradoxical moment of simultaneous delight and horror Psyche beholds the beautiful winged Eros, who she has now betrayed.

Here we have the supreme paradoxical moment of our story, which is both a sacrifice and a birth. If it is the birth of consciousness, it is also the loss of a sustaining illusion; if it is an expansion of consciousness for Psyche who has now illuminated her lover, it is also a humiliation and narrowing of consciousness for the God. In the language of Sabina Speilrein's paper (1984), it is truly "Destruction as a Cause of Coming Into Being." The ambivalence of this moment is also embodied in the winged daimon-lover who is both devouring monster and inspiring god. Viewed from the "outside" – the perspectives of Psyche's human sisters – this figure is truly a snake or a dragon, ensnaring her in illusions which dissociate her from life in reality. But, looked upon from "inside" – the perspective of Psyche herself – the daimon-lover is also a savior-god. He pulls her out of life-in-the-world, but this life, because of her trauma, was a false one. For Jung, this ambivalent imagery portrays the ambivalence of the libido itself – one part is "progressive" and strives for life in the world; another part is "regressive" and when necessary becomes "seductive" enough to pull the ego back into the crystal palace in order to transform it. Jung once said that the "fundamental thesis" of his book *Wandlungen und Symbole der Libido* was "the splitting of the libido into a positive and negative current" (Jung, 1925: 26), but this crucial point, with which Freud disagreed, has largely been lost to Jung's interpreters.

Around this sacrificial moment in our story, there cluster a series of negative emotions: envy (the sisters'), rage (Aphrodite's), woundedness (Eros') and despair (Psyche's). Almost all major psychoanalytic theorists have found in this pivotal moment a major threshold in psychological development. Winnicott called it the "moment of destruction" which separates object-relating from object-use. Melanie Klein called it the "depressive position." Freud saw in it the universal crisis of the Oedipal renunciation which, if resolved, led to a capacity for symbolic internalization. And Jung called it the moment of the inflated ego's *sacrifice* – the dismemberment of the "old king" or the god to begin the renewal of the human. "Sacrifice" means to make sacred, and however we conceptualize this "moment," the ego that emerges from it is a *sacralized* ego – one that holds the connection between the human and the divine.

The slow *sacralization* of the ego in our story can be seen in the way Eros "cooperates" with reality by letting the sisters in. He foresees the consequences of this intrusion, but lets it happen. This is an image of his continuing self-sacrifice in the interest of an ultimate relationship between "his world" and the human world of Psyche. The sacralization process is also symbolized by Psyche's pregnancy. The regression into total dependence has worked. The strong medicine of Eros' dissolving love has taken. This suggests nothing less than the birth of an internal world. In other words, Psyche takes an inner "image" of their relationship out with her after the bubble is broken. The "bubble," so to speak, is now her fertile womb in which joy (Voluptas) is gestating. Simultaneously, Eros is wounded by the hot oil of illumination and retires to Aphrodite's chamber to nurse his injury. Yet this wound is also his "happy fault," the *dismemberment* of a god through contact with the human which Jung saw in the universal mythic theme of God's sacrifice for man's redemption. All the healing gods are wounded gods.

EROS AND PSYCHE: PART 2

With Eros' departure, the pregnant Psyche was in suicidal despair. She tried to drown herself in a river, unsuccessfully "because the river knew Eros." But then, the goat-footed god Pan advised her to "cease from her grief and address Eros with fervent prayer, winning him by tender submission." With this, Psyche set off in search of Eros. Meanwhile, Aphrodite discovered what the two lovers had done and, now enraged at Psyche, roamed the land hoping to kill her. So ravaged was the world by Aphrodite's rage that Psyche could find no refuge, even in the sanctuaries of gods, and was returned again to the verge of despair.

Then, in a moment of true self-reflection and acceptance of her fate, Psyche came to herself, saying "Come then, take heart of grace! Your poor hopes are shattered. Renounce them boldly and yield of your own free will to your mistress (Aphrodite) and assuage the fierce onset of her wrath by submission, late though it be. Who knows but you may even find the husband you have sought so long, there in his mother's house!" (38)

At this point, Psyche prepared for the uncertain fate of her submission. Aphrodite's first torture was to unleash her handmaidens Trouble and Sorrow on poor Psyche who received their scourging with whips and other torments. Then Aphrodite herself beat Psyche cruelly. Her rage satisfied, Aphrodite then set a series of humiliating tasks for her subject, the first being to sort a huge pile of seeds. As Psyche sat in despair and stupefaction at this task, ants swarmed over the seeds and sorted them for her. Seeing this, Aphrodite threw her a crust of bread. The second impossible task – to gather fleece from terrible man-eating sheep – was also made possible by supernatural intervention, this time by a green reed who told Psyche how to accomplish this. And a third impossible task – to bring black water from a dragon-invested Stygian spring – was also performed by supernatural forces – this time by Zeus' Eagle. Finally a fourth task was assigned – to descend into Tartarus itself and bring back some of Persephone's beauty ointment in a box for Aphrodite. Again Psyche despaired and prepared to commit suicide from a tower, but the tower spoke to her and advised her how to proceed. But carrying her box with its special contents out of Tartarus, Psyche was again "overwhelmed with rash curiosity." She opened the box and found no beauty ointment therein but only a Stygian sleep which overcame her.

Meanwhile Eros, now recovered from his wound came again to the spell-bound Psyche and this time was able to awaken her with a harmless prick from one of his arrows. Now deeply in love and reunited with his beloved Psyche, yet fearing his mother's wrath, Eros sought help from Zeus who, after hearing his case blessed Eros' marriage to Psyche and even brought the new bride to heaven to make her immortal. The nuptial banquet was set forth with all the gods and goddesses in attendance, and soon thereafter a daughter was born to them: in the language of mortals she is called Joy (53).

RAGE AND THE RESISTANCE TO INCARNATION

The first thing we note in this part of our story is the rage experienced by Aphrodite as she realizes the betrayal by her son – a rage which parallels the witch's rage in Rapunzel when she finds out about Rapunzel's betrayal. This rage is the inevitable result of a coming together of heretofore dissociated parts of the psyche and it *represents a resistance to incarnation* and to consciousness, which resistance is an inevitable by-product of the archetypal defensive processes we have examined. When the traumatized ego becomes the "client" of a transpersonal daimon or god, this daimon or god protects the stress-ego with the ferocity of a mother bear with her cubs. At this stage in our story, Aphrodite and Eros are an undifferentiated pair, with Aphrodite representing Eros' own rage at Psyche's betrayal. Only after this rage is satisfied, through the various humiliations that follow, is the love of Eros/Aphrodite allowed to prevail. So we must remember that *for the traumatized psyche, integration is the worst imaginable thing* and the self-care system (Aphrodite/Eros), with its numinous caretaking (and persecutory) energies, makes sure that the splitting necessary to adaptation is maintained (even though the gods secretly cooperate in the undoing of that splitting).

There is an interesting mythological amplification of this resistance to incarnation on the part of the archetypal self-care system in the early Christian myth of how the Devil broke away from the Godhead. In one tradition, Lucifer, in a rage, splits off from the Godhead and falls to earth *because God wants to become incarnate as man*. This tradition is found in several Jewish Apocryphal books discovered in the Qumran caves (see Forsyth, 1987: 162) and was elaborated further by Origen who based his exigesis on an early passage in Isaiah (14: 10–15) which alludes to a rebel angel Lucifer, Star of the Morning, who tries to ascend into heaven but is brought down to the Pit of Sheol by his pride, becoming "the prince of this world," – the great Deceiver, Liar, Tempter, and Weaver of Illusions (see O'Grady, 1989: 3–22). We note with interest that these are all aspects of the archetypal defensive system we have been exploring.

Here is an abridged version of Alan Watts' engaging description of Lucifer's fall:

> Now among the angels which God had created, there was one so surpassingly beautiful that he was named Lucifer, the Bearer of Light. . . . One of the first things that Lucifer noticed was the unbelievable grandeur of the being which God had given him. He realized that it would really be impossible for the Almighty to create anything more excellent – that he, Lucifer, was really the crowning triumph of God's handiwork.
>
> He looked again into the heart of the Holy Trinity, and as his gaze went deeper and deeper into that abyss of light he began to share the divine vision of the future. And there, to his complete amazement, he saw that God was preparing a far higher place in heaven for creatures who were coarse and

crude in the extreme. He saw that he was to be outclassed in the hierarchy of heaven by beings with fleshly and hairy bodies – almost animals. He saw that, of all things, a woman was to be his Queen. Far worse than this, he saw that Logos-Sophia, God the Son himself was to become man, and to set one of those "vile bodies" upon the very Throne of Heaven.

At all this Lucifer was inflamed with a mystery called Malice. Out of his own heart, by his own choice, he preferred his own angelic glory to that of the Divine Purpose – which was to "corrupt itself" with humanity. Lucifer could see at once what his malice would involve. Nevertheless, he considered it more noble to rebel and rebel for ever than to surrender the pride of his angelic dignity, and to pay homage to a body less luminous and spiritual than his own. He was convinced that God's wisdom had gone astray and he determined to have no part in such an undignified aberration in the otherwise beautiful scheme of creation. Certainly he would have to submit to the utmost wrath, to complete rejection from That which was, after all, the Being of his being.

Along with Lucifer, there were many other angels who felt the same way – and all together, with Lucifer at their head, they turned their backs on the Beatific Vision, flying and falling from the Godhead towards that ever-receding twilight where Being borders upon Nothing, to the Outer Darkness. It was thus that they put themselves in the service of Nothing rather than the service of Being, and so became the nihilists who were to do their utmost to frustrate the creative handiwork of God, and most especially to corrupt the fleshly humanity which he intended to honour. In this manner a whole host of the angels became devils, and their prince became Satan, the Adversary and Beelzebub, the Lord of Flies.

(abridged from Watts, 1954: 41–3)

This mythical tradition gives us amplificatory evidence of what happens to the whole Self and its integrated connection to the ego as "affiliate" (see Neumann, 1976) when trauma makes embodiment impossible. The Self's darkness cannot remain connected to its light and is retained in archaic, unhumanized form as fierce, rebellious Will (resistance to change). Only as affect-tolerance grows through the psychotherapeutic process is embodiment possible, and at this point the dark and light sides of the Self begin to integrate. But the process is stormy – like Aphrodite's wrath at the discovery that her divine son has stooped to love a mere mortal.

VOLUNTARY SACRIFICE AND EMBODIMENT

The next thing we notice in this part of our story is the way Psyche finally "comes to herself" and voluntarily submits to the wrath of Aphrodite, whom she has offended. Here Psyche is making the final atonement for the hubris with which our tale began. All the beauty and esteem she had "stolen" from the goddess then, Psyche now symbolically gives back to its rightful "object." This is the moment of "voluntary sacrifice" that so interested Jung. It initates a process of humanization in which bodily pain and humiliation are experienced (scourging and beating). The suffering of impossible difficulties (tasks) is undertaken, but *now the "sacralized" ego comes under the guidance of the divine.* Each impossible task is made possible by a miraculous intervention from the "divine" side of life so that the transpersonal is now cooperating in the ego's development. This can only happen after the sacrifice of an *identification* with divinity.

A moment similar to Psyche's voluntary sacrifice is found in Christ's crucifixion. Of this moment, Jung once said:

> the utter failure came at the crucifixion in the tragic words "My God, My God, why hast Thou forsaken me?" If you want to understand the full tragedy of those words you must realize that they meant that Christ saw that his whole life, sincerely devoted to the truth according to his best conviction, had really been a terrible illusion. He had lived his life absolutely devotedly to its full and had made his honest experiment, but . . . on the cross his mission deserted him.

> (Jung, 1937a)

Despite Christ's and Psyche's "disillusionment", this paradoxical moment is pre-eminently an *integrating* moment initiating suffering in the service of an ultimate unity between the human and divine which has been severed. Theologian Jurgen Moltmann points out that the last cry of Jesus means "not only 'My God, why hast thou forsaken me?' but at the same time, 'My God, why hast thou forsaken *thyself*?'" (Moltmann, 1974: 151; emphasis added). This is also paradoxically, Lucifer's cry when he realizes God's intention to become incarnate, and represents the cosmic protest of the spiritually identified ego who, until this moment, refuses to embody. If God is by nature relationship between the divine and human, then this moment is not a forsaking of God by God, but the very beginning of the incarnation.

After these theological speculations, let us return to our story. Psyche's attitude of humility and vulnerability in the face of the divine wrath of the offended goddess tempers Aphrodite's sadism and, like Yahweh, faced with Job's humble suffering, secretly she begins to cooperate in Psyche's evolving struggle towards eventual reunion with Eros. We see this cooperation in her bemused acceptance of Psyche's successful completion of her impossible tasks and in the way the positive side of the numinosum constellates every time Psyche despairs of her ability to do what she is assigned. In Winnicott's language, omnipotence is slowly given up as each time Aphrodite (our story's infantile queen) "destroys" her object, and the object (Psyche) "is there to receive the communication." Aphrodite can then say "Hullo object! I destroyed you. I love you. You have value for me because of your survival of my destruction of you" (Winnicott, 1969: 222).

181

JOY AND THE HUMAN/DIVINE RELATIONSHIP

An additional sign that the trauma defense, with which our story started, is now in a process of healing, is the fact that Psyche is pregnant. This child, whose name will be Joy, constitutes the missing third or, in Ogden's language, that missing capacity for the symbolic which was nowhere to be found in the seamlessly interwoven "twoness in oneness" enjoyed by our couple in crystal palace of Psyche's daimon-lover. So while Psyche's impossible tasks involve self-doubt and suffering, there is now a sense of inner sustainment. She is operating, as it were, out of a deeper center in pursuit of her goal, which is the recovery of a relationship with her lost capacity for love, and this means a relationship between the human and the divine which had "collapsed" in the traumatic circumstances of our tale's beginning.

However, the tension between Psyche's compliance with her divine mistress' instructions and her human – all too human – curiosity (ego-willfuness) can be seen in her last and final task, where, in carrying out of Hades the box with Persephone's beauty inside, she cannot resist her curiosity once again. But this time the revenge of the gods is mild – a sleep from which Eros – now transformed and "humanized" by his wound can easily awaken her.

The final act of our drama is one which cements the relationship between the personal and transpersonal worlds in the ultimate symbolic aim of our story – a divine/human marriage. Eros seeks the blessing and aid of Zeus toward this end and Zeus replies, to our great delight:

> My son and master, you have never shown me the honor decreed me by the gods, but with continued blows have wounded this heart of mine . . . and have brought shame upon me by often causing me to fall into earthly lusts; you have hurt my good name and fame by tempting me to base adulteries in defiance of public law and order, why, you have even led me to transgress the Julian law itself; you have made me foully to disfigure my serene countenance by taking upon me the likeness of serpents, fire, wild beasts, birds, and cattle of the field. Yet, notwithstanding, . . . remembering that you have grown up in my arms, I will grant you all your suit on one condition. You shall be on your guard against your rivals and, if there be on earth a girl of surpassing beauty, shall repay my present bounty by making her mine.
>
> (Neumann, 1956: 52)

In this hilarious admission of helplessness in the face of Eros' power to compel the gods to involve themselves with the human world, including embodiment as animals and so on (a helplessness Zeus insists on experiencing again if an attractive maiden turns up!), we see how important Eros is in drawing God down into the human heart and how much the divine ostensibly needs the human in order to become real.

In the final act of our story, Zeus summons all the Oympian Gods to a banquet, where he presents the young Eros, announcing the limits he is about to set for him:

I have thought fit at last to set some curb upon the wild passions of [the young stripling whom you see before you]. Long enough he has been the daily talk and scandal of all the world ... the wanton spirit of boyhood must be enchained in the fetters of wedlock. He has chosen a maiden, and robbed her of her honor. Let him keep her, let her be his forever, let him enjoy his love and hold Psyche in his arms to all eternity.

(ibid.)

Then, Zeus sends Hermes to fetch Psyche to heaven where he gives her a goblet of ambrosia, making her immortal, thus assuring that her marriage will endure forever. Soon after the nuptial banquet, a daughter is born to them and the myth tells us that "in the language of mortals she is called Joy" (ibid.: 53). With Psyche now immortalized, we might ask whether Joy is human or divine. Here we must remember Eros' warning to Psyche – that if his visage were ever "illuminated" in her presence – if she ever really saw him as "other" in the crystal palace, her child would be a mortal. In other words, she could assure her child's divinity (and that of her lover) only by remaining unconscious. Yet Psyche did risk the destruction of her divine lover by uncovering its daimonic aspect, and this does not prevent her from being elevated to Olympian stature. Our tale is thus a poignant warning that the gods must not always be heeded especially when their presence as archetypal self-care figures cuts us off from living. Our story leaves this issue unresolved – a paradox, in fact. It says that Joy is both human and divine, not either/or, and that the way to this Joy is a passion of ecstasy (Psyche) and humiliation (Eros) in which both the human and divine are transformed, through the agonies of human relationship, into love.

9

FITCHER'S BIRD AND THE DARK SIDE OF THE SELF

This story and the one following in Chapter 10 called "Prince Lindworm" is typical of the so-called "maiden-murderer tales" where an evil wizard, diabolical stranger, or monstrous dragon seduces or capures innocent maidens and murders or eats them until finally the source of his power is revealed, leading to his defeat or transformation. Unlike Rapunzel, where the caretaking part of the self-care system was relatively benign, these tales present an evil, diabolical "caretaker," personifying total destructive aggression. Because aggression is part of defense, both these stories have something to teach us about the nature of the self-care system in early trauma, and especially about the persecutory side of our Protector/Persecutor and how he or she functions as a personification of the psyche's primitive aggressive energies, all directed back at the self. When the Protector/Persecutor is present in the inner world, aggression that would normally be available to the ego for separation/differentiation is cut off from consciousness and appears in daimonic form, attacking from within.

The story of Fitcher's Bird and its related equivalent in the Blue Beard cycle of tales has been the subject of several theoretical/clinical studies by Jungian authors, most notably, by Kathrin Asper (1991) and Verena Kast (1992), both of whom focus on the self-destructive energy in this figure. Asper interprets the diabolical wizard in Fitcher's Bird as the *negative animus* of a woman, that inner masculine figure who "chops and tears her self to pieces" (Asper, 1991: 125). She sees such a figure as a symptom of a deep disturbance in the mother–child relationship, especially leading to narcissistic personality disorder. She also believes this diabolical figure can appear in male dreams as the "negative shadow" (ibid.: 128). The approach we are taking to this figure as a personification of defenses of the primal ambivalent Self is somewhat different from Asper's more classical Jungian metapsychology.

In an interesting variation on the classical approach, and closer to the present analysis of this figure, Verena Kast describes the case of a male analysand in which a tyrannical sadistic "giant" seemed to possess her young male patient from within – erupting into the transference and terrifying both the patient and his analyst. At one point, her patient, as if possessed said:

> You made me cry last time. Don't do that!.... I'll whip you with
> chains! I'll tie you up in chains and beat you! I'll take an iron rod and beat
> you some more! Your blood will flow ... I'll drive you before me like
> an animal.
>
> (Kast, 1992: 183)

At this point, Kast herself became frightened and stopped her patient, whose face
suddenly showed great fear – fear of the fantasy that had possessed him. In the
discussion that followed, the patient said:

> Please forgive me. You know it's not I who made those fantasies. It's a very
> big man who makes them... sort of like a giant, very serious, very
> demanding. He wants me not to cry, he wants me to have a good job, he
> wants me not to be afraid... he terrorizes me.
>
> (ibid.: 184)

Kast interpreted this patient's inner "terrorist" as a "destructive fantasy of
omnipotence" and related it to borderline psychopathology, especially primal
aggression appearing to defend the self at moments of extreme vulnerability. We
have seen precisely this "counter-dependent" self-attack in the cases reported in
Chapters 1 and 2. Now let us turn to our story to see how mythology represents
the diabolical side of our archetypal self-care system.

FITCHER'S BIRD

Our story starts, like Rapunzel, with the two worlds of reality and imagination
separated – not by a wall this time, but by great distance and a dark forest which
separates the mundane human world of the "daughters" and the "bewitched"
world of the wizard. As we have seen from our case examples, on a personal level,
this separation is the inevitable result of a traumatic failure in those "transitional
processes" of good-enough parental support in early childhood. With this failure,
primal affects of the archetypal psyche do not become personalized and transmuted from their original undifferentiated "magical" form into toned down,
modified human form. As we have also seen, after such a failure in transitional
processes, the imaginal world always presents itself "negatively" and personifies
itself as a diabolical figure who casts a spell over some representative of the
reality-bound ego. So our tale begins with a series of *bewitchments* which we might
think of as the imaginal world's "efforts" to drag the reality-bound ego
(like Persephone's abduction by Hades) into some form of intercourse with the
unconscious. However, without an adequate ego to stand its ground, this inevitably
leads to self-destruction, and there is no more gruesome image of this destruction
than that in the story of Fitcher's Bird. The following is a slightly abridged version
which we will go through in two parts.

THE STORY[1]: PART 1

There was once a wizard who used to take the form of a poor man. He went to houses and begged, and caught pretty girls. No one knew whither he carried them, for they were never seen again. One day he appeared before the door of a man who had three pretty daughters; he looked like a poor weak beggar, and carried a basket on his back, as if he meant to collect charitable gifts in it. He begged for a little food, and when the eldest daughter came out and was just handing him a piece of bread, he did but touch her, and she was forced to jump into his basket. Thereupon he hurried away with long strides, and carried her away into a dark forest to his house, which stood in the midst of it. Everything in the house was magnificent; he gave her whatsoever she could possibly desire and said: "My darling, you will certainly be happy with me, for you have everything your heart can wish for." This lasted a few days, and then he said: "I must journey forth, and leave you alone for a short time; here are the keys of the house; you may go everywhere and look at everything except into one room, which this little key opens and there I forbid you to go on pain of death." He likewise gave her an egg and said: "Preserve the egg carefully for me, and carry it continually about with you, for a great misfortune would arise from the loss of it."

She took the keys and the egg, and promised to obey him in everything. When he was gone, she went all round the house from the bottom to the top, and examined everything. The rooms shone with silver and gold, and she thought she had never seen such great splendor. At length she came to the forbidden door; she wished to pass it by, but curiosity let her have no rest. She examined the key, it looked just like any other; she put it in the keyhole and turned it a little, and the door sprang open. But what did she see when she went in? A great bloody basin stood in the middle of the room, and therein lay human beings, dead and hewn to pieces, and hard by was a block of wood, and a gleaming axe lay upon it. She was so terribly alarmed that the egg which she held in her hand fell into the basin. She got it out and wiped the blood off, but in vain, it appeared again in a moment. She washed and scrubbed, but she could not get it off.

It was not long before the man came back from his journey, and the first things which he asked for were the key and the egg. She gave them to him, but she trembled as she did so, and he saw at once by the red spots that she had been in the bloody chamber. "Since you have gone into the room against my will," said he, "you shall go back into it against your own. Your life is ended." He threw her down, dragged her along by her hair, cut her head off on the block, and hewed her in pieces so that her blood ran on the ground. Then he threw her into the basin with the rest.

"Now I will fetch myself the second," said the wizard, and again he went to the house in the shape of a poor man and begged and caught the second daughter who, like the first, allowed herself to be led away by her curiosity, opened the door of the bloody chamber, looked in, and had to atone for it with her life on the wizard's return. Then he went and brought the third sister, but she was clever and wily. When he had given her the keys and the egg, and had left her, she first put the egg away with great care, and then she examined the house, and at last went into the forbidden room. Alas, what did she behold! Both her dear sisters lay there in the basin, cruelly murdered, and cut into pieces. But she began to gather their limbs together and put them in order, head, body, arms, and legs. And when nothing further was wanting the limbs began to move and unite themselves together, and both the maidens opened their eyes and were once more alive. Then they rejoiced and kissed and caressed each other.

On his arrival, the man at once demanded the keys and the egg, and as he could perceive no trace of any blood on it, he said: "You have stood the test, you shall be my bride." He now had no longer any power over her, and was forced to do whatsoever she desired.

So here we have an archetypal story in which a major role is played by a sadistic, dismembering figure who seems to be an image of unregenerate evil, desiring nothing more than the annihilation of everything human. And yet there are certain interesting features about this wizard that complicate this simple interpretation. The wizard gives his victims an egg, a symbol of life potential, and asks them to protect it. Only the third daughter does this, and setting aside the egg has everything to do with her surviving the bloody chamber and reassembling her dismembered sisters. This egg is an important symbol in the story and appears in many other fairy tales and myths as well. Usually it represents the life principle in its wholeness – the undifferentiated totality, with its potential for creative being, resurrection (Easter) and hope – hope for life in this world (see Cooper, 1978: 60).

One example of the egg as a symbol can be found in a Lithuanian tale called *How the Woodcutter Outwits the Devil and Gets the Princess* (see von Franz, 1974: 227–9) where the egg serves as an important link between the imaginal and real worlds and is somehow related to being able to live creatively in both worlds at the same time. A woodcutter rescues the King's daughter from the Devil deep within the underworld where he is keeping her in a kind of crystal palace similar to the magnificent "gilded cage" in which our wizard keeps his three wives before the crisis moment when their curiosity gets the best of them and they disobey his orders. The woodcutter in the tale transforms himself into an ant and slips into the depths to find the princess. When he finds her she is sitting in the window of the crystal palace. The princess is overjoyed to see him, but then the question becomes (as it does for Rapunzel) how to get out. Finally the princess remembers that in reading the Devil's book, she had remembered that in a certain tree was a diamond egg and if one brought that to the upper world, the crystal palace would come too. (We might think of this as an image of rescuing the imagination from its captivity in the underworld, i.e., in its defensive function as fantasy disconnected from reality.) The woodcutter transforms himself first into various animals in order to rescue the egg and when, finally, this happens, the crystal palace appears, together with the King's daughter. Afterward, they are married and live happily in the crystal palace (here the connection between the imaginal and the real has been made).

Says von Franz,

> the diamond egg is the indestructible thing, par excellence; it is a symbol
> of the Self in its highest indestructability both in Eastern and Western

alchemy and philosophy. . . the egg is in the hands of a destructive underworld. . . it has to be brought up. . . the princess helps. She has read the devil's books on magic and so knows where the egg is and how it can be brought to the surface of the earth.

(ibid.: 234)

In the story of Fitcher's Bird, the evil wizard gives his bewitched wives the key to their own rescue. He tells them to preserve the egg carefully for him and says they should carry it about with them at all times, for a great misfortune would result from the loss of it. The wizard is not, therefore, totally evil, but seems to want someone to survive his own destructiveness. In terms of his own transformation, we might say that the wizard's "test" conceals a secret hope that someday he will find someone strong enough to liberate him from his ghastly power and turn him into a human being! This reminds us that wizards and witches in mythology live a disembodied "daimonic" existence, always isolated from the community, always out of time and space in a magical world, stuck in "enchantment." Consequently, they are always trying, so to speak, to capture real-life humans – usually children or beautiful (vulnerable) maidens because it is their very invulnerability that keeps them perpetually disembodied. We might say they are trying to "embody" – to enter time and space and limitation. Unable to become incarnate except through possession of somebody real, our wizard keeps abducting daughters, desperately seeking embodiment. But true to his nature, he keeps dismembering them, disembodying them again in destructive fantasy, until finally someone meets his cannyness with her own. Somehow, the third daughter's capacity to gain power over the wizard has to do with having taken back some of his split-off aggressive energy (the bloody chamber) without herself being destroyed by it. And he helps make this possible by giving her the egg.

The fact that the wizard provides the key to his own transformation and the transformation of the third wife supports the idea that he is a symbol of what Jung called the "archaic ambivalent Self," before it has been adequately humanized. In the dyadic form of wizard/helpless, innocent wives, the Self in our story is heavily weighted on the side of evil. It is what Erich Neumann calls a "negativized Self" (Neumann, 1976) and its function seems to be a splitting (dismemberment) of the personality rather than its integration. This is not the usual way we think of the Self in Jungian theory. The Self is usually understood to be the ordering and unifying center of the psyche, associated with images of wholeness (circle) or the union of opposites within a superordinate totality (mandala). Experienced as awesome or numinous, the Self is usually identified in Jungian theory with the positive side of the numinosum, manifesting in a full range of symbols associated with the divine in human experience. As coordinator of psychological development, it is seen as the inner agency that organizes the individuation process with the ego as its affiliate. This more optimistic formulation about the Self is all true *except where there has been severe trauma.*

One of the central points in this book has been that the above optimistic understanding of the Self must be modified by an understanding of what happens in the inner world when trauma interrupts normal "incarnational" processes. With trauma, the Self has no chance for transmuting humanization and thus remains archaic. The Self then appears in the form of radical opposites which are at war with one another; good vs. bad, love vs. hate, healing vs. destruction. This way of understanding brings Jungian theory into line with object-relations, with the important addition of Jung's awareness of the numinous dimension of the Self's archaic dynamisms on the one hand, and their mythological equivalents on the other.

In our story, the wizard represents the dark aspect of the Self, although his benevolent light aspect is hinted at in his gesture of providing the egg – also evidence for his apparent wish for transformation. So he is an antinomy – a conjunction of opposites – ambivalent. In mythology, archetypal representatives of the archaic Self's ambivalent nature are always Tricksters. Hermes/Mercurius was Jung's favorite example. *The Trickster is ideally suited to be an agent of transformation because he/she carries both sides of a split in the psyche.* The Trickster is evil and good, loving and hateful, male and female, and thus holds the opposites together while also keeping them differentiated. Shape-shifting at will, he/she is the transformer who also gets transformed.

In those psychologies and mythologies where the mediating Trickster has not yet materialized, the benevolent and malevolent aspects of the Self are split into two figures, black and white, while a third intermediary (often the hero(ine) of the tale) struggles back and forth to create a whole. We see this, for example, in the Greek story of Demeter/Persephone, where Zeus, the sky god, with his spirit-bird the Eagle represents the positive side of the Self and Hades, the captor of souls represents the negative side, with Demeter's daughter Persephone representing (with the help of Mercury) the mediating links between these two opposites. In our Christian tradition the split is between the Heavenly Father or Logos on the one hand and a fallen humanity, in the grip of that fallen angel Lucifer, on the other; Christ himself is the go-between followed by the Holy Spirit. This trinitarian dynamism is repeated in the Egyptian Pantheon, where Osiris represents the positive or light side of the Self, his brother Seth the malignant or dark side, and Isis, the winged feminine principle, with her son Horus provide the mediating links. Like the mediating third daughter of our tale, Isis is also a healer of a dismembered Osiris. She collects his scattered fragments, unites them and inseminates herself, Horus being the issue of this union.

These great archetypal stories give us rich imagery about the process through which the Self unifies and becomes incarnate in history. Throughout, the basic idea is that the Self cannot accomplish this without suffering the opposites on the human level of consciousness. That is to say, it is only in the life of the individual that these great archetypal dynamisms can integrate.

LOVE AND AGGRESSION IN THE EVOLUTION OF THE HEALTHY EGO: WINNICOTT

In non-Jungian psychoanalytic theory we have a different language for this achievement, as we have seen. D. W. Winnicott's understanding of the *processes* in human life which bring about this tremendous accomplishment will help us to understand several aspects of our story – especially how the third wife eventually tricks the wizard by pretending to be a bird, i.e., "Fitcher's Bird."

For depth psychology the basic developmental question is "how does the child develop from the stage of primary unconscious identification to the stage of self–object differentiation?" In Winnicott's language: "How does the child develop a capacity for transitional living, intermediate between reality and fantasy, where symbolic language and play define healthy ego-capacity?" In Freud's language: "How does the child get from omnipotent illusion – the Pleasure Principle – to the Reality Principle?" In Jungian language: "How does the ego separate from the numinous energies of the Self, while still retaining a connection to the Self?" These are the major developmental questions of all depth psychologies, and the answers to these questions have profound clinical implications.

For Winnicott, this achievement seems to depend upon whether both the *libidinal* and the *aggressive* components of the true self have been mirrored as the child matures. In his early writing, Winnicott focuses on the mother's loving devotion and accuracy of empathy in meeting the child's *need* (the libidinal side). In later writing Winnicott emphasizes the crucial importance of the child's *destructive impulses* (the aggressive side) for growing out of an omnipotent symbiosis.

Love

The loving, need-satisfying aspect of this process goes something like this. The newborn infant establishes a need-satisfying union between itself and the mother by suckling at the breast or bottle while being securely held by the pleasurable sensations of the mother's smell, warm touch, tender sounds and adoring gaze. This blissful loving state soon runs into frustration and periods of discomfort owing to the mother's less-than-perfect attention. For example, some feedings are less pleasurable than others – the milk is too cold in the bottle, or the mother is interrupted while feeding the child. Gradually, the infant begins to organize its blissful "good" feeling-experiences around one image of the mother/self and its "bad" feeling-experiences around another image of the mother/self. (In Jungian terms we would say that the archetype is split or ambivalent.) Love or "libidinal need" characterizes the good mother/self and aggression or persecution character-ize the "bad" mother/self. During this process, frustration must not be excessive and "good" feeling-experiences and the good mother archetype must pre-dominate. Because the ego is immature, good and bad feelings cannot be allowed toward the same mother. Only gradually can this occur.

The "good-enough" mother must mirror both love and aggression. When speaking of the loving (libidinal) part of the true self, Winnicott says that the mother mirrors the baby's spontaneous gesture so accurately that "the infant begins to believe in external reality which appears and behaves as if by magic . . . and does not clash [too sharply] with the infant's omnipotence" (Winnicott, 1960a: 146). The hungry baby hallucinates the mother's breast and the mother places her breast exactly in the place of the baby's hallucination.

> When this happens, the infant begins to believe in external reality which appears and behaves as if by magic, and which acts in a way that does not clash with the infant's omnipotence. On this basis the infant can gradually abrogate omnipotence. The True Self has a spontaneity and this has been joined up with the world's events. The infant can now begin to enjoy the illusion of omnipotent creating and controlling and then can gradually come to recognize the illusory element, the fact of playing and imagining. Here is the basis for the symbol which at first is both the infant's spontaneity or hallucination and also the external object created and ultimately cathected.
>
> (Winnicott, 1960a: 146)

When the mother is "good enough," the infant enjoys the illusion of complete correspondence between external reality and the infant's own capacity to create. There is an interpenetrating mix-up between what the mother supplies and what the child initiates from within his own spontaneity. Says Winnicott:

> it is a matter of agreement between us and the baby that we will never ask the question: "Did you conceive of this or was it presented to you from without?" The important point is that no decision on this point is expected. The question is not to be formulated.
>
> (Winnicott, 1951: 12)

Once this primary omnipotence has been experienced adequately, then it is the mother's main task to disillusion the infant, and if the first stage has been "good enough," then the infant can actually come to gain from the experience of frustration, since incomplete adaptation to need makes objects real, that is to say, hated as well as loved.

Winnicott makes clear that this process is not just limited to infancy, but is the project of a lifetime, and we have already suggested that fairy tales are pre-eminently concerned with it.

> the task of reality-acceptance is never completed . . . no human being is free from the strain of relating inner and outer reality. . . .Relief from this strain is provided by an intermediate area of experience. . . which is not challenged (arts, religion, etc.); this intermediate area is in direct continuity with the play area of the small child who is "lost" in play.
>
> (ibid.: 13)

This intermediate area of experience emerges in Part II of the story of Fitcher's Bird, as the third wife gains power over the wizard's diabolical energies and is able to trick the Trickster by pretending to be a bird. The wizard, in turn, seems to go along with these tricks and thereby participates in his own demise in the final fire which burns him up.

Aggression

When he is talking about the aggressive aspect of the infant/mother dyad, Winnicott calls the state from which the infant is moving the state of omnipotence or "object relating." This stage is based entirely on illusory projective identifications. He calls the state toward which the baby is moving "object use" by which he means the capacity of the child to make use of an object "out there" (Winnicott, 1969: 218–28).

Destructiveness is an important part of this differentiation. As the mother begins to separate from the baby, the baby has an impulse to destroy the mother. The question is, will the mother survive the child's ruthlessness without retaliating (survival for Winnicott means simply not changing one's attitude in the face of destructive anger). Here is Winnicott's by now famous description:

> after "subject relates to object" come "subject destroys object" (as it becomes external); and then may come "object survives destruction by the subject." But there may or may not be survival. A new feature thus arrives in the theory of object-relating. The subject says to the object: "I destroyed you," and the object is there to receive the communication. From now on the subject says: 'Hullo object!" "I destroyed you." "I love you." "You have value for me because of your survival of my destruction of you." "While I am loving you I am all the time destroying you in (unconscious) fantasy." Here fantasy begins for the individual. The subject can now use the object that has survived.
>
> (ibid.: 90)

In Winnicott's model, an interior world develops alongside an outer world that can enrich the interior world. The object world can be of use to the baby. He or she can get fat by taking in food from the outside. The baby has relinquished the omnipotent illusion of self-sufficiency by letting his or her love and hate be felt toward the mother. The baby now has "binocular" vision. Depth perspective has suddenly come into being and separation/individuation is occurring.

Love and aggression together

Now, if the same mother can both survive the attack of the aggressive infant and mirror the spontaneous gesture of the loving infant then something miraculous happens. Winnicott would say that the outer world and an interior world are born simultaneously. In other papers, as we have already seen, he described this accomplishment as a process of personalization or "indwelling" (Winnicott, 1970). Winnicott does not speculate about what exactly comes to "dwell" within the body, but we have speculated in these pages about what "it" is, namely, the inviolable personal spirit (daimon) of the individual.

However we describe this process, it clearly has to do with transpersonal, archetypal energies and their gradual, stormy incarnation . Fitcher's Bird is a story about this process. The wizard initially represents the primal archaic infant-Self in both its creative and (here, primarily) destructive aspects. His "magnificent" house in the deep forest is a fantasy palace, representing the split-off positive side of the numinous – still disincarnate but providing a self-soothing refuge for the beleaguered reality-bound ego represented by the man and his three daughters. The problem is that this "refuge" has a hidden room, and therein lies all the evil typical of the dark side of the numinous in its unregenerate form. These two sides of the archaic Self must come together in the "suffering" of the tale's daughters and we see how this happens – two of them are chopped to pieces. Yet somehow the third daughter is able to make use of the positive side of the wizard's numinous energies – the loving "wholeness" dimension provided in his gift of the egg, and this enables her to suffer the dark side of the numinous depicted in his diabolical room without falling prey to its destructive energy.

In our story, the wizard is equivalent to the infantile destructiveness of Winnicott's primary undifferentiated state – a destructiveness turned diabolical by traumatic frustration or abuse (like Yahweh in the Job story). The third wife is in the role of the omnipotent infant's "object" – she is the one who must survive his destruction (as Job did Yahweh's). She does this by finding an advocate within the wizard against himself (as Job did with Yahweh), i.e., she makes use of his egg and his advice about it. She sets it aside, i.e., she preserves her wholeness and her center without splitting as she enters the realm of archetypal destructive affects represented by the terrible hidden room. This centeredness allows her to survive the destruction. The wizard can say "Hullo object – I destroyed you; but you have value for me because you have survived my destruction of you. . . . I love you. . . . you will be my wife."

CLINICAL EXAMPLE

Examples of this quick change from destructivness to "love" are frequently encountered in the clinical situation. A married woman consulted me and told me her husband kept torturing her about an affair she'd had twenty years earlier, claiming that she never made him feel loved or special, and this harping of his was so relentless that it had her in an agitated state where she began actually to develop asthma (she had a tendency to feel guilty for everything). She tried everything to meet his needs and make him feel the special feelings he claimed she denied him. As this did nothing but temporarily assuage his complaints and his cold withdrawals, she began to despair of ever saving her marriage. This went on for a long time until finally through therapy (an egg), she began to realize that separate from the husband's complaints, there was a self-attacking wizard in her own psyche and a hideous room in which she was dismembered regularly by his axe. The husband's complaints, she realized, were merely the outer occasion for a diabolical inner attack against which she was defenseless. Each outer complaint was amplified by the wizard's axe inside herself and thus the husband spoke "the truth" about her – i.e., that she was a bad person! It began to dawn on this compliant patient that if the problem were to be solved with the husband, she would have to first break the spell of this self-destructive inner figure.

Slowly, with the help of psychotherapy, she began to get in touch with her own aggression, i.e., she began to peek into her own hideous room. This meant losing her "innocence" as the divine victim of an unreasonable husband who criticized her all the time, and it meant taking responsibility for her own rage and aggression. Slowly and incrementally, she reached into her own forbidden room, and took some of the dark wizard's energy back into herself. She told her husband that his constant complaints were no longer tolerable and that she wouldn't stay with him if he continued this barrage of blame. She candidly stated that he ought to take some responsibility for his own feelings for her and stop hiding his own lack of feeling behind these whining inflated complaints about not being made to feel special. To my patient's amazement, this newfound assertiveness completely ended his power over her. All his imperious rage evaporated and he suddenly felt very human and loving toward her – as though he had needed her to liberate him from his own inflated bullying wizard.

THE DUAL NATURE OF SACRIFICE IN THE TRANSORMATION OF THE SELF-CARE SYSTEM

In our story the potential marriage between wizard and third daughter represents – as it did in the marriage of the bewitched Rapunzel and her Prince – an ultimate (transitional) relationship between the archetypal world and the human. According to our story, however, this relationship has not been fully realized with the third wife's triumph over the horrible room. This is a beginning, but not the full transformation of the self-care system. The wizard requires more transformation and the third daughter is still caught in his "magnificent" house with her (secretly) reconstituted sisters, i.e., she is still subject to his inflating bewitchment. She must find a way out of this inflated "magnificence" and back into human reality. This struggle is represented in Part II of the story.

We know from observing psychological development in children as well as from the clinical situation, that this process of moving from a traumatically generated inflated "bewitchment" to a realistically anchored human ego is a stormy affair and represents a process in which inflated energies of the archaic Self must be sacrificed. All the world's great religions describe this sacrifice. Usually it is the God who sacrifices himself for man by "coming down" out of the all-embracing plenitude and becoming incarnate in time and space. This also requires reciprocal sacrifices by the God-identified ego (for Jung, the Self-identified ego).

In Jungian language, we talk about the gradual humanization of the archetypal

194

world as participation mystique gives way to consciousness. Edward Edinger envisions this as a cyclical process in which the child's inflated ego is repeatedly confronted by parental discipline, retreats in humiliation, and then is restored to intimate union with the parents. The process goes round and round: inflated act, punishment, humiliation and suffering, restoration of love. Gradually, a differentiated ego – capable of holding the opposites – results (see Edinger, 1972: 41).

It is both a loving and a hateful affair. The child "loves" to expand his human ego-capacities and consciousness, but also "hates" sacrificing the God-like omnipotence of the archetypal realm with which his ego was identified. Marie Louise Von Franz has commented on how this process is simultaneously

> an expansion of consciousness for the ego ... but for the god it is a narrowing experience. In the mirror process it means pulling down a brilliant all-omnipotent god into the miserable cage of human existence. One concept in the Christian theology illustrates this: the process of *Kenosis* (Greek-to-empty) which means that Christ (when with the Father, before His incarnation as the Logos, the Johannist Logos) had the plenitude of the Father, the all pervading oneness with the divine world, without definiteness. As St. Paul writes: He emptied himself – *ekonose heauton* (Philippians II: 7 R.S.V.). He emptied himself to become a mortal, emptied Himself of his all-embracing plenitude and one-ness to become definite.
>
> (von Franz, 1970: 10)

In other words, ego-growth entails a dual sacrifice – both infantile and inflated trends at the same time. In the dyad of our wizard and his "innocent" childlike wives living in unknowing magnificence, we might say that both sides must undergo a sacrifice. We have seen that this dyadic structure of Protector/Persecutor and innocent child-client is the basic architecture of the self-care system. Its energies are, on the one hand, incredibly inflated, imperious, and "royal" – a king or a queen and, on the other, equally infantile, innocent and victimized – a divine victim. As this "king/baby" structure undergoes integration, both sides of it are sacrificed to an intermediate humanity – limited, and capable of personal responsibility. The daughter's spellbound "innocence" is lost in the hideous room, the wizard's spell-casting powers are lost as the third daughter re-members her sisters and through this act, now gains "total power over him."

FITCHER'S BIRD: PART 2

"Oh, very well," said the third daughter "you shall first take a basketful of gold to my father and mother, and carry it yourself on your back; in the meantime I will prepare for the wedding." Then she ran to her sisters, whom she had hidden in a little chamber, and said "The moment has come when I can save you. The wretch shall himself carry you home again, but as soon as you are at home send help to me." She put both of them in a basket and covered them quite over with gold, so that nothing of them was to be seen. Then she called in the wizard and said to him: "Now carry the basket away, but I shall look through my little window and watch to see if you stop on the way to stand or to rest."

The wizard raised the basket on his back and went away with it, but it weighed him down so heavily that the sweat streamed from his face. Then he sat down and wanted to rest awhile, but immediately one of the girls in the basket cried: "I am looking through my little window, and I see that you are resting. Will you go on at once?" He thought it was his bride who was talking to him; and he got up on his legs again. Once more he was going to sit down, but instantly she cried: "I am looking through my little window, and I see that you are resting. Will you go on directly?" And whenever he stood still, she cried this, and then he was forced to go onwards, until at last, groaning and out of breath, he took the basket with the gold and the two maidens into their parents' house. At home, however, the bride prepared the marriage-feast, and sent invitations to the friends of the wizard. Then she took a skull with grinning teeth, put some ornaments on it and a wreath of flowers, carried it upstairs to the garret-window, and let it look out from thence. When all was ready, she got into a barrel of honey, and then cut the feather-bed open and rolled herself in it, until she looked like a wondrous bird, and no one could recognize her. Then she went out of the house, and on her way she met some of the wedding-guests, who asked:

"O, Fitcher's bird, how com'st thou here?"
"I come from Fitcher's house quite near."
"And what may the young bride be doing?"
"From cellar to garret she's swept all clean,
And now from the window she's peeping, I ween."

At last she met the bridegroom, who was coming slowly back. He, like the others, asked:

"O, Fitcher's bird . . . etc."
. . . .
"And now from the window she's peeping, I ween."

The bridegroom looked up, saw the decked-out skull, thought it was his bride, and nodded to her, greeting her kindly. But when he and his guests had all gone into the house, the brothers and kinsmen of the bride, who had been sent to rescue her, arrived. They locked all the doors of the house, that no one might escape, set fire to it, and the wizard and all his crew had to burn.

This part of the story describes the final transformation of the self-care system and its two constituent personifications, the third daughter and her bridegroom the wizard. The third daughter is liberated and the wizard immolated in the fire. We note with interest that the Trickster element, heretofore the prerogative of the wizard, now defines the bride' way of operating. First there is her trick of hiding the sisters under gold in his basket, then her trick of the voice harrassing him from afar on his journey, then her trick of luring all the wizard's friends into the house with wedding invitations, the trick of the decorated skull in the window, and finally her trick of honey and feathers which disguises her as Fitcher's Bird so she can

196

escape. If we wish to understand this second part of the tale, we will therefore have to come to terms with the psychological meaning of this Trickster element and its function as both disguise and defense in transmuting the terrible energies of the archetypal dimension into human form.

We have already explored the dynamic significance of the Trickster archetype in Chapter 1 in our discussion of Mary and her food daimon. There we saw primarily the diabolical side of the Trickster – his capacity for splitting in two (dissociation), for trance, for attacking the connections (links) among the components of experience, and in general, for self-destructive regression. However, we also noted that the Trickster, as a threshold deity, is equally concerned with mediating two sides of a paradox and, therefore, in his positive incarnation, might be thought of as a kind of dynamic personification of what Winnicott called "transitional phenomena." As an antinomy, he holds together a pair of opposites and constitutes the missing "third." He is ideally suited, therefore, to the task of *mediating* the opposing archetypal dynamisms that sweep over the psyche after trauma. In short, he is both *diabolical* (splitting) and *symbolical* (integrating) in his function. In his diabolical form, he severs connections in the inner world in order to prevent the unbearable from being experienced. In his symbolical form, he makes whole what was previously fragmented and does this by linking up the unconscious world with the ego through the symbol. Provided that the previously traumatized ego is now strong enough to "bear in mind" the full impact of its experience, the Trickster is freed of his diabolical dismembering role and now contributes to individuation and creative living.

In Part II of our fairy tale, the Trickster's positive, mediating function is emphasized as the third wife, now strong enough to have power over the wizard, is able to employ tricks and disguises in order to link her diabolical husband's bewitched world with her own world of reality. She sends her re-membered sisters back to her parents' home on the back of the wizard who dismembered them in the first place – and in a basket – the same basket into which these daughters jumped at the beginning when he "did but touch them." Psychologically, this is an example of how the very power which threatens the immature or weak ego is, at a later time, employed in its service.

The wizard's suffering during his trip with the heavy basket is a humorous reversal of the suffering he has caused the sisters and represents the gradual sacrifice of his transpersonal powers. Now he must sweat and struggle, knees buckling under the load, carrying his "cross," as it were, to his final destiny in the immolating fire. And all the while the "voice" of his bride, with her new-found power over him, harasses him and goads him on, meting out brutality to the brutal, meanness to the mean. Psychologically, this "voice" in its negative form is what Jung called the "negative animus" and is frequently experienced as an overcritical, perfectionistic inner taskmaster that drives a person forward and is never satisfied with human imperfection. This is the voice which, like the negative animus, "chops a woman to pieces" (see Asper, 1991), and so the wizard, who previously personified this negative force in the psyche now falls victim to the same critical harassment.

The hidden sisters in the basket of gold are supposed to send help to the third daughter, still in the bewitched mansion of the wizard. So the two sisters become the link between the encapsulated world of the wizard's lair and the world of reality. The help they eventually bring (brothers and kinsmen) we might think of as the positive side of the masculine They lock the wizard in his own house with all his guests and set it on fire. This is positive masculine aggression in the service of ego-development, and this positive side of the masculine has been notably missing in our story, just as it was in the story of Rapunzel. The father of our three daughters has apparently left them extremely vulnerable to enchantment by the negative, diabolical side of the masculine with its archetypal aggression. Psychologically, this is the inevitable legacy of either outright neglect by the father or his failure to set limits on the daughters and thereby provide the opportunity for working through aggression interpersonally. In other words, both love and aggression must be experienced toward the same father if a woman is to have a "whole" image of the masculine and hence be "immunized" from infection by the negative masculine in the form of bewitchment.

OVERCOMING THE WIZARD WITH THE SYMBOL

By far the most intriguing trick played on the wizard by the third daughter is her "transformation" of herself into a bird – Fitcher's Bird – in order to escape the bewitched mansion. First, she puts a decorated skull in the window to represent a decoy of herself to the wizard and guests. The idea that they all mistake a bridal "death's head" for the bride makes the story's point that to be a bride of this wizard is to be dead. As the wizard and his guests all represent death, they recognize one of their own, so to speak, and think that the bride is at home, when in reality she is making her escape, disguised as a bird.

Covered with honey and feathers, the true bride is "unrecognizable" except as Fitcher's Bird – a bird who converses with the guests and wizard on the road that connects the world of bewitchment and the world of reality. It is important to realize that the third daughter has not transformed herself into a bird here (as Asper suggests) but is *pretending* to be a bird, and a miraculous talking bird at that. In her bird form she is neither human nor bird but both. Embodying the symbolic function of transitional reality, she participates in both reality and fantasy. When she meets the wizard and his guests on the road, they do not question whether she is a human or a bird. They take her transitional form for granted. As Winnicott says, you do not ask the baby whether he found the breast or created it – as transitional reality it is always both.

In this shape-shifting fantasy bird form, the third daughter successfully tricks the wizard and makes her escape homeward. Psychologically, this suggests that in dealing with the terrible energies of the archetypal psyche, transitional forms and symbolic processes are essential. The storms of affect emerging from the archaic layers of the psyche are only transformed if the tension between reality and imagination can be held by the ego and, if this is accomplished, then a creative image (symbol) may provide the transitional link between the two worlds, i.e., may provide a meaning which allows us to "escape" the splitting dynamisms of the archetypal world and find our way "home" to a human world, graced with the vital energies of the imaginal world.

This process, which is everyone's struggle to individuate, is especially difficult after trauma has set the psyche off in the direction of archaic splitting and rendered the ego weak. Malignant forms of transference-regression develop and threaten to undermine the patient's growth. None the less, the process gets some important help from what Jung called the "transcendent function" of the psyche itself. By this he meant the innate tendency of the psyche to give form to undifferentiated, chaotic "stuff" from the primary process and to represent it to consciousness in the form of dreams and other imaginal products. So, for Jung, transitional processes occurred not only between infant and mother, or even patient and therapist; they define the inner relations between ego and Self. Unfortunately, the inner process is never successful if there has not been a "good-enough" outer one. When trauma prevents this, transitional relatedness must be reconstituted in psychotherapy.

A crucial element in this reconstituted transitional relatedness is a playful, imaginal space between therapist and patient. Expressive arts of all kinds must be used in therapy with victims of trauma – not just talk-therapy oriented to recovering insight and memory. The work must be aligned with the psyche's natural integrative linking of affect and image. When we have the affect, we look for an image... when we have the image, we seek its associated affect. In order to do this we have to be able to play with the patient in a variety of modalities – not just verbal ones.

Jung came to this understanding as far back as 1916 when his patients would bring in a certain mood or present a confusing dissociated affect which did not seem to make sense in light of current experience. Jung said:

> I therefore took up a dream image or an association of the patient's, and, with this as a point of departure, set him the task of elaborating or developing his theme by giving free rein to his fantasy. This, according to individual taste and talent, could be done in any number of ways, dramatic, dialectic, visual, acoustic, or in the form of dancing, painting, drawing, or modeling. [Finally] I was able to recognize that in this method I was witnessing the spontaneous manifestation of an unconscious process which was merely assisted by the technical ability of the patient, and to which I later gave the name "individuation process".... In many cases, this brought a large measure of therapeutic success, which encouraged both myself and the patient to press forward despite the baffling nature of the results. I felt bound to insist that they were baffling, if only to stop myself from framing, on the basis of certain theoretical assumptions, interpretations which I felt were

not only inadequate but liable to prejudice the ingenious productions of the patient. . . . And so it is with the hand that guides the crayon or brush, the foot that executes the dance-step, with the eye and the ear, with the word and the thought: a dark impulse is the ultimate arbiter of the pattern, an unconscious a priori precipitates itself into plastic form. . . . Over the whole procedure there seems to reign a dim foreknowledge not only of the pattern but of its meaning. Image and meaning are identical; and as the first takes shape, so the latter becomes clear. . . the pattern needs no interpretation: it portrays its own meaning.

(Jung, 1947: paras 400–2)

To return to our story, we find the third daughter embodying this transcendent function as Fitcher's Bird. Why, we might ask, as a bird? The first thing that occurs to us is that the bird is a natural development from the egg. If the egg represents potential life in its original, primordial, undifferentiated wholeness, then the bird clearly represents a differentiation of that original wholeness and a transcendence of it as transcendent personal spirit. Cooper reminds us that fabulous birds depict the celestial spiritual realms and those powers opposing the chthonic serpent – in other words, they are thieromorphic images associated (mostly) with the positive side of the Self, opposing its negative, diabolical or chthonic side as depicted in our wizard (see Cooper, 1978).

In other mythology, birds are messengers of the gods, always associated with the light, positive side of the numinous. The Christ child often is depicted as holding a bird and, according to Virgil (Aeneid, 6. 242), the entrance to the underworld is called "Aornos" (birdless land) by the Greeks. Because of the bird's significance as a transitional being, plying the space between the human world and the divine, bird robes and feathers were frequently worn by shamans in their mediumistic rites. In Egyptian mythology, the Ka-soul represented as a bird with human head, is depicted leaving the mouths of the dying, and souls in the underworld wear garments of bird-feathers (see de Vries, 1984: 48).

So our heroine, the third daughter, makes her escape disguised as the magical symbol of transcendence itself – the winged personal spirit – both real and imaginal, human and divine. In this evocative symbolic form she links the two worlds that were originally separated in our tale: the mundane human world on the one hand, and the magical primordial world in its negative "bewitched" form, on the other. The formation of this link (re-ligeo) is coincident with the final sacrifice of the dark side of the Self's energies in the fire – that "agent of transmutation," according to Heraclitus, from which all things derive and to which all things return. In the personal development of the individual, this development represents that moment when the unconscious begins to constellate positively and the sacralized ego, now liberated from the Self's protective/persecutory defenses, comes under the guidance of the whole Self and begins the process of creative living.

10

PRINCE LINDWORM AND TRANSFORMATION OF THE DAIMONIC THROUGH SACRIFICE AND CHOICE

This story, like the story of Fitcher's Bird, depicts a dreadful diabolical form of the Self in its role as archetypal defense or self-care system, and concerns itself with how that defense can be (1) survived, and (2) transformed by the feminine – again in this case, by the feminine appearing as the "third." Our story has been discussed by von Franz as depicting possession by the Self "such as is found in borderline cases where the complex of the ego and the archetype of the Self have been contaminated, so that both become blurred. . . and there is no adequate polarization of the psyche" (von Franz, 1980b: 79, 83). While this description is true as far as it goes, there is no mention in von Franz's analysis of archetypal defenses and no developmental theory to describe how this "contamination" with the dark side of the Self happens and what its implications are for clinical practice. We hope to illuminate these issues in the pages that follow.

PRINCE LINDWORM[1]: THE STORY

There was once a King and his lovely Queen, who lived in blissful happiness, but for one thing. They had no children. One day the Queen, in great sorrow, consulted an old crone who lived in the forest and was told the remedy for her sterility. She should place a small goblet upside down in her garden, the crone said, and the next morning she would find two roses, one white and one red growing underneath it on a single stalk. If she ate the red rose she would have a boy; if the white rose, a girl. In any case she had to choose one or the other. If she ate both a catastrophe would result.

The Queen was ecstatic and did as the old woman said, but after eating the white rose, she got greedy, forgot her promise, and ate the second rose also. When it came time for the birth, twins were born, but the first-born was a hideous Lindworm or serpent. The Queen was terribly frightened when she saw him, but he snaked out of sight with one quick lithe movement, so that no-one else saw him. Besides, right after the Lindworm came a fine son who was so wonderful and handsome and made everyone so happy that the Queen lived her life as though the Lindworm had never been.

Many blissful years later, the handsome Prince set off in a royal coach in search

201

of adventure and a wife. No sooner had he reached the crossroads, however, than an enormous Lindworm, its fangs more deadly than lightning, reared before him and hissed, "A bride for me before a bride for you!" (7) The Prince fled back to the castle and the King was about to send out an army of men to fight the beast, when the Queen thought it time to confess that the Lindworm had only claimed what was rightfully his – he was the elder child and had a right to marry first.

Thereupon began a "nine days' wonder and a ten-day debate" (7) after which the King concluded that if the Prince was ever to marry, they'd better find a bride for Prince Lindworm first. This was easier said than done, but the King sent to the most distant countries he could think of in search of a Princess. The first princess arrived and unknowingly got involved in the wedding festivities until it was too late to back out, and when morning came there was nothing left of her and the Lindworm had the look of one sleeping off a good meal. "After a short but respectful period" (7) the Prince rode out again, only to be confronted once again by the Lindworm, more impatient than ever! Again a Princess was found and she too was not permitted to see her bridegroom till it was too late. After the wedding night, she too was only a bulge in the Lindworm's belly. Again the Prince rode out and again at the crossroads was stopped by his brother Lindworm. By this time the King was beside himself. No more princesses could be found and the King in desperation, decided to ask one of his lowly shepherds who lived in a tumbledown cottage for his daughter as the Lindworm's next wife. The shepherd refused but the King would not take no for an answer so the lovely girl was told of her fate.

The shepherd's daughter was beside herself with grief. She wept and ran through the woods bleeding and desolate until she came to an old crone – seemingly the same one who had advised the Queen in her sorrow twenty years earlier – and to this old woman she poured out her plight. "Dry your eyes, my child – and do exactly as I tell you," said the crone. "When the wedding is over, you must ask to be attired in ten silken shifts and when the Lindworm asks you to take off your shift, you must bid him shed a skin. When this happens nine times, he will be nothing but a writhing mass of flesh and you must then whip him soundly with whips dipped in lye. When this is done, bathe him in sweet milk, and lastly you must take him in your arms and hold him close, if only for one brief moment" (11). "Ugh," cried the shepherd's daughter, "I can never do that!" "It is that or be eaten," chided the crone and she disappeared.

So when the wedding was over and the horror of the Lindworm was there before her in the bedchamber – half man, half snake, the repulsive creature turned to her and said "fair maiden, shed a shift." "Prince Lindworm," she replied, "cast a skin!" "No one has dared tell me to do that before," he hissed angrily, and for a moment she thought he would swallow her down, but instead he began to moan and groan and writhe until a long strong snakeskin lay on the floor. She drew off her first shift and spread it on top of the skin. And so it went, despite his protests and his groans and his writhing and slobbering until in the end he was a raw, thick, slimy mass, "now rearing, now rolling, now slithering all over the floor" (14). Then the shepherd's daughter took the whips, dipped them in lye as she was told and whipped him with all her might and main. When she was exhausted, she washed him in fresh milk and then took him grovelling in her arms and held him close for one brief moment before she fell asleep.

Next morning the King and his courtiers came in sorrow to the wedding chamber – afraid to enter. At length the King opened the door. There was the lovely shepherd's daughter, all dewy with the dawn. And in her arms was no Lindworm, "but a quicksilver Prince as Handsome as the grass is green." The palace echoed with happiness at this discovery and after the rejoicing came a wedding celebration such as had never been seen before or since. Thereafter, the Prince and his new Princess reigned happily ever after.

THE MOTIF OF THE CHILD AND CHILDLESSNESS

Our story, like that of Rapunzel and many other tales, begins in a state of childlessness which gives rise to grief and longing. Jung has dealt extensively with the psychology of the child archetype, where he makes clear that the motif of the child, when it appears in symbolic material such as our story, means far more than the concrete, literal "child." The *child motif*, says Jung, is almost always associated with something miraculous or divine – the wonder-child whose origins are extraordinary (virgin birth) and whose deeds are somehow associated with redemption of the darkness and recovery of the light. As such, says Jung,

> it is a symbol which unites the opposites; a mediator, bringer of healing, that is, one who makes whole.... It represents the strongest, the most ineluctable urge in every being, namely the urge to realize itself. It is, as it were, an incarnation of *the inability to do otherwise*.
>
> (Jung, 1949; paras 278, 289; emphasis in original)

So the child, then, is a boundary concept, stretching between the potential wholeness of the Self and its *actualization* in the ego's world of reality. It represents the eternal in time. It links up the real and imaginal worlds and holds the promise that the imperishable numinous world might find life in this world. It is for this reason that the child is mythology's almost universal answer to the question "Does God manifest himself in history?" As Moses, as Christ, as Bhudda, as Krishna, the answer is always the divine child. In terms of our previous discussion, we could say that it represents symbolically the potential for realization of the inviolable personal spirit or Self in "this life," i.e., in the personal history of the individual.

So it is no wonder, then, that so many fairy tales begin with the desire for a child. With the world of reality separated from the psychoid, magical world in which transpersonal powers reside, there is no spontaneity, no life, and no genuine possibility for personal growth. Things dry up. There is no depth, no hope. We have seen that precisely this split between ego and Self is the legacy of early trauma.

Our story reports that in this condition, the barren Queen consults the old lcrone, representing the ancient prophetic wisdom of the psyche in its archaic "uncivilized" form. We note that not only the Queen's womb is barren, but her whole attitude is shot through with despair. She complains to the old crone, "Alas,

There is no one in the world can help me." The old crone replies that "no ill is without its remedy" – a statement which itself embodies the hope symbolized by the longed-for child.

Here the Queen's attitude is typical of those traumatized patients who arrive in the analyst's office depressed and forsaken by those in their lives who, as children, they desperately needed to depend upon. In this situation, the therapist holds out the same hope as the old crone – "no ill is without its remedy." This hope in a trusted companion, is often just enough to get the barren psyche dreaming again, even though this renewed sense of the possible is only the first stage in a two-stage process, as we have seen in our previous analysis. Unfortunately, in the second stage, the hope generated in the first stage must eventually be "disillusioned" if a full incarnation of the personal spirit is to occur and a complete working through of the patient's early wounding is to be achieved.

REFUSAL TO CHOOSE

The first thing the old crone tells the Queen is that if she wants a child, *she will have to choose* between the two roses that she will find growing on a single stalk under a goblet the next morning. This task seems simple enough, but the Queen "forgets" her promise, and proceeds to "have her cake and eat it too" – she eats the second rose also. Choice means limitation in time and space, and in the Queen's action, we have a refusal of such limitation and a preference for the seemingly unlimited possibilities of the situation; perhaps she will have both a boy and girl. This is tantamount to a preference for fantasy as Winnicott defines it (as distinct from imagination), and we have already seen how regularly the psyche turns diabolical when the link with real living is severed in the traumatized patient's preference for fantasy. A preference for fantasy is perhaps the core problem in all addictions. For our Queen it was "one more rose," for the addict it may be one more drink, or vial of cocaine. This compulsive preference for self-soothing fantasy and a concomitant refusal to live within human reality and to suffer its limitations constellate the unconscious negatively and bring on the daimon.

We saw this same issue of choice and its daimonic consequences in the story of Eros and Psyche, where Eros admonishes the pregnant Psyche, who is blissfully unconscious in his crystal palace, not to tell her sisters anything about his true identity: "If you keep my secret in silence, your child shall be a god; if you divulge it, a mortal" (Neumann, 1956: 18). In other words, you must choose whether to stay in the fantasy world of the gods or not. There are consequences. Like the Queen of our story, Psyche initially has trouble making the choice that would rupture her "oneness" with the fantasy world of Eros and the potential "divinity" of her child. She too prefers the endless possibilities of numinous fantasy, until finally she chooses mortality with its knowledge of evil as well as good. This comes about, as we have seen, through an encounter with the dark side of the numinous, i.e., by realizing its devouring snake-like aspect – the price one pays for not choosing to live.

The connection between a failure to choose and the takeover of psychic life by daimons is given beautiful expression in some remarks made by author Isaac Beshevis Singer in an interview for *Parabola* Magazine. Singer remarks:

I would say that behind all my ideas . . . is the freedom of choice. I feel that the freedom of choice is the very essence of life. We have one great gift from God and this is to choose. And we always indulge in choosing. If we pay attention to one thing, we have chosen to pay attention to it. If we love somebody, we have chosen this person for love. This is in every act of humanity. To me, God is freedom. And nature, to me, is necessity. . . . When people leave free choice, the demons appear. The demons are in a way the dark side of nature which we choose. If we stop completely believing in our power [of choice], then other powers can come upon us. In other words, the demon to me is a negative side of free choice. Demons come when people resign themselves . . . when people say to themselves, "I'm not going to make any choices anymore. I will just let the powers work for themselves." It is then that the demon is bound to appear. The danger is always there – like a medical doctor who will tell you that the microbes are always there in your mouth and in your stomach, and if you become weak, they begin to multiply and become very strong. . . . Just as we are medically surrounded by dangerous microbes, so our spirit has always to fight melancholy and disbelief and viciousness and cruelty and all kinds of things.

At this point the interviewer asks, "Why melancholy?" and Singer replies:

Oh, but the very essence of demons is melancholy. Because it's the very opposite of hope. . . . I have sympathy for everyone who suffers and lives. Because we are all living in a great, great struggle, whether we realize it or not. Sometimes we realize it. This is a very difficult thing – we very often say how difficult life is. . . . We have to go through this kind of struggle. In a way, the hope is that life does not last forever, the crisis does not last forever, and behind all this crisis, behind all this darkness, there is a great light. We have to struggle, but we are not lost, because the powers which have created us are actually great and benign powers.

(Singer, 1981: 73)

THE MELANCHOLIC WORLD OF FANTASY IN THE SELF-CARE SYSTEM

Like the Queen who refuses to choose and embodies a melancholic disposition, we often find in psychotherapy with the victims of early trauma, a kind of inner addiction to fantasy which leaves them in a permanent state of melancholy. In these patients, aggressive energies which should be available for adaptation are thwarted in their outward expression and take the form of archaic self-attack and self-criticism. Thus, suffering from terrible and incessant inner persecution, these patients seek out "heavenly" states, such as fusional identification with others, or they "space out" into diffused undifferentiated states of melancholic self-soothing in order to stay unembodied and away from the traumatic affect. These patients often spend time alone crying, but their tears are a peculiar form of self-soothing. They are crying and holding themselves at the same time. They do not know how to cry with others. Sadness and wistful longing are a continual ache in their hearts. But none of this ever brings any empathy from outside because *these patients often do not know what they are crying about* and whenever they try to communicate it to others, it breaks down. It is all a very complicated, intricately nuanced sad story they are telling themselves but it remains self-contained, inflated, disembodied ,and one-dimensional. And the tragic irony is that all this suffering is designed to prevent another kind of suffering – the suffering of coming into being in time and space which always entails a *sacrifice* of fantasy.

JULIA KRISTEVA AND THE "BLACK SUN"

Julia Kristeva, the French linguist and Lacanian psychoanalyst has chillingly described the melancholy state engineered by our self-care system as a "presence" in the inner world of depressed patients. She uses the image of the "Black Sun" to describe it (Kristeva, 1989). This inner presence, she says, is really an *absence*, a "light without representation" (ibid.: 13), a sadness which is "the most archaic expression of an unsymbolizable unnameable narcissistic wound" (ibid.: 14) which becomes the depressed person's sole object of attachment . . . an object they tame and cherish for lack of another. She calls this non-object "The Thing." Describing patients who exploit this "Thing" Kristeva says:

> [all symbolic] language starts with [entails] a negation [transcendence] (*Verneinung*) of loss, along with the depression occasioned by mourning. "I have lost an essential object . . . (my mother)" is what the speaking being seems to be saying. "But no, I have found her again in signs, or rather since I consent to lose her I have not lost her (that is the negation), I can recover her in language."
>
> (ibid.: 43)

> Depressed persons, on the contrary, disavow the negation: they cancel it out, suspend it, and nostalgically fall back on the real object of their loss [what Kristeva calls "The Thing" – the "non-lost object"] . . . . The denial (*Verleugnung*) of negation would thus be the exercise of an impossible mourning, the setting up of a fundamental sadness and an artificial, unbelievable language, cut out of the painful background that is not accessible to any signifier. The result is that traumatic memories are not

repressed but constantly evoked as the denial of negation prevents the work of repression. . . [and symbol-formation, which depends upon the psyche's creative elaboration].

(ibid.: 46)

Persons in despair become hyperlucid by nullifying negation. [Words] will appear to them as heavily, violently arbitrary . . . . The depressed speak of nothing, they have nothing to speak of.

(ibid.: 51)

The dead language they speak, which foreshadows their suicide, conceals a Thing buried alive. The latter, however, will not be translated in order that it not be betrayed; it shall remain walled up within the crypt of the inexpressible affect, anally harnessed, with no way out.

(ibid.: 53)

I have assumed depressed persons to be atheistic – deprived of meaning, deprived of values. . . . Nevertheless, those in despair are mystic – adhering to the preobject, not believing in Thou, but mute and steadfast devotees of their own inexpressible container. It is to this fringe of strangeness that they devote their tears and jouissance.

(ibid.: 14)

EXCURSUS ON THE DEFENSIVE USES OF THE NUMINOUS

Kristeva's comment that depressed patients are really "mystical devotees" to their own inexpressible "Thing" provides us with the opportunity to discuss one of the most important aspects of the so-called "schizoid" defense, namely, the access it provides to numinous experience. Jung himself based his definition of religion on Rudolf Otto's apt term "the numinosum," which is that peculiar alteration in consciousness brought about by the ego's contact with transpersonal psychic energies which overwhelm it – whether these energies be daimonic or sublime. For Jung, the experience of the numinous was much more than the "oceanic experience," or the "primary process" described by Freud. It was not only an artefact of early infantile mental processes but a category of experience central to the deepest apprehension of human existence and central to all healing and transformation. Man and woman, for Jung, were not *homo sapiens* but *homo religiosus*.

This acknowledgement of the numinous as a category of humankind's archetypal experience is at once Jungian psychology's greatest strength and, simultaneously, its greatest weakness and a source of endless misunderstanding – even by some Jungian analysts. Jung was fond of talking about the numinous and distinguishing his method in reference to it. In a letter, for example, he says:

the main interest in my work is not concerned with the treatment of neuroses but rather with the approach to the numinous. But the fact is that the approach to the numinous is the real therapy and inasmuch as you attain to the numinous experiences you are released from the curse of pathology.

(Jung, 1973: 376–7)

This statement stands in need of some critical reflection and clarification. What does Jung mean when he says that if you "attain to numinous experiences you are released from the curse of pathology"? This seems to imply that if we could just find a way to tap into the transpersonal realm, healing would occur. Yet we know full well that many troubled people are positively addicted to the positive, light-giving side of numinous experience (and equally terrified of the numinous's dark aspect). Numinous experience dissolves ego-boundaries and therefore many people with shaky ego-boundaries (or perhaps ego-boundaries that were falsely established to begin with) seek it out to escape the pain and humiliation that inevitably accompany the disillusioning process of coming into being as a limited, time-bound, mortal, definite, embodied individual.

We would call this a defensive use of the numinous and we have seen how prominent a feature this is in the establishment of the archetypal self-care system. It has been my intention to show that this defense is in itself a rather miraculous creation, but a deadly one as well. Jung did not sufficiently emphasize this daimonic, diabolical side of the numinous and its insidious, corrosive effect within the world of fantasy. He described it beautifully as the ambivalence of the archaic Godhead, but left the problem in the realm of religion, with its clinical applications to be worked out by those of us who follow.

Fortunately, Jung says, the "approach to the numinous" is the real therapy (not the numinous itself), and we have tried to indicate that this approach is, for the traumatized patient, a two-stage process in which the negative, daimonic side of the numinous is experienced first (as bewitchment) and that only later, after the secret daimonic element in the self-care system has been unmasked and confronted, can the positive numinous dimension of life enter a relationship with the ego. In our story of Eros and Psyche, this "third" (symbolic) possibility is named "Joy" and it defines a new birth at the end of a great struggle involving many sacrifices – sacrifices of identification with numinous, archetypal realities. Such is psychotherapy with those individuals whose archetypal self-care system has managed to assure their survival but which now must be given up if the reality ego is to be strengthened. In this work, ultimately we hope to promote the growth of an ego strong enough to house a *relationship* to the numinous *as a whole*, light and dark – a relationship which honors the sacred dimension of our spiritual as well as our material/physical lives.

Freud said the task of analysis was to transform neurotic suffering (with its domination by the pleasure principle) into everyday misery. Freud was right, but, as Jung saw, this is only half the story. What Freud did not realize is that bound up in the wishful fantasies and blissful longings of the neurotic's unrealistic hopes are also universal (archetypal) unconscious fantasies, and these are both angelic

208

and daimonic. Granted, the traumatized ego is initially identified with and inflated by these in an archetypal self-care system, but these universal inner "persons" are the first incarnational stages of the inviolable personal spirit's longing for embodiment and incarnation in "this world." The sacrifice of identification with these structures, which both Freud and Jung understood as essential, does not unmask the numinous as an *illusion* (Freud), but breaks the husk of the inflated ego's *identity* with the numinous and opens the way for surrender, gratitude, and a *relationship* with the numinous – both dark and light – which is the essence of the religious life.

PRINCE LINDWORM AS A TWIN

Returning now to our story, we notice that after the Queen's failure to choose one rose or the other, not one child, but a very aberrant pair of twins is born. It is of interest that most famous twins in mythology are the product of an immortal father and a mortal mother, so twins represent a link (*hieros gamos*) between heaven and earth. Apollo–Artemis, Castor–Pollux, Romulus–Remus are all products of such a union and for this reason they were understood to have special powers, giving them a numinous quality, so the potential ego–Self relationship is already intimated in the new twin-birth, although in the present form this dual unity is grotesque and will have to be transformed.

We also note with interest that in mythology, the birth of the divine child is almost always accompanied by the simultaneous emergence of a daimonic killing factor that wants to prevent the child from living. In our story, this daimonic killer, born alongside the "good" child is the Lindworm himself, but in many myths it is a diabolical king or wicked ruler whose "old order" is threatened, such as King Herod at the birth of the Christ child. Similar threats to the new life of the hero or divine child can be found in the birth legends of Dionysus, Perseus, Oedipus, Moses, Krishna, and others. This archetypal motif describes the diabolical side of our self-care system – that resistance to change embodied in the dark side of the Self, which must slowly be transformed if renewal is to occur.

In our story, the Lindworm side of the twinship duality carries the loathsome aspects of the Self and he is ignored by the mother, who prefers only the positive aspects of the emerging numinous "child." In this state of unknowing bliss, she lives for many years with her handsome new son – just as Psyche lived for many years with Eros in his crystal palace, enjoying the nectar of his love but never confronting his dragon-like imprisonment of her, lulled as she was by the trance of his love – until finally she lights a lamp and prepares to kill her snake-like imprisonment.

This idea of a one-dimensional happiness on the surface with a secret death-dealing Lindworm underneath is the condition of denial in which every addicted personality finds itself. It is precisely described in all the fairy tales we have examined – in Rapunzel's tower, Psyche's crystal palace, the wizard's miraculous cottage, and now in the twenty years of bliss during which the Queen avoids the responsibility for the choices (or failed choices) she has made. Busily making wedding plans for her second-born son, the Queen forgets that her whole life is hemmed in by the repressed and by now grotesque aggressive power of the daimon-Lindworm snaked around an oak tree on the threshold of her kingdom. With him on the threshold nothing can get out into life and nothing can come in either. Things are sterile all over again. Everything is made to appear as if the daimon does not exist, but sooner or later his destructive effects must be confronted.

This crucial moment happens in our tale when finally the second son rides off to be married, is confronted by his Lindworm brother, and reports all this to his father. It is interesting that only when someone wants to leave the happy kingdom behind, i.e., *separate*, does the Lindworm become a problem. This is the seductive aspect of the self-care system. As long as the insular world overseen by the diabolical part of the self-care system is maintained, everything is OK, except for the already noted chronic state of melancholy. But separation/individuation is another story. This requires aggression and, if aggression is missing in the ego, then it involves a confrontation with aggression coming from the archetypal level of the unconscious. Such is the nature of our Lindworm. He does nothing but hiss and gnash his terrible teeth and block the passage out of the kingdom.

When the second son comes back hastily from the gates of the kingdom with his story, the Lindworm can be denied no longer. The Queen finally confesses both his existence and his first-born rights as heir to the throne. This is the critical "moment" in our story – equivalent in importance to Psyche lighting her lamp, because it represents a full recognition of the dark side of the Self and its rightful place in the overall scheme of things. In general, this moment also brings up a great deal of grief, because, usually, many years of life have gone by and nothing has been able to leave the inner sanctum of illusion.

The Queen's admission sets the kingdom in an uproar, with everyone scrambling around trying to figure out how to appease the Daimon-Prince and find him a lover. And the first two pretty Princesses do not do the trick. Their loss would correspond to the tremendous rage and destructivness that first erupts from a part of the personality denied its birthright for decades. We saw this also in Aphrodite's rage in the Eros and Psyche tale and saw what it took (by way of changed attitudes) to transform this rage into something constructive. In our current tale, the first two Princesses are excessively compliant and ingratiating – always trying to please the inflated, imperious worm-Prince who behaves, now that he has everyone's attention, like an *enfant terrible* – he just gulps them down.

THE WORM-PRINCE AND THE KING OR QUEEN/BABY DYAD

The worm-Prince of our story, bulging with his swallowed first two wives, is a perfect example of that inner structure within the self-care system that we have already recognized as both excessively infantile and also incredibly inflated – a sort of imperious, royal queen/ or king/baby. This combination of infantility (inferiority) and "royalty" (inflation) expresses the regressed and the progressed sides of the self simultaneously and represents our self-care system in all of its simultaneous maturity and immaturity. As we have repeatedly seen in our clinical

210

material, with trauma, the humanization of this archaic dual structure is developmentally interrupted and the primitive king/ or queen/baby dyad is retained in the unconscious as an anti-individuating force – albeit with one eye on the future. As self-care system, it can be either an overly protective or an overly persecutory caretaker, and almost always it is both. The resulting energies of the system are thus sado-masochistic. The archetypal defense protects the innocent "baby" part of the self as long as it does not want to grow or change, but at the first sign of hope or individuating desire for the world, it attacks and persecutes the host personality. The result is the perpetuation of trauma in the internal world together with the conviction in the patient of his or her own "badness."

SHEPHERD'S DAUGHTER AND CRONE AS POSITIVE DYAD OF THE SELF

To return now to our story, we find that Prince Lindworm has already devoured two princesses and has the whole kingdom intimidated. In other words, he is behaving like an imperious, royal baby. Presumably, he would just keep eating princesses were it not for a fundamental change of attitude at this point. We find this attitude first in the shepherd girl's father. He refuses the unreasonable demands of the King and will not be bought off. He has to capitulate in the end, but it is his attitude that matters to our understanding of the tale. Similarly, his daughter rants and raves, tears her clothes and objects vigorously to the destiny announced for her by the King. She runs through the woods, scratches herself in the briars to a bloody pulp and only in her despair does she blunder into the old crone's lair and get some help.

Almost always in these tales, genuine suffering and mortification must be undergone by the ego before supernatural aid arrives, and this involves genuine rage and objection to one's "destiny." Just as in the tale of Eros and Psyche, the heroine must be beside herself with the sheer impossibility of her situation before the ants come and help her with the seeds or the reed speaks to her, etc. This represents a necessary humbling of the ego before the unbearable conflict prescribed by destiny – a real wrestling with the unknown, but then an acknowledgment of limitation, a surrender to it, a "turning it over," as is commonly said in Alcoholics Anonymous. But this must not occur prematurely, nor must it be done with passive acceptance.

In our story the heroine's faith comes from the crone who tells her, just as she told the Queen, twenty years earlier, "I have helped those who were not less unhappy than you," and then proceeds to give the shepherd's daughter the elaborate instructions necessary to transform the Lindworm. The fact that this crone is the same toothless old lady who advised the Queen earlier shows that a transpersonal control point is "producing" the whole drama, so to speak. We might think of this as that urgency in the psyche which wants the opposite sides of the ambivalent Self to integrate, a kind of superordinate urgency towards wholeness that stands behind the original ambivalent antinomial Self of the archetypal defense. It is as if the old crone, representing the psyche's transpersonal core herself "wants" to incarnate in the human world but can do so (given the traumatic splitting we hypothesize) only through the transformation drama that unfolds through her agency. Looked at in this way, we might say that the Self first enters the world through the paradoxical lowly but inflated form of the Lindworm – a perfect image of infantile omnipotence – lowly and slimy, but righteous and terrifying. Ego and Self in this constellation are identified and the ego is correspondingly inflated and cut off from life. In other words, at this stage in the story, the Self can only devour or possess its human counterpart. It cannot relate to it. But as a first stage of the Self's incarnation, the Lindworm is the "best" that the old crone can do under the circumstances. Her next task is to find another more humble heroine to transform this Prince-in-disguise into his true form – not a destructive transformation this time, for he is to be transformed constructively into a form related to human affairs.

Once contact is made (a second time and a second stage) between the shepherd's daughter and the old crone, the sacralized ego is on a path of its own individuation process, and the "faith" necessary to enter a life-conflict and struggle with it is present. In the clinical situation this means the development of affect-tolerance, and especially the tolerance of conflicting affects within the transference. The patient must have a taste of both love and hate toward the same person and be able to admit both love and hate toward the self as well. The shepherd's daughter has to know that there is a Prince underneath the snake, i.e., that goodness exists within the diabolical Worm. This means a giving up of illusions and, in our story, actual contact with the slimy, disgusting shadow-side of the Self.

> "You must take him in your arms and hold him close, if only for one brief moment," says the Crone. "Ugh," cried the shepherd's daughter, "I can never do that!" And her heart turned right over inside her as she thought how cold and wet and slimy the Lindworm must be, and how horrible it would feel to embrace him. "It is that or be eaten," chided the crone.
>
> (Jones, 1975: 11)

Again, a choice!

It is typical of many fairy tales that the heroine must embrace a repulsive loathsome beast. In the tale of Beauty and the Beast, for example, Beauty finally overcomes her weak-kneed revulsion and consents, out of great compassion, to marry poor Beast and leave her (incestuous) father. At this moment Beast transforms into the Prince. In many of the stories the Beast is a snake or a frog or an ass or a crocodile and the heroine can only manage to kiss him with supernatural aid or inspiration as happens here with the help of the old crone in the forest. In clinical terms, this means embracing all the aggressive, sexual and "chthonic" energies which lie unredeemed under the "nice, compliant" false self of childhood – something easier said than done and often requiring the continued encouragement of the therapist who, like the crone, has a faith in the complexities of life that the traumatized patient does not.

RAGE AND THE TRANSFORMATION OF PRINCE LINDWORM

We come then, in our story, to the nuptial bed where Prince Lindworm is licking his chops and preparing for a third meal. Despite his diabolical "intent," however, we see something in this scene that we previously observed in the tale of Fitcher's Bird, where the diabolical wizard partly cooperates with his own transformation. The shepherd's daughter, now protected by her ten shifts and prepared by the old crone to trick her partner out of his God-like power, repeatedly demands that he shed a skin each time she disrobes. Although the Lindworm objects to this each time, he nevertheless follows her orders instead of eating her. Finally he is completely vulnerable – a writhing, slimy mass of raw flesh – and our heroine must then dish out some of his own cruelty, i.e., she must whip him with sticks dipped in lye.

In our tale, it is not enough that the heroine love her daimon-lover as in Beauty and the Beast. After he is exposed and vulnerable, she must thrash him. This apparent mercilessness might be thought of as confronting his aggression on its own terms but consciously – not being overcome by compassion and pity before the transformation is complete. Most of us as therapists are so caught up in the need to provide empathic mirroring and healing acceptance that we have trouble probing a wound that is open. And yet, as we know from medical practice, deep healing cannot come about unless a recently opened wound is thoroughly cleaned. Our heroine does this with controlled aggression, ritually coordinated, as it were, by a transpersonal control point (the old crone)

What follows is a true crucifixion scene – a dismemberment experience and is part of the Self-identified ego's sacrifice of itself in the interest of incarnation – painful though it is. Under normal developmental circumstances, this sacrifice of the "all-embracing plenitude" of the inflated Ego occurs incrementally as the child's inflated expectations are "disillusioned" by the parents' normal frustrations and failures in empathy.

But in trauma, the situation is different. The archaic Self in its terrible as well as benevolent form has not transformed and therefore when it does the result is a crisis. We see this in the multiple layers of "skin" on the Lindworm. The snake shedding its skin is a classic image of growth and transformation. But in our story it is as though the Lindworm, split off from consciousness for twenty years, has been unable to grow or transform and has to go through his nine incarnations all at once – ending up a slimy blob. During this process, our heroine must be very well protected so that she does not reveal herself in her nakedness, i.e., her true vulnerability too soon. She is dealing here with archetypal aggression and, until it transforms, she must hold herself back. Still, she is empathic, i.e, she mirrors her partner, shedding a skin every time he does, and she does not succumb to his threats or objections.

A MOMENT OF COMPASSION

Then comes the reconciling bath in milk – the mother's nourishment and the momentary embrace – which turns into an all-night affair. This is the moment of *coniunctio* in our narrative and the important thing is that it is truly a *coniunctio oppositorum* – a union that follows separation and dis-identification between ego and Self. Only such unions are transformative according to mythology.

Our story says that the bath of milk and the momentary embrace by the third wife transform the diabolical Lindworm into the Prince. Psychologically, we might understand this as the moment when a central split in the primal duplex Self-figure, serving as the self-care defense, is healed through human compassion. This is an experience of "wholeness" and unity which does not deny the body, i.e., it transcends the experience of "oneness" that we have seen earlier in that splitting of the numinous that constitutes a religious defense. As "Lindworm" only, the snake-bridegroom represents the negative side of the (here) masculine Self, the positive side being completely unconscious and unavailable – non-existent except as a *potential*, a potential perhaps known only to the old crone in the forest. Only human compassion can activate the integrative potential of the Self when its energies have been diverted into evil and hate by unbearable trauma and its inevitable archetypal self-care system.

Moments such as this can happen in psychotherapy through the "tough compassion" of the therapist who "sees" – for just one moment – the grief and woundedness buried inside the patient's self-care system. Such a moment was described, for example, in Chapter 2 at the time when my patient Lenore suddenly "saw" her suffering little girl and felt a wave of compassion well up in herself. When this patient had walked into the session that day, her ego was completely identified with the critical voices of her snake-like self-care system, exacerbated by her husband's cruel announcement that he was filing for divorce. As she sat despondently in the session, her stomach convulsed and full of self-loathing for her "failure" once again, I asked her simply to attend to her pain and let it speak to us through an image or fantasy. She suddenly burst into tears, having "seen" her "little girl," and she felt a sudden wave of compassion for this suffering innocent child inside herself. We might say that her ego, previously identified with the hateful angry side of the maternal Self-figure suddenly switched radically to the positive loving side of this same inner "mother." Now she could feel compassion for herself. The positive side of the Self could constellate, flowing through her in a truly transformative moment – a moment analogous to the "switch" from Lindworm to Prince through the medium of the third wife's compassion in our tale. We might also describe this "flowing through" as the return of her personal spirit to its "home" in the body.

This experience helped my patient sort out something that had confused her all her life. She had always thought that her real mother was the "good" mother and that she had nothing but "badness" in herself. Now she experienced her own deep capacities for loving (or, we might say, the Self's loving energies flowing through her) and she realized that she could be a "good" mother to her own wounded child. The "goodness now" was inside her. She had turned, as it were, from Worm into Prince, and all it took was one "moment" of compassionate attention to the pain in her belly. This was not, however, compassion she could give herself.

CONCLUDING REMARKS

This leads us to a final speculation about the old crone in our story. We have noted that she seems to "stand behind" the unfolding drama which evolves from a state of *sterility* to *bewitchment* by the dark side of the Self (paramount in the self-care defense of trauma), through *suffering* and death, to a moment of human *compassion*, leading to *enchantment* or an experience of the whole Self and its embodied incarnation. In this process, whether good or evil triumphs depends to a frightening degree upon whether human compassion can mediate the volcanic archetypal energies of the psyche. The Self "itself" seems indifferent to this singularly human dilemma, and if constellated negatively as a survival-Self, it will keep on devouring the person's life (one wife after another) *ad nauseum*.

And yet, if our hypothesis is correct, even this diabolical destructiveness has a meaning in the overall scheme of things. And this meaning seems to have to do with the old crone and her ultimate relationship to what we have called the inviolable personal spirit. I like to think of her as a kind of "spirit-bank," who keeps this personal spirit inviolate in "her world" when it has found no place in "this world," and in her toothless scheming and dreaming she wants desperately for this spirit to find a home in the lives of those who suffer enough to blunder into her lair. Ultimately "she" is the author of our story and of our lives. She cannot incarnate in a trauma-ridden world except as a monster, but she needs a human person to give birth to this monster and then another one to redeem it. She can do none of this herself. After all she is only a "spirit." But she can nudge the struggling and broken ego along, and when both her evil and good have a chance to be held by human compassion, she comes happily down into the world and makes it a beautiful place in which to live.

NOTES

INTRODUCTION

1 The "mythopoetic" function of the unconscious was a term originally coined by classical scholar Fredrick Myers in the latter part of the nineteenth century. Myers believed that the unconscious was continually creating mythic fantasies which manifested themselves in dreams, somnambulism, hypnosis, possession and the trance-states of mediums. Ellenberger (1970: 318), in his monumental survey of the unconscious in contemporary psychiatry, regrets that this promising notion was never more fully investigated by theorists other than Flournoy and Jung.

2 Jung's researches led him to the concept of the Self as the ordering and unifying center of the whole personality, whereas the ego was understood to be the ordering center of consciousness alone. For Jung the Self was equivalent to the *imago Dei* in the psyche and therefore of transpersonal origins. He himself never capitalized it, but I have chosen to do so throughout the text in order to distinguish Jung's concept from descriptions of the self by other theorists where the numinous, spiritual dimension of the term is not included.

3 The numinosum is a category of experience described by Rudolph Otto characterizing humankind's encounter with the *mysterium tremendum* or the *wholly other* or the *daimonic* (Otto, 1958). It is accompanied by the ego's sense of being seized by a mysterious power greater than or "beyond" itself, over and against which it stands in *awe, fascination, or dread*. Positive constellations of the numinosum inspire humility, gratitude, religious devotion, and worship, whereas negative experiences inspire fear, dread (shudder, tremor), and horror. Throughout this book, the intimate relationship between trauma and the numinous will be emphasized. When the ego falls through the abyss of trauma into the darkness of the unconscious psyche, it falls into an archetypal world which is experienced by the ego as numinous – dark or light. Unfortunately for the trauma victim, the numinous usually constellates negatively.

4 One important exception is Emmett Early's recent book on psychological trauma (Early, 1993) which begins with a chapter on a Jungian approach to the subject. Early emphasizes what he calls the "trauma complex" and points out that dissociation is the psyche's normal way of coping with traumatic events. Although he recognizes the archetypal dimension of trauma and discusses the role of the Trickster archetype, Early interprets the diabolical figures with which this book is concerned as literal representations of "death" (116) or as "unwanted consciousness" (26) thereby losing the role of these figures as archaic defenses against unbearable experience.

CHAPTER 1 THE INNER WORLD OF TRAUMA IN ITS DIABOLICAL FORM

1 For this distinction I am indebted to Robin van Loben Sels, who discusses this difference in her recent paper "Dreams as Daily Bread," delivered at Temenos Institute, Westport, Connecticut, in October, 1993.

2 The reader is referred to Michael Balint's illuminating discussion on the differences between "malignant" and "benign" forms of regression and their clinical implications (see Balint, 1979).

3 Leonard Shengold presents an interesting discussion of how severely traumatized patients (he calls severe trauma "soul murder") utilize auto-hypnosis as a defense against unbearable anxiety. These patients, he says, become experts at hypnotizing themselves (see Shengold, 1989).

4 James Masterson has especially emphasized how the Rewarding Object Relations Part Unit (RORU) forms a pathological alliance with the patient's weak ego and in this way keeps it weak. All individuative urges are escaped into the self-soothing regressive gratification of the interior Rewarding Object, thus obviating the patient's need to struggle with reality and suffer his or her own anxiety and responsibility (see Masterson, 1981).

5 Of course, one could argue that the evil Trickster-doctor in the zombie-hospital is an image of me in the transference. Some analysts might say that Mary unconsciously experienced my offer of the phone number as a trick, colluding with her own defenses, and therefore her dream represented me as diabolical – delivering de-humanizing serum. This interpretation cannot be discarded out of hand. The dangers of collusion with the false-self of the patient are very real. As I have suggested already, to the extent that I was trying to "help" Mary not to feel the full impact of her despair and anxiety during previous years of her therapy, I would have been in collusion with the diabolical side of her Trickster. In this way, the material shows us the diabolical underside of our therapeutic *good intentions* – always present to seduce the therapist as well as the patient out of the work of analysis. Such seduction is a special danger when the black magician appears in the context of an eroticized transference.

Alternatively, from a more classical slant, one could interpret the injecting doctor sexually, i.e., that underneath my "nice exterior" in the transference I was envisioned by Mary's dream as planning to inject her with my penis and turn her into a zombie. Neither of these interpretations is "wrong." Each is just too facile and too reductive, translating the dream image back into the concrete reality of the analyst from its "disguised" form in the unconscious, as though the unconscious were preoccupied only with the transference. If we stay with the image, we notice that the Trickster-doctor and Mary's Food Daimon seem to share the same "intention." Both seduce her out of "her world" into "their world," where she ends up in an altered state, "spaced out" or "a zombie." These are basically non-feeling states. So our diabolical figure's "purpose" seems to be to get her into a "numb" de-personalized state. Why would he do this? In order to prevent Mary's ego from experiencing what he envisioned as a threat to her "sanity," namely, a real relationship in which she might begin to trust again, only to be massacred. He would massacre her first in the inner world.

CHAPTER 3 FREUD AND JUNG'S DIALOGUE ABOUT TRAUMA'S INNER WORLD

1 This case is reported in two places in Jung's works. In his autobiography (Jung, 1963) and in his paper "Schizophrenia" (Jung, 1958) contained in *Collected Works, Vol. 3*. The following description is a compilation of these two accounts.

CHAPTER 7 RAPUNZEL AND THE SELF-CARE SYSTEM

1 This version of the story comes from *The Complete Grimms' Fairy Tales*, (1972) where it appears as number 12, pp. 73–7.

CHAPTER 8 PSYCHE AND HER DAIMON-LOVER

1 This version of the story is abridged from Neumann's (1956) text. Page numbers appear in parentheses where phrases are quoted directly.

CHAPTER 9 FITCHER'S BIRD AND THE DARK SIDE OF THE SELF

1 This story is taken from the *The Complete Grimms' Fairy Tales* (1972), where it appears as tale number 46., pp. 216–20.

CHAPTER 10 PRINCE LINDWORM AND TRANSFORMATION OF THE DAIMONIC THROUGH SACRIFICE AND CHOICE

1 This version of the story is abridged from *Prince Lindworm* as retold by Gwyn Jones in *Scandinavian Legends and Folk-tales* (1975), where it appears on pp. 3–15. Page numbers appear in parentheses where phrases are quoted directly.

BIBLIOGRAPHY

Anonymous, (1994) "Body Work" in *To Your Health: The Magazine of Healing and Hope* 6 (8).

Asper, K. (1991) "Fitcher's Bird: Illustrations of the Negative Animus and Shadow in Persons with Narcissistic Disturbances," in M. Stein and L. Corbett (eds) *Psyche's Stories: Modern Jungian Interpretations of Fairy Tales, Vol I*, Wilmette, Ill.: Chiron Publications: 121–40.

Balint, M. (1979) *The Basic Fault: Therapeutic Aspects of Regression*, Evanston, Ill.: Northwestern Universities Press.

Beebe, J. (1993) "Comment to Issue on Borderline Patients," *Journal of Analytical Psychology* 38: 101–3.

Bergler, E. (1959) *Principles of Self-Damage*, Madison, Conn.: International Universities Press.

Bion, W. (1959) "Attacks on Linking," in W. Bion *Second Thoughts*, New York: Jason Aronson (1967).

Bion, W. (1962a) *Learning from Experience*, London: Heinemann; reprinted in paperback, Maresfield Reprints, London: H. Karnac Books (1984).

Bion, W. (1962b) "A Theory of Thinking," in W. Bion *Second Thoughts*, New York: Jason Aronson (1967).

Blatt, S. (1995) "The Destructiveness of Perfectionism," *American Psychologist* 50(12): 1003–20.

Bollas, C. (1987) *The Shadow of the Object*, New York: Columbia University Press.

Braun, B. G. (1988) "The BASK Model of Dissociation," *Dissociation* 1: 16–23.

Bunster, J. (1993) "The Patient Difficult to Reach," *Journal of Analytical Psychology* 38 (1): 37–44.

Cooper, J.C. (1978) *Illustrated Encyclopaedia of Traditional Symbols*, London: Thames & Hudson.

Corrigan, E., and Gordon, P.E. (eds) (1995) *The Mind Object*, New Jersey: Jason Aronson Inc.

Davies, J. and Frawley, M. (1994) *Treating the Adult Survivor of Childhood Sexual Abuse: A Psychoanalytic Perspective*, New York: Basic Books.

Early, E. (1993) *The Raven's Return: The Influences of Psychological Trauma on Individuals and Culture*, Willmette, Ill.: Chiron Publications.

Edinger, E. (1972) *Ego and Archetype*, New York: Penguin Books.

Edinger, E. (1985) *Anatomy of the Psyche: Alchemical Symbolism in Psychotherapy*, La Salle, Ill.: Open Court.

Edinger, E. (1986) *The Bible and the Psyche*, Toronto: Inner City Books.

Edinger, E. (1992) *Transformation of the God-image: An Elucidation of Jung's Answer to Job*, Toronto: Inner City Books.

Eigen, M. (1995) "Mystical Precocity and Psychic Short Circuits," in E. Corrigan and P.E. Gordon (eds) *The Mind Object*, New Jersey: Jason Aronson Inc: 109–34.

Ellenberger, H. (1970) *The Discovery of the Unconscious*, New York: Basic Books.

Fairbairn, R. (1981) *Psychoanalytic Studies of the Personality*, London: Routledge and Kegan Paul.

Ferenczi, S. (1933) "Confusion of Tongues Between Adults and the Child," in M. Balint (ed.) *Final Contributions to the Problems and Methods of Psycho-Analysis*, New York: Brunner/Mazel: 156–67.

Ferenczi, S. (1988) *The Clinical Diary of Sandor Ferenczi*, ed. J. Dupont, Cambridge Mass.,: Harvard University Press.

Fordham, M. (1974) "Defences of the Self," *Journal of Analytical Psychology* 19 (2): 192–9.

Fordham, M. (1976) *The Self and Autism, (Library of Analytical Psychology, vol. 3)*, London: Heinemann.

Forsyth, N. (1987) *The Old Enemy: Satan and the Combat Myth*, Princeton, N.J.: Princeton University Press.

Freud, S. (1966) *The Standard Edition of the Complete Psychological Works of Sigmund Freud*, London: Hogarth Press, 24 vols.

Freud, S. (1893) *On the Psychical Mechanism of Hysterical Phenomena: Preliminary Communication, Standard Edition II*.

Freud, S. (1894) *The Neuro-Psychoses of Defence, Standard Edition III*.

Freud, S. (1896) *The Aetiology of Hysteria, Standard Edition III*.

Freud, S. (1917) *Mourning and Melancholia, Standard Edition XIV*.

Freud, S. (1919) *The Uncanny, Standard Edition XVII*.

Freud, S. (1920a) *Civilization and its Discontents, Standard Edition XXI*.

Freud, S. (1920b) *Beyond the Pleasure Principle, Standard Edition XVIII*.

Freud, S. (1923) *The Ego and the Id, Standard Edition XIX*.

Freud, S. (1924) *The Economic Problem of Masochism, Standard Edition XIX*.

Freud, S. (1926) *Inhibitions, Symptoms and Anxiety, Standard Edition XX*.

Freud, S. (1933) *New Introductory Lectures, Standard Edition XXII*.

Freud, S. (1937) *Analysis Terminable and Interminable, Standard Edition XXIII*.

Freud, S. (1954) *The Origins of Psychoanalysis: Letters to Wilhelm Fliess*, Trans. Mosbacher and Strachey, New York: Basic Books.

Garfield, D. (1995) *Unbearable Affect*, New York: John Wiley and Sons Inc.

Goethe, J. W. von. (1941) *Faust*, trans. G. M. Priest, New York: Knopf.

Gordon. R. (1987) "Masochism: The Shadow Side of the Archetypal Need to Venerate and Worship," *Journal of Analytical Psychology*, 32(3): 227–40.

Graves, R. (1955) *The Greek Myths*, New York: Penguin.

Grotstein, J. (1981) *Splitting and Projective Identification*, New York: Jason Aronson.

Grotstein, J. (1984) "Forgery of the Soul," in C. Nelson and M. Eigen (eds) *Evil, Self and Culture*, New York: Human Sciences Press: 203–26.

Grotstein, J. (1987) "An Object-relations Perspective on Resistance in Narcissistic Patients," in J. Grostein *Techniques of Working with Resistance*, New York: Jason Aronson: 317–39.

Guntrip, H. (1969) *Schizoid Phenomena, Object Relations and the Self*, New York: International Universities Press.

Guntrip, H. (1971) *Psychoanalytic Theory, Therapy and the Self*, New York: Basic Books.

Harpur, P. (1994) *Daimonic Reality: A Field Guide to the Other World*, New York: Viking–Penguin Books.

Haule, J. (1992) *Pilgrimage of the Heart: The Path of Romantic Love*, Boston, Mass.: Shambhala.

Henderson, J. (1990) *Shadow and Self*, Wilmette, Ill.: Chiron Publications.

Hill, D. (1970) "The Trickster," in R. Cavendish (ed.) *Man, Myth and Magic: An*

Illustrated Encyclopedia of the Supernatural, vol. 21, New York: Cavendish Corporation: 2881–5.

Hillman, J. (1972) *The Myth of Analysis*, Evanston, Ill.: Northwestern University Press.

Hillman, J. (1979) "Senex and Puer," in *Puer Papers*, Dallas, Tex.: Spring Publications: 3–53.

Hillman, J. (1983) "The Bad Mother," *Spring*, Dallas, Tex.: Spring Publications: 165–81.

Hubback, J. (1991) "The Changing Person and the Unchanging Archetype," in M. Matoon (ed.) *Proceedings of the Eleventh International Congress for Analytical Psychology, Paris, 1989*, Einsedeln: Daimon Verlag: 35–50.

Jones, G, (1975) "Prince Lindworm," as retold in *Scandinavian Legends and Folk-tales*, Oxford: Oxford University Press: 3–15.

Jung, C. G. (1963) *Memories, Dreams, Reflections*, New York: Random House.

Jung, C. G. (1973) *Letters Vol 1, 1906–1950*, ed. G. Adler, Princeton, N.J.: Princeton University Press.

Jung, C. G. (1953–79) *The Collected Works* (Bollingen Series XX), trans. R. F. C. Hull: eds. H. Read, M. Fordham, and G. Adler, Princeton, N.J.: Princeton University Press, 20 vols.

Jung, C. G. (1904) *Studies in Word Association, Collected Works 2*.

Jung, C. G. (1907) *The Psychology of Dementia Praecox, Collected Works 3*.

Jung, C. G. (1912a) *The Theory of Psychoanalysis, Collected Works 4*.

Jung, C. G. (1912b) *Symbols of Transformation, Collected Works 5*.

Jung, C. G. (1913) *On the Doctrine of Complexes, Collected Works 2*.

Jung, C. G. (1916) *The Psychology of the Unconscious, Collected Works 7*.

Jung, C. G. (1925) *Notes on the Seminar Given in 1925*, ed. Wm. McGuire, Princeton, N. J.: Princeton University Press (1989).

Jung, C. G. (1926) *Spirit and Life, Collected Works 8*.

Jung, C. G. (1928a) *The Therapeutic Value of Abreaction, Collected Works 16*.

Jung, C. G. (1928b) *The Psychological Foundations of Belief in Spirits, Collected Works 8*.

Jung, C. G. (1928c) *Mental Disease and the Psyche, Collected Works 3*.

Jung, C. G. (1934a) *The Relations Between the Ego and the Unconscious, Collected Works 7*.

Jung, C. G. (1934b) *Review of the Complex Theory, Collected Works 8*.

Jung, C. G. (1937a) "A Farewell Speech," given to the Analytical Psychology Club of New York on Oct. 26, 1937 (unpublished). Available in the Kristine Mann Library, 28 E. 39th St., New York, N. Y. 10016.

Jung, C. G. (1937b) *Psychology and Religion, Collected Works 11*.

Jung, C. G. (1946) *Psychology of the Transference, Collected Works 16*.

Jung, C. G. (1947) *On the Nature of the Psyche Collected Works, 8*.

Jung, C. G. (1949) *The Psychology of the Child Archetype, Collected Works 9/1*.

Jung, C. G. (1951) *Aion, Collected Works 9/2*

Jung, C. G. (1952) *Answer to Job, Collected Works 11*.

Jung, C. G. (1954) *On the Nature of the Psyche, Collected Works 8*.

Jung, C. G. (1955) *Mysterium Coniunctionis, Collected Works 14*.

Jung, C. G. (1958) *Schizophrenia, Collected Works 3*.

Jung, C. G. (1977) *C. G. Jung Speaking*, ed. Wm. McGuire and R.F.C. Hull, Princeton, N.J.: Princeton University Press.

Jung, C. G. (1989) Notes of the Seminar Given in 1925, ed. Wm. McGuire, Princeton, N.J.: Princeton University Press.

Kalsched, D. (1980) "Narcissism and the Search for Interiority," *Quadrant* 13(2): 46–74.

Kalsched, D. (1981) "Limbo and the Lost Soul in Psychotherapy," *Union Seminary Quarterly Review*, XXXVLI (2 and 3): 95–107.

Kalsched, D. (1985) "Fire from the Gods: How Will Prometheus Be Bound – an Essay on Soviet-American Relations," *Quadrant* 18(2): 71–92.

Kalsched, D. (1991) "The Limits of Desire and the Desire for Limits in Psychoanalytic Theory and Practice," in F. Halligan and J. Shay (eds) *Fires of Desire: Erotic Energies and the Spiritual Quest*, New York: Crossroads Press.

Kast, V. (1992) *The Dynamics of Symbols: Fundamentals of Jungian Psychotherapy*, trans. S. Schwarz, New York: Fromm Publications.

Kavaler-Adler, S. (1993) *The Compulsion to Create: A Psychoanalytic Study of Women Artists*, New York: Routledge.

Kernberg, O., Selzer, M., Koenigsberg, H., Carr, A. and Appelbaum, A. (1989) *Psychodynamic Psychotherapy of Borderline Patients*, New York: Basic Books.

Kerr, J. (1993) *A Most Dangerous Method: The Story of Jung, Freud, and Sabina Speilrein*, New York: Alfred Knopf.

Khan, M. (1963) "The Concept of Cumulative Trauma," in M. Khan *The Privacy of the Self*, New York: International Universities Press: 42–58.

Khan, M. (1974) "Towards an Epistemology of Cure," in M. Khan *The Privacy of the Self*, New York: International Universities Press: 93–8.

Khan, M. (1983) "Beyond the Dreaming Experience," in M. Khan *Hidden Selves*, New York: International Universities Press: 42–50.

Klein, M. (1934) "A Contribution to the Psychogenesis of Manic-depressive States," in M. Klein *Contributions to Psychoanalysis 1921–1945*, London: Hogarth Press: 282–310.

Klein, M. (1946) "The Early Development of the Conscience in the Child," in M. Klein *Contributions to Psychoanalysis*, London: Hogarth Press: 67–74.

Kohut, H. (1971) *The Analysis of the Self*, New York: International Universities Press.

Kohut, H. (1977) *The Restoration of the Self*, New York: International Universities Press.

Kohut, H. (1984) *How Does Analysis Cure?* ed. A. Goldberg, Chicago, Ill.: University of Chicago Press.

Kristeva, J. (1989) *Black Sun: Depression and Melancholia*, New York: Columbia University Press.

Krystal, H. (1988) *Integration and Self Healing*, New Jersey: The Analytic Press.

Kugler, P. (1986) "Childhood Seduction: Physical and Emotional," *Spring*, Dallas: Spring Publications: 40–60.

Langs, R. (1976) *The Bipersonal Field*, New York: Jason Aronson.

Leonard, L.S. (1985) *The Wounded Woman: Healing the Father–Daughter Relationship*, Boston, Mass.: Shambhala Press.

Leonard, L.S. (1986) *On the Way to the Wedding*, Boston, Mass.: Shambhala Press.

Leonard, L.S. (1989) *Witness to the Fire: Creativity and the Veil of Addiction*, Boston, Mass.: Shambhala Press.

Leonard, L.S. (1993) *Meeting the Madwoman*, New York: Bantam Books.

Masson, J. (1984) *The Assault on Truth: Freud's Suppression of the Seduction Theory*, New York: Farrar, Strauss & Giroux.

Masterson, J. (1976) *Psychotherapy of the Borderline Adult*, New York: Brunner Mazel.

Masterson, J. (1981) *The Narcissistic and Borderline Disorders: An Integrated Developmental Approach*, New York: Brunner Mazel.

McGuire, W. (1974) (ed.) *The Freud/Jung Letters*, trans. R. Manheim and R.F.C. Hull, Princeton, N.J.: Princeton University Press.

McDougall, J. (1985) *Theaters of the Mind*, New York: Basic Books.

McDougall, J. (1989) *Theaters of the Body*, New York: W.W. Norton & Co.

Mead, G.R.S. (1967) *The Doctrine of the Subtle Body in Western Tradition*, Wheaton, Ill.: Theosophical Publishing House for Quest Books.

Modell, A. (1958) "The Theoretical Implications of Hallucinatory Experiences in Schizophrenia," *Journal of the American Psychoanalytic Association* 6: 442–80.

Modell, A. (1976) "The Holding Environment and the Therapeutic Action of Psychoanalysis," *Journal of the American Psychoanalytic Association* 24: 285–307.

Mogenson, G. (1989) *God is a Trauma: Vicarious Religion and Soul-Making*, Dallas, Tex.: Spring Publications.

Moltmann, J. (1974) *The Crucified God*, SCM Press, p. 151, quoted in Garrison, J. *The Darkness of God: Theology after Hiroshima*, Grand Rapids, Mich.: William B. Eerdman's Publishing Co. (1982).

Mudd, P. (1989) "The Dark Self: Death as a Transferential Factor" in *Proceedings of the 11th International Congress of Analytical Psychology, Paris, 1989*, Einsiedeln: Daimon Verlag: 103–18.

Neumann, E. (1956) *Amor and Psyche: The Psychic Development of the Feminine*, trans. R. Manheim, Princeton, N.J.: Princeton University Press.

Neumann, E. (1969) *Depth Psychology and a New Ethic*, New York: Harper Torchbooks.

Neumann, E. (1976) *The Child*, New York: Harper Colophon Books.

Nunberg, H. (1932) *The Principles of Psychoanalysis*, New York: International Universities Press.

Odier, C. (1956) *Anxiety and Magic Thinking*, trans. M-L. Schoelly and M. Sherfey, New York: International Universities Press.

Ogden, T.H. (1986), *The Matrix of the Mind: Object Relations and the Psychoanalytic Dialogue*, New Jersey: Jason Aronson.

O'Grady, J. (1989), *The Prince of Darkness*, Longmead: Element Books.

Otto, R. (1958) *The Idea of the Holy*, trans. J. Harvey, New York: Oxford University Press.

Palmer, R.E.A. (1970) "Janus," in R. Cavendish (ed.) *Man, Myth and Magic: An Illustrated Encyclopedia of the Supernatural*, New York: Cavendish Corporation (1970): 483–4.

Perry, J. W. (1976) *Roots of Renewal in Myth and Madness*, San Francisco: Jossey-Bass.

Pinkola Estes, C. (1992) *Women Who Run with the Wolves*, New York: Ballantine Books.

Plaut, F. (1966) "Reflections About Not Being Able to Imagine," in *Analytical Psychology: A Modern Science* (*Library of Analytical Psychology, vol. 1*), London: Heinemann (1973): 128–44.

Proner, B. (1988) "Envy of Oneself, Adhesive Identification and Pseudo-Adult States," *Journal of Analytical Psychology*, 33: 143–63.

Proner, B. (1986) "Defenses of the Self and Envy of Oneself," *Journal of Analytical Psychology*, 31: 275–9.

Radin, P. (1976) *The Trickster: A Study in American Indian Mythology*, New York: Schocken Books.

Redfearn, J. (1992) *The Exploding Self: The Creative and Destructive Nucleus of the Personality*, Wilmette, Ill.: Chiron Publications.

Ross, C. (1989) *Multiple Personality Disorder: Diagnosis, Clinical Features, and Treatment*, New York: John Wiley & Sons.

Ross, L, (1991) "Cupid and Psyche; Birth of a New Consciousness" in M. Stein and L. Corbett (eds) *Psyche's Stories: Modern Jungian Interpretations of Fairy Tales*, Wilmette, Ill.: Chiron Publications: 65–90.

Rossi, E. L. (1986) *The Psychobiology of Mind–Body Healing: New Concepts in Therapeutic Hypnosis*, New York: W. W. Norton.

Salman, S. (1986) *The Horned God: Masculine Dynamics of Power and Soul*, Quadrant, Fall: 7–25.

Samuels, A. (1989) *The Plural Psyche: Personality, Morality, and the Father*, London: Routledge.

Sandner, D. and Beebe, J. (1982) "Psychopathology and Analysis," in M. Stein (ed.) *Jungian Analysis*, La Salle, Open Court: 294–334.

Satinover, J. (1985) "At the Mercy of Another: Abandonment and Restitution in Psychosis and Psychotic Character," in *Abandonment*, Wilmette, Ill.: Chiron.

Savitz, C. (1991) "Immersions in Ambiguity: The Labyrinth and the Analytic Process," *Journal of Analytical Psychology* 36: 461–81.

Schaefer, R. (1960) "The Loving and Beloved Superego in Freud's Structural Theory," *The Psychoanalytic Study of the Child* 15: 163–88.

Schwartz-Salant, N. (1989) *The Borderline Personality: Vision and Healing*, Wilmette, Ill.: Chiron.

Seinfeld, J. (1990) *The Bad Object*, Northvale, N.J.: Jason Aronson.

Semrad, E. and Van Buskirk, D. (1969) *Teaching Psychotherapy of Psychotic Patients*, New York: Grune & Stratton.

Shengold, L. (1989) *Soul Murder: The Effects of Childhood Abuse and Deprivation*, New York: Fawcett Columbine.

Sidoli, M. (1993) "When the Meaning Gets Lost in the Body," *Journal of Analytical Psychology*, 38: 175–90.

Singer, I. B. (1981) "Demons by Choice: An Interview with *Parabola* Magazine," in *Parabola* 4(4): 68–74.

Speilrein, S. (1984) "Destruction as a Cause of Coming Into Being," *Journal of Analytical Psychology*, 39: 155–86.

Stein, L. (1967) "Introducing Not-Self," *Journal of Analytical Psychology*, 12 (2): 97–113.

Terr, L. (1990) *Too Scared to Cry: Psychic Trauma in Childhood*, New York: Harper & Row.

The Complete Grimm's Fairy Tales (1972) New York: Random House, Pantheon Books,

Tripp, E. (1970) *Classical Mythology*, New York: Meridian Books.

Tustin, F. (1990) *The Protective Shell in Children and Adults*, London: Karnac Books.

Ulanov, A. (1971) *The Feminine in Jungian Psychology and in Christian Theology*, Evanston, Ill.: Northwestern University Press.

Ulanov, A. and Ulanov, B., (1987) *The Witch and the Clown: Two Archetypes of Human Sexuality*, Wilmette, Ill.: Chiron.

von Franz, M.-L. (1970) *A Psychological Interpretation of the Gold Ass of Apuleius*, Zurich: Spring Publications.

von Franz, M.-L (1974) *Shadow and Evil in Fairy Tales*, Zurich: Spring Publications.

von Franz, M.-L. (1980a) *Projection and Re-collection in Jungian Psychology: Reflections on the Soul*, trans. W.H. Kennedy, London: Open Court, reprinted in *Parabola* 4(4): 36–44.

von Franz, M.-L (1980) *The Psychological Meaning of Redemption Motifs in Fairytales*, Toronto: Inner City Books.

de Vries, A. (1984) *Dictionary of Symbols and Imagery*, Amsterdam: North-Holland Publishing Co.

Watts, A. (1954) *Myth and Ritual in Christianity*, London: Thames & Hudson.

Weil, S. (1987) *Gravity and Grace*, London: Routledge and Kegan Paul.

Whitmont, E.C. (1969) *The Symbolic Quest*, New York: Harper Colophon Books.

Wilmer, H. (1986) "The Healing Nightmare: A Study of the War Dreams of Vietnam Combat Veterans," *Quadrant*, Spring: 47–62.

Winnicott, D. W. (1949) "Mind and its Relation to the Psyche-Soma," in D.W. Winnicott *Through Paediatrics to Psychoanalysis*, New York: Basic Books: 243–54.

Winnicott, D. W. (1951) "Transitional Objects and Transitional Phenomena," *Playing and Reality*, New York: Basic Books, 1971: 1–25.

Winnicott, D. W. (1960a) "Ego Distortion in Terms of True and False Self," in D. W. Winnicott *The Maturational Processes and the Facilitating Environment*, London: Hogarth Press, 1965: 140–52.

Winnicott, D. W. (1960b) "The Theory of the Parent–Child Relationship," D. W. Winnicott *The Maturational Processes and the Facilitating Environment*, London: Hogarth Press, 1965.

Winnicott, D. W. (1963) "Fear of Breakdown," in C. Winnicott, R. Shepherd, and M. Davis (eds) *Psychoanalytic Explorations*, Cambridge, Mass.: Harvard University Press, 1989: 87–95.

Winnicott, D. W. (1965) "The Concept of Trauma in Relation to the Development of the Individual within the Family," in C. Winnicott, R. Shepherd, and M. Davis, (eds) *Psychoanalytic Explorations*, Cambridge, Mass.: Harvard University Press, 1989: 130–48.

Winnicott, D. W. (1969) "The Use of an Object and Relating Through Identifications," in C. Winnicott, R. Shepherd, and M. Davis, (eds) *Psychoanalytic Explorations*, Cambridge, Mass.: Harvard University Press, 1989: 218–27.

Winnicott, D. W. (1970) "On the Basis for Self in Body," in C. Winnicott, R. Shepherd, and M. Davis (eds) *Psychoanalytic Explorations*, Cambridge, Mass.: Harvard University Press, 1989: 261–83.

Winnicott, D. W. (1971a) "Dreaming, Fantasying, and Living", in D. W. Winnicott *Playing and Reality*, New York: Basic Books: 26–37.

Winnicott, D. W. (1971b) "The Location of Cultural Experience," in D. W. Winnicott *Playing and Reality*, New York: Basic Books: 95–103.

Woodman, M. (1982) *Addiction to Perfection: The Still Unravished Bride*, Toronto: Inner City Books.

Woodman, M. (1985) *The Pregnant Virgin: A Process of Psychological Transformation*, Toronto: Inner City Books.

INDEX